Designing Learning Opportunities

A PRACTICAL

HANDBOOK

FOR

EDUCATORS

Liesel Knaack

Library and Archives Canada Cataloguing in Publication

Knaack, Liesel Charmaine, 1966-
    A practical handbook for educators : designing learning opportunities / Liesel Knaack.

ISBN 978-1-897160-47-3

1. Effective teaching--Handbooks, manuals, etc.
2. Learning strategies--Handbooks, manuals, etc. I. Title.

LB1025.3.K63 2011   371.102   C2011-902663-5

Cover design by de Sitter Publications and Liesel Knaack
Cover image and content pictures are licensed from fotolia.com and istock.com
Content design and layout by Liesel Knaack and de Sitter Publications

de Sitter Publications
111 Bell Dr., Whitby, ON, L1N 2T1
CANADA

deSitterPublications.com
289-987-0656
info@desitterpublications.com

Designing Learning Opportunities

About the Author

Liesel Knaack is the Director of Vancouver Island University's teaching, learning, and technology centre in British Columbia, Canada. She has been teaching for 25 years. She was an Associate Professor at the University of Ontario Institute of Technology (UOIT) working in the Faculty of Education as a teacher educator.

Liesel has taught school teachers, university professors and college instructors about teaching and learning methods, incorporating assessment and evaluation components, making learning accessible to all learners, as well as integrating technology into learning environments.

Her research interests are in curriculum and instructional design, engagement of students, development and evaluation of web-based learning tools, integrating technology tools and employing effective questioning techniques. Prior to her post-secondary teaching, she taught in the public school system and in outdoor education centres.

Liesel was awarded UOIT's Faculty Teaching Award in 2006. She has a PhD in Curriculum, Teaching and Learning, a Master of Education in Curriculum and a Bachelor of Education.

Liesel Knaack

Brief Contents

Contents

Chapter 5: Preparing Your Useful Syllabus

Section II: Creating and Designing Learning Opportunities and Experiences   91

Chapter 6: Making Learning Accessible

Chapter 7: Choosing Teaching & Learning Strategies

Chapter 8: Planning Your Classes

Chapter 13: Writing Well-Constructed Test Questions

Chapter 14: Designing Digital & Print Materials

Chapter 15: Ending the Last Class on a Strong Note

Handbook Overview

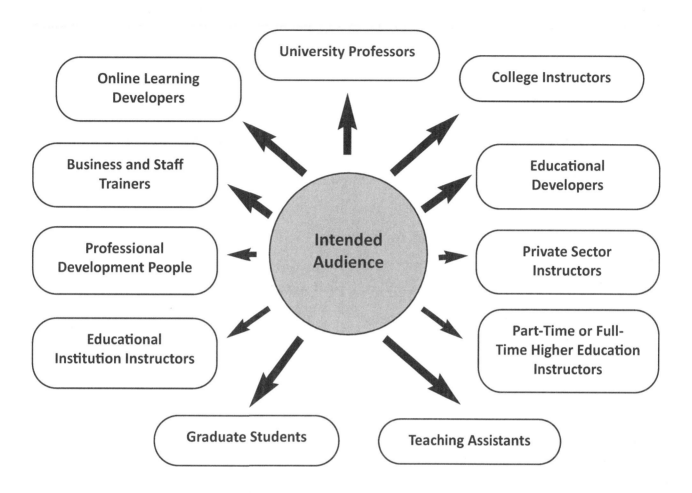

Purpose of Handbook

- To **distill** and **consolidate** the **many recommended practices** about teaching and learning that fill the pages of books, journals, magazines, and research articles and present them in a practical handbook of ideas that can be used effectively and immediately

- To provide essential strategies for **designing and creating effective teaching and learning opportunities**

- To **support new** and **experienced instructors** with a **process** for revamping an existing course/class or developing a new course/class that provides steps, questions, clear outlines and concepts to consider

- To provide **examples** and **information** about how to make **learning accessible** to the greatest number of people through effectively designing documents, web pages, questions, online courses, presentations, assignments, and so on.

Handbook Design

This handbook aims to cover the steps an instructor would go through in planning a course or upgrading an existing course along with strategies for creating effective learning opportunities and tips for refining teaching practices.

The handbook is divided into three sections, each with five chapters. Each section is ordered in a somewhat chronological manner. The chapters progress from the course planning process, to strategies for class implementation, and then to suggestions for refinement once a course is underway. It is important for each chapter to have a distinct theme and include related sub-sections so that users can access a chapter with ease when looking for a specific topic. All chapter sub-sections are listed at the beginning of each chapter in a format showing the relationship among the chapter contents.

Section I: Preparing and Planning Your Course

1: Understanding Your Course & Students
2: Determining Goals & Learning Objectives
3: Aligning Assessment & Evaluation
4: Developing Course Content & Structure
5: Preparing Your Useful Syllabus

The **first five chapters** delineate a common set of steps to plan or re-design a course before stepping into the classroom. The focus of these beginning chapters is based on determining what an instructor wants his or her students to know and be able to do by the end of the course and then working backward to plan how to get them there.

Instructors need to understand the nature of a course and the students who will be taking it. Writing learning objectives and then choosing appropriate assessment and evaluation methods ensures a course is focused on student learning and is using measurable and observable methods to assess that learning. Putting all this pre-planning into an organized schedule allows for easy syllabus, or course outline development before an instructor delves into lesson details.

The first five chapters contain steps that are often missed, skipped over, or not given enough attention by instructors. These chapters provide instructors with helpful information, important questions to ask themselves, thoughts to ponder, and strategies to help organize course content before they even meet their students. When a course is well thought-out and planned, there is a higher rate of success and accomplishment for students and instructors.

Section II: Creating and Designing Learning Opportunities and Experiences

The **middle five chapters** focus on the mechanics of planning and delivering a class along with how to interact with students. Chapters 6, 7, and 8 delve into more detailed planning and course design while taking into account the needs of students.

6: Making Learning Accessible
7: Choosing Teaching & Learning Strategies
8: Planning Your Classes
9: Starting with a Full First Day
10: Building Rapport & Managing the Class

This section begins with a unique chapter on making learning accessible and utilizes a variety of principles and practices to make content, concepts, and class activities available to more learners. Next, a comprehensive chapter on teaching and learning activities demonstrates that lecturing is only one strategy and there exist so many more ways to engage students in powerful learning experiences. The template introduced in the class planning chapter gives instructors a framework for organizing and developing learning activities.

Often, inexperienced instructors squander the first class by just handing out the syllabus, talking a bit about the course, and then letting students out early. The chapter on the first class outlines why the first day is so important and how imperative it is to set the correct tone and expectations related to how the course will be conducted. The last chapter in this section provides many tips and ideas for building rapport with students. The greater the rapport an instructor has with his or her class the easier it is to manage when challenging situations, problems, and unexpected circumstances arise.

Section III: Refining and Improving Strategies and Resources

The **last five chapters** focus on topics that an instructor can read after they have a good solid start to teaching.

Chapter 11 focuses on supporting students through small and easy-to-implement additions to the class. This chapter also represents a fairly unique component rarely found in

11: Supporting Student Success
12: Honing Skills for Effective Questioning
13: Writing Well-Constructed Test Questions
14: Designing Digital & Print Materials
15: Ending the Last Class on a Strong Note

instructor handbooks. With so many unprepared and at-risk students in today's classrooms, this chapter outlines simple tips and ideas for instructors to implement to help support them in their learning. So often the literature focuses on the out-of-classroom support and institutional academic support centers that exist for students, rather than on the strategies that can be used within the class. Ideas on how to structure a class to support effective note-taking, concept acquisition, and creation of study notes will help all students in their learning. These simple ideas are not hard to add to a teaching repertoire and will benefit students in so many ways!

The other chapters, dealing with topics such honing skills in asking effective questions and writing solid test questions, are important but come after the basics have been established. Additionally, there is a chapter on designing print and digital materials to assist instructors with instructional design principles as they relate to learning and how the brain understands images, text and digital media. Finally, there is a chapter on the last class. Often forgotten about or used solely to conduct course/instructor evaluations, the last class should be used to consolidate course information.

Chapter Design & Layout

Each chapter begins with an overview that briefly explains the content of the chapter. Near the end of each chapter is a top ten takeaway section which summarizes ten key ideas from the chapter. Also included are some steps to start implementing ideas from the chapter. Resources and links are provided at the end of each chapter for further learning.

The book is intentionally visual in nature with a reduced use of paragraphs and prose than is found in current books and resources. People learn better and with more ease when there are accompanying graphic elements and page designs that allow the reader to skim content. Text is often arranged in bullets or short phrases, chunked in smaller sections and has relevant visual images to help the reader understand the concepts. There are charts and tables, arrows and boxes, circles and triangles, concept maps and quotation bubbles among the various visual components. These are included to provide variety in the way information is presented and make this handbook more useful.

Engagement Activities

Additionally, most chapters include checklists, matching activities, true-false statements and questions to help the reader apply what they are learning and intentionally engage with the content of the book. The interactive component of this book is not common in other resources.

Effective learning happens when students have a chance to interact and think about the content. Similarly, effective learning about teaching happens when instructors have that same chance; rather than skimming over large chapters or paragraphs of text, instructors need critical questions to ponder, case scenarios to solve, and quizzes to explore their understanding and where more time is required for learning.

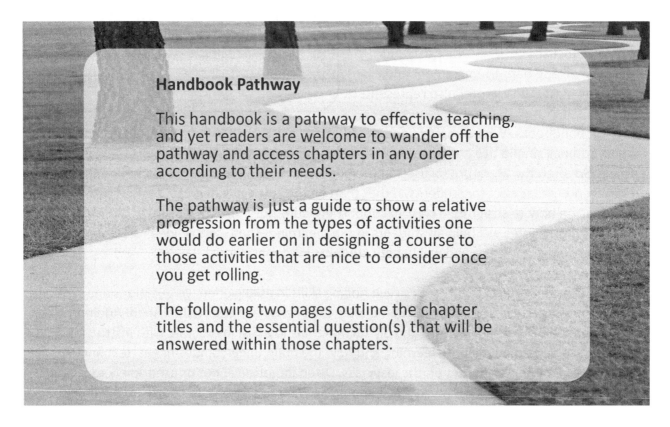

Handbook Pathway

This handbook is a pathway to effective teaching, and yet readers are welcome to wander off the pathway and access chapters in any order according to their needs.

The pathway is just a guide to show a relative progression from the types of activities one would do earlier on in designing a course to those activities that are nice to consider once you get rolling.

The following two pages outline the chapter titles and the essential question(s) that will be answered within those chapters.

1: Understanding Your Course & Students
What do you know about your course and your students?

2: Determining Goals & Objectives
What do you want students to be able to know, value, and do by the end of the course?

3: Aligning Assessment & Evaluation
What will students demonstrate to indicate they have accomplished the learning objectives?

4: Developing Course Content & Structure
What topics will you include and what structure will the course and online components take?

5: Preparing Your Useful Syllabus
How do you prepare the syllabus so that students can access important details?

6: Making Learning Accessible
How can you design learning opportunities that are accessible to most students?

7: Choosing Teaching & Learning Strategies
What will students do in and out of class to apply and learn the content?

8: Planning Your Classes
What components are necessary for a successful and well planned class?

Section I: Preparing and Planning Your Course

Chapter 1: Understanding Your Course & Students

Chapter Overview

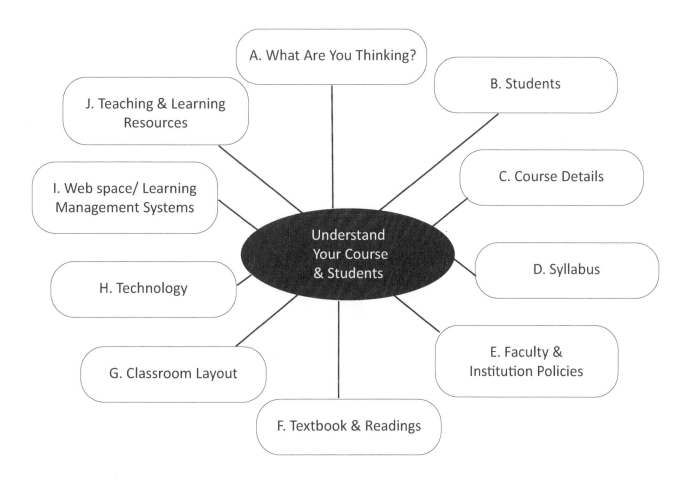

You have signed the contract as a new staff member or you have been told by your supervisor that you are teaching a new course or updating an existing one – what is next? Most often instructors skip over the content from this chapter and head right into the syllabus or course outline. This is not a good move. Some investigative questioning can help you get off to the right start and settle into planning the course much quicker.

Beginning a new course or updating an existing one, whether you have teaching experience or not, is a daunting task. Most often those who take the time to plan and scope out valuable information are those who end up with more successful courses and better organized learning opportunities. It does not take a lot of time—but the time invested is going to be worth it in the long run.

Jump right in. This chapter contains some key topics to get you thinking and asking the right questions. Now let's get moving and find out some information to help you with your course.

A. What Are You Thinking?

Activity: Consider the following thoughts about starting a course. Check off the questions you know an answer to or you have undertaken already. This provides a framework for the rest of the chapter where each thought (cloud) will be briefly explained along with some tips.

Course Details

Is this course a core course or an elective? Are there prerequisites for admittance? How long has it been offered? Who has taught it?

Students

What is the academic background of a typical student (age, experience, ability)? Why do they take the course?

Textbook & Readings

Is there a textbook for this course? Do you have a copy? Do you need to consider a textbook or a collection of readings instead?

Classroom Layout

What does your classroom look like? How are seats arranged? Have you visited your classroom?

Faculty & Institution Policies

Do you know about assessment, academic misconduct, attendance and other policies affecting your teaching?

Web Space/Learning Management Software

Do you have a web environment in which to post materials and have class discussions?

Syllabus or Course Outline

Do you have access to a previous syllabus/course outline? Can you find a similar syllabus online to get ideas? Can you alter the syllabus?

Technology

Do you have a laptop to take to class? Is there capability to show videos in class? Are there data projectors you can sign out for use in classroom?

Teaching & Learning Resources

What resources do you already have for this course? What can you borrow? What is available in the library?

B. Students

Why it is Important To Understand your Students?

To start planning, you need to have a good understanding of your students. So often instructors plan a course without really thinking of their audience and the vital role they play in the whole planning process. If you are unfamiliar with the demographics and abilities of typical students in your class, it would be helpful to seek out someone who can give you some insights. You can get a good picture of students' abilities, experiences and expectations of the course if you ask the right people and dig deep enough. Students will appreciate you taking the time to plan learning experiences that meet their needs.

Where to Find More Info:

- Other instructors in your department

- Students who have taken the course

- Department head about the student demographics

- Academic advisors/Counselors

Questions to Ask:

- What courses have students typically taken prior to your course?

- What are the students' strengths and weaknesses?

- What did students struggle with in previous offerings of this course?

- What assignments and projects did students like the most?

- How did students typically do on mid-terms and final exams?

- What other demands do the students have at the same time as taking your course?

- What are some of their basic demographic variables (e.g., age, ethnicity, gender etc.)

- What percentage of students will be bringing laptops to the classroom to take notes?

- How technologically competent are students?

- What are your students' abilities with proper note-taking, research, and study skills?

From your students' perspectives, here are some thoughts about the learners in your classroom.

I have a learning disability and require supports to aid in my success in the classroom. Are you aware of how you can help me?

I have some prior knowledge, skills, and beliefs about your course. Do you know how to find this out?

I learn best by visuals. Anytime you can include an image, graphic, or chart to explain a concept, I would appreciate it!

I am part of the Net Generation and love social networking opportunities and the ability to use the Internet and computer for my studies. How will you address my generation?

I learn best by actively engaging in the class. Are you able to provide varied learning experiences for me?

I work a part time job 15 hours a week, look after my ailing grandmother and am a leader in my youth group. I come to your class wanting to learn but have a busy life beyond class.

I have a different cultural background than my peers and this affects my learning. Are you prepared to address a variety of cultures in the classroom?

C. Course Details

Why are Course Details Important?

It is important to have an understanding of the course and its history. Knowing how the course fits into the bigger picture of the program will allow you to tailor content and assignments to meet students' needs and graduation requirements. If you conduct a short investigation into the course background, you can find a lot of information and resources that will help you in planning.

Where to Find More Info:

- Department heads and supervisors will be able to give you a good overview of the course

- Faculty who have been in the department for a number of years

- Administrative personnel

- Academic advisors as they will know about the course from the student perspective

Questions to Ask:

- Is this a course revision or a brand new course design?

- How long has this course been offered?

- Who has taught the course in the past?

- What sort of feedback do students give on the course?

- Is this a core course or an elective course?

- In what semesters has the course been typically offered?

- How does this course stack up against other courses in the students' timetables (e.g., is it typically a heavier course on readings, is it a more practical course or more a theory-oriented course)?

- How many students will likely be enrolled in your course?

- What day of the week and what time during the day is your class being offered?

- Is there content that you must cover in order to prepare students for other courses?

- Is this course being taught by other instructors who may need to work with you on achieving some consistencies?

- Does this course come with TAs (Teaching Assistants) or GAs (Graduate Assistants)?

- What role would a TA/GA play in terms of instruction and grading?

- Is there someone in the department who can assist you in course design?

D. Syllabus (Course Outline)

Why is the Syllabus (Course Outline) Important?

It is important to get a copy of the syllabus or course outline for the course you are about to plan. Often syllabi or outlines have to be turned into the office to be kept on file for legal and academic purposes. Copies can often be given to instructors. It helps to have a starting point. The syllabus lets you know what textbooks are used, what types of topics are covered and how the assessment is organized. If you have designed the course or know the syllabus very well, it is helpful to re-examine at it and consider if changes should be happening given the time that has passed since its design. The syllabus is like a contract between the student and the instructor and contains all the key information for the course. Obtaining other syllabi from your department will also show you formatting standards, policies and phrasing to include.

Where to Find More Info:

- Administrative assistants

- Department heads

- Instructor who previously taught the course
  (or is co-teaching the course with you)

Questions to Ask:

- Could you have a copy of the syllabus?

- Is it possible to alter the syllabus or is the content unable to be changed?

- When does the syllabus have to be submitted?

- Does someone have to approve the syllabus? What timeframe exists for approvals?

- Are there similar courses that might have an online syllabus to give you some ideas?

- Do you have to work with another faculty member to plan the syllabus?

- Are there standard pieces to the syllabus you must include?

- Can the syllabus be put online and not photocopied?

- Is there a specific format for the syllabus for your department/Faculty?

E. Faculty and Institution Policies

Why is it Important to Know about Faculty and Institution Policies?

It is important to know about all faculty and institutional policies as they pertain to teaching and learning. Sometimes new instructors are not aware of such policies and mid-way through the term encounter an issue and have to backtrack and learn about the policy. Oftentimes, policies are not shared or are forgotten, so it is important to be proactive and seek out the information ahead of time. Some faculties require reference to policies or the actual wording to appear in course syllabi and so once again it is necessary to be a sleuth and find out all you can.

Where to Find More Info:

- Department/faculty or institution web site

- Administrative personnel

- Institution academic calendar (some policies have to be approved by senior administration and shared with students through the calendar)

- Instructors who teach in your department

- Teaching and Learning Centres (they will often know about plagiarism and academic misconduct issues and policies)

Questions to Ask:

- **Plagiarism**: What are the policies on first and subsequent offenses?
  - Can you use a software tool to test for plagiarism?
  - Are there forms students must sign to have plagiarism checked?

- **Cheating:** What are the policies on catching students cheating? What are the steps you must take to deal with cheaters?
  - What are some tips for preventing cheating during mid-terms and exams?
  - What are the policies about students leaving exams and tests to use the washroom?
  - Can students use calculators or other resources during exams and tests?

- **Academic and professional misconduct:** What do the academic regulations say about students who violate safety regulations, harass others, or infringe on freedom and rights of other students?
  - How do you handle such offenses in your classroom?
  - To whom do you report such offenses?

- **Attendance/Absences:** Is there any policy or informal statement on how to deal with excessive absence in your class?
  - What are your expectations for dealing with students who have missed tests and need make-up opportunities?
  - Is there someone whom students need to see if they are going to miss a large chunk of your class?

- **Grading**: What are the policies around giving marks, submissions, and final grades?
  - Are there department or faculty percentage breakdowns for different types of assessment that happens during the course?
  - What is the grade appeal process?

- Can students repeat courses if they fail?
- Are there any set mid-terms or exams you need to use?
- Do you have to have a final exam in your course? If so, what are the policies on the type, length, and layout of your questions and the scheduling of your exam?

- **Autonomy:** What role will you have in shaping the course content and design?
  - Can you select the text and readings for this course or are they already pre-selected?

F. Textbook and Readings

Why are Textbook and Readings Important?

It is important to inquire about textbooks or course packs as it often takes months to obtain permissions and order materials. If you are hired at the last minute, this is an area to investigate immediately. Maybe the textbook has already been ordered? If it has been ordered, this will impact your design and implementation of the course. It is also important to find out about readings or course packs as they may take time to alter or create an updated version. Lastly, you will find it helpful to contact publishers and find out about online versions of the text and any supporting teacher/student materials.

Where to Find More Info:

- Administrative personnel or faculty
- Syllabus from previous instructor
- Bookstore (often they will know if a textbook has been ordered and the date it is expected to be on the shelves for purchasing)
- Publisher (often provide instructor with a free desk copy to have for planning and in advance of the bookstore shipment)

Questions to Ask:

- Has there been a textbook for this course before?
- What is the textbook information? (e.g., author(s), version/edition, publisher)?
- Is the textbook available online (or a portion of it) along with any additional teaching/learning materials to enhance content?
  - Is the publisher able to provide web-enhanced portions, notes, chapter summaries, and other digital material?
- What is the student cost of the textbook once taxes and institutional costs are considered?
- Are there additional readings or a course pack of readings for this course?
- What are the procedures for ordering textbooks (from publisher and institution bookstore) and who are the people you need to speak to?
- How was the textbook used in the course when it was offered before?

- Is it the main source of information or is it used as supplementary reading?

- Is it necessary to have a textbook for the course? (sometimes we assume that everyone needs a textbook but there are other options for teaching without texts)
  - Does the publisher offer alternatives for student materials (e.g., chapters from selected texts bundled into one unique textbook)?
  - Can your institutional bookstore bundle together readings that fit within copyright policies and sell the 'course pack' to students?

G. Classroom Layout

Why is Classroom Layout Important?

It is important to know where you will be teaching. The layout and design of the room could affect how you plan for group work, student presentations, and how you will interact with the students. It is important to know the room location and conduct a little trip to check it out. Even if this is a room you know well, it is prudent to double check on any additions or upgrades. It is also important to check your room at least two weeks prior to start of class and the day or two prior. Things can change at the last minute (e.g., chairs missing or a microphone not working) and it is helpful to find solutions and plan accordingly.

Where to Find More Info:

- Administrative personnel or faculty

- Scheduling Department often has specifications on rooms and can inform you about capacity, equipment, layout etc.

- Audio Visual Department can also give you insights into how your room functions in terms of data projectors, audio, screens etc.

Questions to Ask:

- Is this a classroom with desks/chairs on various levels or are all on the same level?

- Do the desks move or are they affixed to the floor?

- What audio visual elements are included in the classroom (e.g., data projector, lighting, overhead projector, DVD/CD player, wireless microphone, screen, etc)?
  - Are there passwords or keys required to open cabinets to access material?
  - Are there training sessions to use more sophisticated AV materials?

- Is there any natural sunlight entering the room?
  - Are there blinds to block out the light?

- ▪ Can windows be opened to let in fresh air?
- Is there a podium or an instructor area?
  - ▪ What do you need to bring that isn't there (e.g., whiteboard markers, erasers, chalk, plugs, network cable, laptop, etc.)? Where and how do you sign out or gain access to these resources if you do not have them?
  - ▪ How does an instructor connect to the data projector?
- Is there Internet access in your classroom?
  - ▪ Will students be able to access wired or wireless connectivity?
  - ▪ Where are the plugs in the classroom for power or do you have to use battery power?

H. Technology

Why is Technology Important?

It is important to find out about technology as it is a pervasive teaching and learning tool today. It takes time to acquire specific technologies for teaching in the classroom and time to learn new hardware and software. Being aware of some of the questions will help you decide how you will use technology in your course.

Where to Find More Info:

- Faculty in department
- Department Head or supervisor
- Audio Visual/Technology Department
- Teaching and Learning Centers

Questions to Ask:

- Is there a computer in the classroom in which I will be teaching?
  - ▪ What is required to access any computer hardware/software?
  - ▪ Who do I call if there is a problem while I am teaching?
- Can I bring my own laptop (or institution laptop) into the classroom and have success in connecting to all the audio and visual components?
  - ▪ Are there any passwords, firewalls, or special access I need for getting the Internet on my personal laptop (or institution laptop) in the class?
  - ▪ Who do I call if I am having problems connecting my laptop?
  - ▪ Are there instructors available to help or are there training sessions I can attend?
- How robust will the Internet connection be at the time I am teaching?

- Can I access my files from a central location while at home/teaching?
  - Is there a VPN (virtual private network) access?
- Are there any policies or requirements for using technology in teaching?

I. Web Space and Learning Management Software

Why is Web Space and Learning Management Software Important?

Most institutions have a learning management system (LMS) or an online portal for hosting course content, discussion boards and messaging systems for students. Blackboard, Moodle and Desire2Learn are some of the common systems. It is important to find out about the LMS at your institution and the policies and parameters about its use, as it will take time to gain access, put up content and learn about all the details. If you have good web page design skills, you might want to consider creating your own course web site. Not taking this section to heart could mean your students may see you as not being prepared or organized in your teaching.

Where to Find More Info:

- Teaching and Learning Centers often offer workshops on getting started with online learning systems
- Technology departments are often in charge of hosting the software and ensuring all are able to gain access
- Faculty in your department are excellent people — they are the front line users and will know the ins and outs of using the system

Questions to Ask?

- Is there a learning management system (LMS) component (e.g., Blackboard, Moodle, etc.) associated with your course?
  - What are the department/institutional expectations about using the LMS?
- When will you be able to gain access to design the environment and upload materials?
- Are there training sessions available for faculty needing assistance?
- Are there any instructors who might be willing to help with quick questions concerning any digital uploading, online course design, or troubleshooting?
- How much space do you have for uploading content?
- Can you gain access to faculty web space to upload additional content or create a web site for your course instead of using the LMS or in addition to it?
- How well do videos and heavier digital content work within the LMS?
  - Can the LMS take video files or do you need another server space?
- Will students be emailing you through the LMS or do they normally do it through your insti-

tutional email address?

- How do other instructors use the LMS?
  - Should you consider similar uses of the system to be consistent?

J. Teaching and Learning Resources

Why are Teaching and Learning Resources Important?

It is important to find useful resources for teaching and learning in your course. It will be helpful to source out any previously used resources and ask about any new ones so that you have a good start when planning your course. You may also want to find out if there is any budget set aside for course resources and how you might access them.

Where to Find More Info:

- Syllabus (books, journals, web materials)

- Faculty in your department (there may be resources that are applicable to a variety of courses that you can use)

- Librarians (they are excellent people to talk to about current books, periodicals, and other resources that may assist you in teaching your course or assist your students)

Questions to Ask:

- What resources were used to teach this course before?

- Is there any budget money for this course to purchase additional resources?
  - What is the procedure for requesting resources?

- What resources are being used by other instructors at other institutions who teach similar courses?

- What online resources exist that might be helpful?

- What books, journals, magazines, or digital resources might be available in the library?

Top Ten Takeaways

1. **Importance:** It is important to investigate your course before you get started on planning. Time spent now gathering answers to questions about the course will make planning your course much easier.

2. **Students:** Acquire information about your students. This will help you develop a course that meets their needs and plans for their optimal learning.

3. **Course Details:** Know how the course fits within the whole program. This will allow you to tailor assignments and projects to benefit students and their learning.

4. **Syllabus/Course Outline:** Obtain a copy of the course syllabus or course outline, if you can. This will help you get a head start on possible topics, assessment, and resource ideas.

5. **Faculty and Institutional Policies:** Understand academic regulations and policies about misconduct, plagiarism, cheating, and other issues. This will allow you to include important information in your syllabus/course outline and will help you be prepared should you need to act.

6. **Textbook and Readings:** Gather information about textbooks and readings. This will give you time to order copies, acquaint yourself with content, and incorporate the content effectively into your course.

7. **Classroom Layout:** Know what your classroom looks like. This will help you prepare to have students work with each other, have effective discussions, and will enable you to teach properly within the learning space.

8. **Technology:** Technology is part of every instructor's teaching repertoire. Because of the complexities of using technology, it is advisable to be prepared and know what is possible and not possible to do during your course.

9. **Web Space/Learning Management System:** Most institutions have a learning management system (LMS) or an opportunity to host web pages with course content. Ensure you connect with the technology support staff at your institution to find out how you can get all or parts of your course in a digital format.

10. **Teaching and Learning Resources:** An instructor needs resources for effective teaching and to share with students for their learning. Do a thorough search of all available resources and seek out new and current materials before planning your course.

Next Steps

1. Go through each of the sections and ask the questions.

2. Sit down with a department head and ask some of the more detailed and institutionally related questions.

3. Create a space in your office or at home to collect resources, paperwork, and other materials. Have pre-labeled file folders for each of the sections.

4. Spend some time online finding instructors who teach similar courses and see what they teach, how they teach it, and what sorts of assignments and projects they include in their courses.

5. Take time to think about the answers you get about your course. You will be better able to make well informed course decisions if you consider all the information you have gathered.

References and Resources

Davis, B. G. (2009). *Tools for Teaching*. San Francisco, CA: Jossey-Bass. (see Chapter 1: Designing or Revising a Course for some additional tips and suggestions)

Carnegie Mellon University (n.d.). *Recognize who your students are.* Retrieved November 27, 2009, from http://www.cmu.edu/teaching/designteach/design/yourstudents.html

Carnegie Mellon University (n.d.). *Consider timing and logistics.* Retrieved November 27, 2009, from http://www.cmu.edu/teaching/designteach/design/logistics.html

Carnegie Mellon University (n.d.). *Identify the situational constraints.* Retrieved November 27, 2009, from http://www.cmu.edu/teaching/designteach/design/constraints.html

Chapter 2: Determining Goals & Learning Objectives

Chapter Overview

- **A.** Determining Overall Goals
- **B.** The Basics of Learning Objectives
- **C.** Categories of Learning: Creating a Variety of Objectives
- **D.** Performance Verbs Used in the Creation of Learning Objectives
- **E.** How Do You Write Learning Objectives?
- **F.** Checkpoints for Good Learning Objectives
- **G.** Find the Well-Written Objectives

Chapter 1 focused on gathering facts and details about your course to enable you to effectively look at all the material and begin to create or refine your goals and learning objectives.

The course goals and learning objectives help guide you through planning the course and help students know what is expected of them. This chapter helps you design and develop goals and learning objectives. Many educational institutions place great importance on this step in the course design process. Goals and learning objectives are key components to revisit each time you teach your course.

By taking some time to think through the goals and objectives of your course, you will be giving students a better course. When assessment and evaluation methods are directly linked to course objectives, students are provided with opportunities to demonstrate how their learning matches the intent of the course. Ensure you include learning opportunities for students to demonstrate a wide range of thinking skills. A simple chart is included in the chapter, along with examples and verbs to help you design a greater variety of learning objectives for your course.

The chapter begins by defining overall course goals. The remainder of the chapter will focus on steps to writing effective learning objectives.

A. Determining Overall Goals

After you have gathered all the details and facts about your course, you need to set aside some time to consider a few overall goals for your course. Goals are different than learning objectives. Goals are broader while learning objectives are more specific. Goals are sometimes called aims or outcomes.

Definition:

- Goals describe concepts that act like a large umbrella overarching your whole course

- Goals serve to inform students what 'big picture' content you will be covering

Benefits of Goals:

- assists you in keeping the 'main purpose' of course in mind while planning

- helps students so they know the main ideas for studying

- gives the department head/supervisor and others who read your syllabus a quick overview of the course for discussion and planning purposes

- allows academic planning and program design people to ensure your course fits within degree and diploma requirements

Sample Goals:

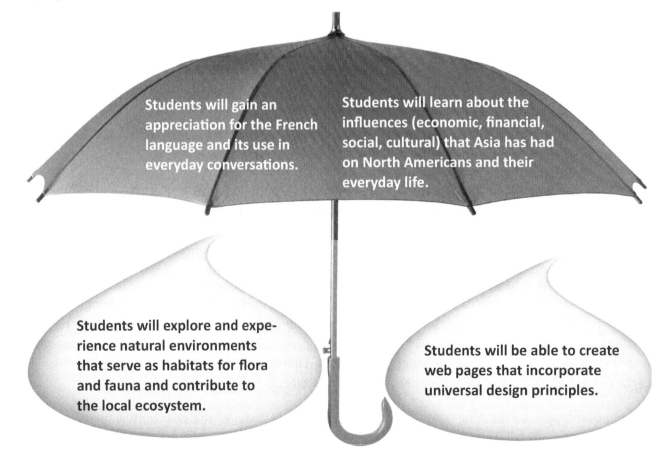

Students will gain an appreciation for the French language and its use in everyday conversations.

Students will learn about the influences (economic, financial, social, cultural) that Asia has had on North Americans and their everyday life.

Students will explore and experience natural environments that serve as habitats for flora and fauna and contribute to the local ecosystem.

Students will be able to create web pages that incorporate universal design principles.

B. The Basics of Learning Objectives

1. What Are They?

Learning objectives are...

- statements about anticipated student learning after the course has been completed

- essential knowledge and skills required by students to demonstrate learning

- like a 'road map' to show the instructor and students where they are headed and what stops they will be making along the way

- written when you are designing or revising courses

- important to include on your syllabus and should always be explained to students

2. How Do They Fit Within The Course Design?

The learning objectives are tied to the assessment and evaluation methods, along with the teaching and learning strategies.

Consider the learning objectives first, before your other methods and strategies are chosen.

Keep the learner front and center at all times during the planning process.

3. What Are The Parts?

A well written learning objective has **three parts:** Performance, Condition, and Criteria.

Part 1: Performance
The student often has to 'perform' something to demonstrate his/her learning. The performance must

- be measurable and observable

- be connected to aligned assessment methods

- easily indicate what the student will know or be able to do

- include an action verb to convey what the students will be doing

It is important to consider a wide variety of learning objectives for your course. Two charts, based on Bloom's Taxonomies (Bloom, 1964) and found later in this chapter in Sections C and D, are helpful resources to assist you in designing learning objectives.

In 1956, Benjamin Bloom and his colleagues developed a framework for organizing learning objectives into three domains (affective, cognitive and psychomotor) (Anderson & Krathwohl, 2001). Most educators have heard about the cognitive domain, but Bloom's other two domains (affective and psychomotor) are presented for a complete chart for developing learning objectives. Ensure you do not just focus on the cognitive domain, but fully consider what you want your students to be able to know and do by the end of the course.

Although this framework is over 50 years old and there are other taxonomies out there, educators world-wide continue to use Bloom's Taxonomy when developing courses and programs. In 2001, Lorin Anderson and David Krathwohl revised Bloom's Taxonomy based on new knowledge and research in education that informed us about how students learn and the connection to teaching, assessment and evaluation strategies. The revisions resulted in a more in depth look at each of the taxonomy categories. Bloom's original work is presented here as it serves the purpose of this chapter, but if you wish to explore this further consult "A Taxonomy for Learning, Learning and Assessing: A Revision of Bloom's Taxonomy of Educational Objectives" (2001).

The following are a few phrases that you should try to avoid when you are writing learning objectives. The following phrases are simply too vague or unable to be measured in terms of learning.

x Appreciation for	x Knows
x Awareness of	x Has knowledge of
x Capable of	x Learns
x Comprehend	x Likes
x Conscious of	x Memorizes
x Familiar with	x Understands
x Shows interest in	x Will be able to

Part 2: Conditions

The learning objective should contain conditions or circumstances for learning to occur such as

- setting/situation/format under which the student will demonstrate the learning (in the classroom, in the field, in a research project, in a written assignment, in a poem)

- materials/tools be used (translation dictionary, library database of journal articles, calculator, web site, reference guide, subject specific software)

Part 3: Criteria

The learning objective should include specific details about the minimum criteria expected for performance such as
- type of performance (written, spoken, visual, graphical)

- quantity of items to include (three pieces of evidence, number of pages, number of sections, length of essay)

- quality of items (choice of resources used, relevancy of items)

- accuracy (spelling and grammar errors)

4. What Might Sample Learning Objectives Look Like?

Here are five examples of well-written learning objectives.

1. By the end of this course, the student will be able to use proper grammar, sentence structure, and spelling on the final essay and exam.

2. By the end of this course, the student will be able to correctly write and balance chemistry equations using chemistry laws.

3. When this course is over, students should be able to outline and explain three tests environmentalists use to determine the level of soil contamination in a former industrial site.

4. By the end of this course, the student will be able to create a rating system, related to ten key instructional design principles, to evaluate five online learning tools.

5. By the end of this course, the student will be able to identify and describe five key impacts the Internet has had on social and business networking activities.

C. Categories of Learning: Creating a Variety of Learning Objectives

	Affective (Feelings/Attitudes)	Cognitive (Mental Skills/Knowledge)	Psychomotor (Manual/Physical Skills)
Lower Levels of Learning	**Overview** The student is aware of the situation and is able to control attention to it. The student also is able to be actively involved in the situation and has appropriate responses. **Examples** *Respectfully listens to group leader. Participates in discussions and suggests new ideas. Assists colleagues with tasks.*	**Overview** The student retrieves and recalls basic information from memory. Students show their ability to construct meaning from material that results in demonstrating comprehension. This knowledge provides the foundation for other kinds of learning. **Examples** *Recites a poem. Translates a foreign language paragraph. Explains in own words how to perform the experiment.*	**Overview** The student uses sensory clues to inform his/her motor activity. The student is ready to act and is set to take on a task. **Examples** *Able to operate a simple tool. Copy or create art after taking lessons from an instructor. Shows basic balance beam movements with some assistance.*
Medium Levels of Learning	**Overview** The student has a set of internalized values and is able to accept and have commitment to a value. **Examples** *Shows sensitivity towards others in awkward situations. Shows problem solving abilities when a situation has arisen.*	**Overview** The student is able to demonstrate an application of knowledge. The student is also able to break down, examine and analyze information. **Examples** *Applies formula to a new set of variables. Uses a spreadsheet to calculate taxes. Compares two magazine design proposals in terms of pros/cons.*	**Overview** The student practices a simple skill under the supervision of instructor. The student moves on to carry out that skill by demonstrating confidence and proficiency. The student moves to handling more complex tasks in a smooth manner. **Examples** *With fewer errors and through co-ordination of many actions, a final video cut is produced with sound and graphics.*
Higher Levels of Learning	**Overview** The student is able to organize values, resolve conflicts and create a new value system. In addition, the student is able to develop a consistent response to a set of values and use them in a variety of situations. **Examples** *Accepts responsibility for one's learning and behavior. Adjusts behavior when new information is presented.*	**Overview** The student is able to problem solve and make judgments through evaluating and supporting information along with creating and designing new knowledge. **Examples** *Designs a new experiment to test a concept. Justifies the choice of a position on an issue. Evaluates and ranks the arguments for immediate climate change.*	**Overview** The student adapts motor responses when encountering new situations and problems. The student is also able to create new motor responses for adapting when new skill sets are required. **Examples** *Demonstrates advanced and natural movements of tennis strokes without having to take time to think and react.*

Clark, D (2010)

D. Performance Verbs Used in the Creation of Learning Objectives

	Affective (Feelings/Attitudes)		Cognitive (Mental Skills/Knowledge)			Psychomotor (Manual/Physical Skills)	
Lower Levels of Learning	Aid Ask Assist Attempt Choose Conform Discuss Follow Give	Identity Locate Name Observe Perform Question Report Request Respond	Cite Define Estimate Find List Name Recognize Rephrase Select State Transfer Acquire	Clarify Describe Explain Identify Locate Outline Record Report Show Summarize Translate Memorize	Choose Draw File Label Match Recall Relate Review Sort Tell Write Repeat	Choose Detect Differentiate Display Distinguish Explain Identify Isolate Link	Listen Observe Point To Proceed React Relate Respond Select Show
Medium Levels of Learning	Accept Appreciate Choose Complete Concern Demonstrate Describe Differentiate	Distinguish Explain Express Invite Join Justify Propose Share	Adjust Apply Classify Differentiate Examine Illustrate Inspect Modify Prepare Question Tabulate Use Survey Contrast Organize	Alter Calculate Compare Discriminate Extract Infer Investigate Order Produce Separate Test Dissect Probe Detect Translate	Analyze Categorize Compute Distinguish Extrapolate Interpret Manipulate Predict Relate Solve Uncover Verify Inquire Deduce	Adjust Assemble Build Calibrate Close Construct Disconnect Dismantle Dissect Draw Duplicate	Grind Heat Load Loosen Manipulate Mend Open Organize Replace Rotate Select Sort
Higher Levels of Learning	Act Arrange Adhere Change Compare Contrast Demonstrate Formulate Generalize	Integrate Influence Mediate Organize Propose Qualify Revise Solve Synthesize	Appraise Assess Compile Choose Construct Design Develop Formulate Implement Justify Propose Rate Reorder Revise Synthesize	Approve Build Compose Conclude Create Devise Diagnose Generate Indicate Organize Prove Rearrange Research Support Transform	Assemble Combine Conceive Confirm Criticize Discover Evaluate Integrate Judge Plan Rank Recommend Resolve Structure Validate	Adapt Alter Build Create Change Combine Compose Construct	Design Devise Initiate Modify Originates Rearrange Reorganize Revise

Gross & MacKeracher. (n.d)

E. How Do You Write Learning Objectives?

Performance: organize and developing

By the end of the course, the student will be able to organize and develop a written seven-step plan for undertaking a small research project.

Criteria: written and it will include seven steps

Condition: framed around a research project

Performance: apply and then analyze

By the end of the course, the student will be able to apply 4 architectural principles (building type, architectural style, materials and technological components) of an analysis of mystery buildings and make evidence-supported hypotheses as to why the buildings were designed in the way they were.

Condition: evidence-supported hypotheses

Criteria: 4 principles

Performance: construct

By the end of the course, the student will be able to construct a timely response to written or spoken message in a manner that ensures effective communication and professional conduct for an office situation.

Criteria: using effective communication and professional conduct, timely manner

Condition: response to a written or spoken message

F. Checkpoints for Good Learning Objectives

Consider the following checklist to see if you have created good learning objectives.

✔ S – Specific

Learning objectives need to be more specific than goals as they indicate exactly what you want the students to be able to do and how they will demonstrate their learning. Being specific also means you focus on one learning activity per each objective.

✔ R – Realistic

Learning objectives need to be realistic and related to the real-world. Students want to know that they are learning things that make sense and will help them after the course.

✔ A –Attainable

Learning objectives need to be attainable so that all students have the opportunity to be successful. In other words, do not make the objectives so difficult or unattainable that most of the students cannot reach them by the end of the course.

✔ M – Measurable

Learning objectives need to be measurable, not vague. This means that you need an assessment method that will measure the level of student success in relation to the learning objective. For example, do not use "students will understand...." Or "students will gain an appreciation of ....." – make your objectives more observable.

✔ A – Active Verbs

Learning objectives should include an action-related verb which will directly relate to what the students are doing. See the chart in Section D (in this chapter) for a list of action verbs that will help you in writing your objectives.

✔ R – Relevant

Learning objectives need to be relevant to the course, to the students, and to the way the learning is going to be structured. Consider the course goals, course content, and the students' interests and abilities to make your learning objectives as relevant as possible.

✔ S – Student-Centered

Learning objectives need to focus on the student at all times. Begin your learning objectives with the phrase "By the end of this course, the student will be able...".

G. Find the Well-Written Learning Objectives

Activity: The following page contains some well-written learning objectives and some poorly written learning objectives. Can you tell the difference? Put a check beside the learning objectives that have been well-written. Consider how you could improve the poorly written objectives. Answers are along the left side.

1. Students will be able to describe broad trends in energy consumption over the past ten years in North America.

2. Students will be able to identify primary and secondary sources of evidence in a written report or paper.

3. You should be able to operate the various saws in the shop in a safe and productive manner without assistance.

4. Students will know all about biology and have an appreciation for how it impacts their lives.

5. By the end of the course the students will be able to identify the countries and culture groups currently existing in the Caribbean.

6. When this course is over you should be able to create and deliver a slideshow presentation following the design guidelines for effective training.

7. By the end of the course students will understand the main concepts of economics, will see how economics impacts their lives and will just know the basic facts.

8. After the course is over, each student will be able to shoot, edit and produce a 5 minute video using current AV equipment and resources.

9. You will be familiar with the processes and products of the gas and oil industry.

10. Students will show an interest in studying the many works of Shakespeare.

Well-written: 1, 2, 5, 6 & 8

Top Ten Takeaways

1. **Goal Definition:** Goals are broad, big picture concepts that act as an umbrella hovering over your course.

2. **Learning Objective Definition:** Learning objectives are more specific statements about the learning of students by the end of the course.

3. **Alignment:** Learning objectives are aligned with the assessment and evaluation methods and the teaching and learning strategies.

4. **Parts of a Learning Objective**: A well-written learning objective has three parts: Performance component (an action verb to describe what students are doing); Condition for learning (a description of the setting, tools or situation under which the learning happens); and Criteria (any specific details about the learning such as the quality, quantity, accuracy, or format of performance).

5. **Categories of Learning:** While there are a number of ways to categorize the types of learning in which students can become engaged, generally most educators work with models that are rooted in Benjamin Bloom's three areas (Affective: feeling/emotions; Cognitive: mental thinking/knowledge; Psychomotor: manual/physical skills).

6. **Psychomotor Category:** Most often instructors just focus on the cognitive area, but if you are teaching courses that require students to perform tasks, operate machinery, demonstrate physical skills, etc., then consider the psychomotor area as well.

7. **Affective Category:** Instructors often shy away from considering the affective area of learning due to the challenge in assessing/evaluating the learning. There is more awareness in education about trying to get students to understand themselves, their learning, their reactions to and emotions associated with certain subjects/jobs.

8. **Action Verbs:** There are verbs that are associated with each of the categories and span the levels from lower thinking objectives to higher thinking objectives. It is prudent to consider a variety of learning levels in a course for optimal learning.

9. **Worth the Effort:** Writing learning objectives takes time but is a very worthwhile activity to help organize your thinking before planning course content, grading schemes and layout of the lessons.

10. **Use Checklist:** Once you have your learning objectives written, there is a checklist you can use to see if your objectives need some tweaking.

Next Steps

1. Read through any goals and objectives you may have already for your course.

2. Spend time thinking about what you truly want students to learn in your course. Jot down some ideas while you are pondering this topic.

3. Consider the goals of your course as big concepts. Are your goals really in tune with today's student, the world we live in and are clearly connected to the course content?

4. Glance over the various learning categories and the lower to higher level thinking verbs and associated examples. Could your course have a broader range of objectives?

5. By looking at the learning objective samples, try writing or rewriting just one or two and see if the objective meets some of the criteria.

References and Resources

Anderson, L.W. & Krathwohl, D. R. (Eds.) (2001). *A taxonomy for learning, teaching and assessing: A revision of Bloom's taxonomy of educational objectives*. New York, NY: Longman.

Bloom, B.S. (1984). *Taxonomy of educational objectives. Book I: Cognitive domain* (revised edition). New York, NY: Longman.

Bloom, B.S., Krathwohl, D.R. & Masia, B.M. (1964). *Taxonomy of educational objectives. Book 2: Affective domain.* New York, NY: Longman.

Clarke, D. R. (2006, May 26). *Bloom's taxonomy of learning domains: The three types of learning*. Retrieved December 17, 2009, from http://www.sos.net/~donclark/hrd/bloom.html

Gross, P. & MacKeracher, D. (n.d.). *Writing learning objectives.* Retrieved April 22, 2011, from http://www.unb.ca/fredericton/cetl/_resources/pdf/writinglearningobjectives.pdf from the Centre for Enhanced Teaching and Learning, UNB Fredericton.

Simpson, E.J. (1972). *The classification of education objectives in the psychomotor domain.* Washington, DC: Gryphon House.

Chapter 3: Aligning Assessment & Evaluation

Chapter Overview

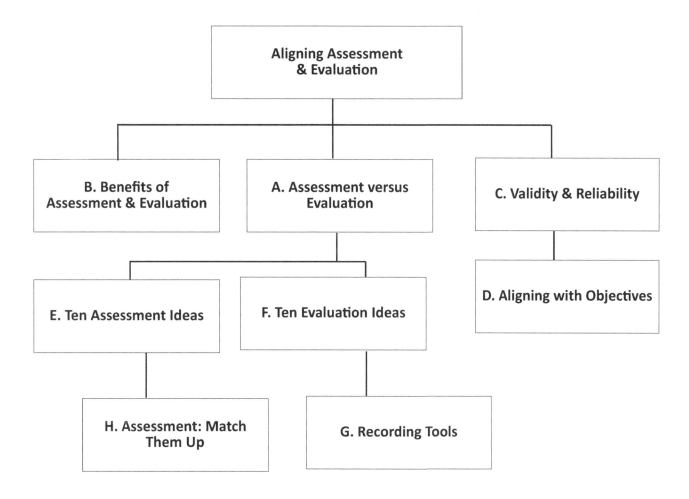

Wiggins and McTighe (2005) have been widely published on the concept of planning with the end in mind, also known as 'backwards planning'. It is 'backwards' because it is the opposite of what most instructors have tended to do, which is often to start with deciding on content, choosing teaching and learning strategies, thinking of objectives, and then designing a test or exam. Backwards planning revolves around planning the assessment first and then deciding on everything else. After learning objectives are solidified, instructors need to determine how they will know if students have learned and what specific demonstrations of learning will be accepted as evidence.

The words assessment and evaluation are often used interchangeably in educational conversations; however, they have very unique characteristics. This chapter begins by exposing those differences and offering examples of ten assessment and ten evaluation methods. A chart has been designed to indicate how you can align the methods with the intended purpose of the objectives. Lastly, this chapter will look at three recording tools (i.e., rating scales, checklists, and rubrics) that will help you gather marks and provide feedback to students.

A. Assessment versus Evaluation: What's the Difference?

Assessment

Sometimes called **formative assessment**

Assessment **as** learning (helping students self-monitor, self-assess)

Assessment **for** learning (to inform instructors about their instruction)

Informal gathering of data for feedback to students and instructor

No marks or **grades** are attached to assessment

More needed in secondary and post-secondary classrooms

Takes **little time** to conduct

Huge impact on student **learning** throughout course

Evaluation

Sometimes called **summative assessment**

Assessment **of** learning (with a purpose of reporting, making decisions)

Formal gathering of data for feedback to students and instructor

Results in the giving of **grades, marks, levels** – giving a value to learning

Frequently done in secondary and post-secondary education

Takes some **time** to conduct

Impact on learning - if evaluation includes **feedback** on where **improvements** could be made and marks/comments are **returned before end of course** then high impact on student learning

B. Benefits of Assessment & Evaluation

The primary purpose of assessment and evaluation is to improve student learning. Here is a short summary of the benefits as they pertain to the students and the instructor.

Students

- Gives student information about how they are doing in the course
- Assessment activities will provide more immediate feedback on a weekly basis
- Provides motivation for further learning
- Opens doors for identifying strengths for future careers

Instructors

- Provides feedback on what is being learned/not learned by students
- Curriculum and instructional strategies are easily adapted with feedback
- Modifications for next class can be quickly made with student input
- Gain information about struggling students and where to direct attention
- Allows for aligning the evaluation more closely with student progress

C. Validity & Reliability

When considering your assessment and evaluation methods, do not overlook the importance of reliability and validity. Here is a summary and example of each.

Validity is the ability of the assessment or evaluation instrument to measure what it is intended to measure. Carefully consider what it is you want students to learn and match that with the appropriate instrument.

Example: If you want to see if students know how to properly operate a specialized microscope...

Good: *...set up lab times for students to come in and demonstrate their knowledge on the actual microscope and how to operate it under certain conditions*

Poor: *...have students fill in the blanks on a diagram of the microscope found on a paper and pencil test*

Reliability is the ability of an assessment or evaluation instrument to be used in various classes with various students and achieve similar results.

Example: If you have designed a multiple choice test with 50 questions, every time you administer the test to your class – over the years...

Good: *...you generally get similar results, final mark breakdown is fairly consistent and there are no vague or poorly worded questions that constantly stump students*

Poor: *...you get varied results, final mark breakdown is not consistent and upon examination you find some vague and poorly worded questions that seem to always cause students to get the same questions incorrect*

D. Aligning with Objectives

The following chart demonstrates how to align your assessment and evaluation with your learning objectives. Keep it handy when you are planning your course.

Performance-related action verbs are in the first column. These come from the learning objectives and would relate to 'what' the students are doing to demonstrate their learning.

Suggested assessment and evaluation methods are in the second and third columns and are more fully explained throughout the rest of the chapter. While there are many other assessment and evaluation methods available, only a maximum of ten are presented for each method.

Learning Objective Focus	Assessment Method	Evaluation Method
Recalling Recognizing Identifying Listing Naming Choosing	➤ Prior Knowledge Survey ➤ Self-Assessment Quiz ➤ Question and Answer Discussion ➤ I am in the Fog About…. ➤ Whiteboard Charades Game ➤ Ticket out the Door	➤ Demonstration / Experiment ➤ Quiz, Test or Exam Questions: Multiple choice, True/False, Matching, Labeling diagrams
Explaining Paraphrasing Summarizing Outlining Describing	➤ Prior Knowledge Survey ➤ Self-Assessment Quiz ➤ Question and Answer Discussion ➤ Operation Outline ➤ I am in the Fog About…. ➤ Whiteboard Charades Game ➤ Ticket out the Door ➤ Conference	➤ Demonstration / Experiment ➤ Learning Log / Blog/ Digital Portfolio ➤ Case Study ➤ Presentation ➤ Essay / Research Paper / Report / Wiki ➤ Quiz, Test or Exam Questions: Multiple choice, Short Answer, Long Answer
Applying Calculating Solving Translating Manipulating	➤ Prior Knowledge Survey ➤ Self-Assessment Quiz ➤ Question and Answer Discussion ➤ Operation Outline ➤ I am in the Fog About…. ➤ Concept Map ➤ Whiteboard Charades Game ➤ Ticket out the Door ➤ Conference	➤ Artistic, Dramatic, Audio/Video, Musical or Web Composition ➤ Model / Diagram / Sketch / Map ➤ Prototype/Working Example ➤ Problem-Based Project ➤ Demonstration / Experiment ➤ Learning Log /Blog / Digital Portfolio ➤ Case Study ➤ Presentation ➤ Essay / Research Paper / Report / Wiki ➤ Quiz, Test or Exam Questions: Multiple Choice, Short or Long Answer

Analyzing Comparing Categorizing Differentiating Uncovering Verifying Organizing	➤ Self-Assessment Quiz ➤ Question and Answer Discussion ➤ Operation Outline ➤ I am in the Fog About…. ➤ Concept Map ➤ Chart it Up ➤ Whiteboard Charades Game ➤ Ticket out the Door ➤ Conference	➤ Artistic, Dramatic, Audio/Video, Musical or Web Composition ➤ Model / Diagram / Sketch / Map ➤ Prototype/Working Example ➤ Problem-Based Project ➤ Demonstration / Experiment ➤ Learning Log / Blog / Digital Portfolio ➤ Case Study ➤ Presentation ➤ Essay / Research Paper/ Report / Wiki ➤ Quiz, Test or Exam Questions: Multiple Choice, Matching, Short or Long Answer
Assessing Evaluating Judging Justifying Recommending Validating	➤ Self-Assessment Quiz ➤ Question and Answer Discussion ➤ Concept Map ➤ Chart it Up ➤ Ticket out the Door ➤ Conference	➤ Artistic, Dramatic, Audio/Video, Musical or Web Composition ➤ Model / Diagram / Sketch / Map ➤ Problem-Based Project ➤ Learning Log / Blog / Digital Portfolio ➤ Case Study ➤ Presentation ➤ Essay / Research Paper / Report / Wiki ➤ Quiz, Test or Exam Questions: Long Answer
Creating Composing Constructing Building Synthesizing Designing Devising Developing	➤ Self-Assessment Quiz ➤ I am in the Fog About…. ➤ Concept Map ➤ Ticket out the Door	➤ Artistic, Dramatic, Audio/Video, Musical or Web Composition ➤ Model / Diagram / Sketch / Map ➤ Prototype / Working Example ➤ Problem-Based Project ➤ Learning Log / Blog / Digital Portfolio ➤ Essay / Research Paper / Report / Wiki

E. Ten Assessment Ideas: Gathering Informal Feedback

Instructors are always encouraged to include more assessment activities in their classes. Assessment should not take a long time to conduct and should provide fairly instant feedback for both students and instructors. Try a few of these ideas the next time in your class. Remember: These activities should not be graded or awarded marks, but rather should become part of the ongoing assessment you conduct for informing students about their learning.

1. Prior Knowledge Survey

This is a short survey you give students at the beginning of your course or before any new unit or topic. It alerts students to topics the course will cover and gives them a chance to share what they already know.

- Focus questions on the level of knowledge in the course (e.g., basic facts, assumptions, understandings, misconceptions)

- Ask about a dozen questions to gauge background in key concepts

- Phrase questions as multiple choice or true/false questions for easy feedback - possibly include a few open-ended questions

- Alternative: Set up an online survey in your learning management system or through a free survey website – it is a fast and easy collection of data

- Share results as soon as you can - students will appreciate knowing the results of their input

2. Self-Assessment Quiz

This is a short quiz you create on previously taught content. It becomes an informal report about student progress.

- Set aside five minutes in class for students to complete

- Ask them to use half a scrap sheet of paper

- Create a few questions for students. Include a rating scale for each question, with 1 being the lowest and 5 being the highest. Students rate how they are feeling about course content, about their understanding on certain topics and how comfortable they feel going into a mid-term or exam.

- Students are creating their own report card as they are really thinking about their own learning and where they need to improve

- Ask students to put their names on the self-assessment quiz and hand in for review

3. Question and Answer – Discussion

When you engage students in a good discussion framed with well-developed questions, you and your students gain a lot of information about what is being learned and where there is a need for further explanation.

- Post questions for students to consider (preferably before class so they can prepare) and display on overhead or slide during discussion

- The small group method is preferable for getting greater participation and makes more students feel comfortable enough to engage more – arrange into groups to discuss questions

- For large classes, have students work in smaller groups: appoint a reporter who will summarize the discussion and share with class

4. Operation Outline

This is a group activity where students work together to fill in the blanks found in an outline/handout you have created that focuses on key topics. It helps in determining how well students are understanding the course and gives students an idea of how to organize a study guide on key concepts.

- Organize students in groups of 4-5

- Allocate about ten minutes to complete this task

- Hand out an incomplete outline related to a recent topic

- To save paper, upload a digital version of the incomplete outline and have one student (with a laptop) download and be the recorder for their group

- The incomplete outline might include sub-titles, key concepts, important facts, and principles

- There has to be important content missing and the outline has to look incomplete

- The group's task is to scour their notes, text book, and possibly the Internet to fill in the outline – they should be able to use any resource to complete the task

- You can choose to take up the outline in class and share the complete version with your students or the you can collect and analyze for reporting on next class

5. I Am In The Fog About.....

This activity gives students an opportunity to express where they are confused, unsure, or feel they need help with concepts and components of the course. Students share with you where 'things are foggy'.

- Near the end of class, pass out a recipe card to each student and ask them to jot down anything they are in 'in the fog about' or require help with

- The responses are open-ended for obtaining any type of response

- By making activity anonymous, students will feel more comfortable to share

- Collect responses and quickly sort through them to identify key ideas

- This activity will help you in reframing future classes and re-emphasizing important concepts

6. Concept Map

Concept maps are wonderful ways for students to organize their understandings of a topic in a visual way. Students are also able to share their conceptual learning. Either on chart paper or in one of the many free concept mapping web sites, students will enjoy working with their peers and being creative with the map.

- Share some examples of a concept map

- Arrange students into small groups of 4-5

- Students depict the major themes and ideas of the course in an organization scheme that they create together

- A representative from each group shares the concept map with the class

- Could ask students to create a rough draft on their own concept map first - this might help the groups progress faster and with more discussion

- Uploading the maps to your course web site is a great way to share with your class

7. Charting It Up

Having students complete a chart is an excellent way to get feedback on what they are learning about conceptual relationships. A chart activity also provides students with another way to look at the course and use as a study guide.

	Concept 1	Concept 2
Similarities		
Differences		

- Arrange your class into small groups

- Give each group a chart which includes only the titles and subtitles for rows and columns

- The chart might be a pro/con chart for a topic, a chronological chart to outline key components according to a timeline, a comparison chart for looking at similarities and differences between concepts etc.

- Give groups a short amount of time to use their notes and Internet to complete the chart

- Charts can be posted around the room. Students get up and look at each chart or one student can summarize his/her group's chart in a presentation to the class

8. Whiteboard Charades Game

This is a fun activity that students always find valuable. Similar to a game show format, there are teams of students trying to guess the answer to a question about course content. It gets students out of their seats and working together. It gives them ideas about what they know well or where they need more work. This game works very well as a review session before a test or exam. Instead of using paper, try using small to medium-sized whiteboards with markers and a rag. You can purchase whiteboards at your office supply store, or head to your home renovation big box store and ask for shower stall lining/melamine sheets to be cut up into 2 foot X 2 foot sizes and you have a cheaper alternative!

- Create 20-30 questions that require a few words or a short phrase to answer

- Base the questions on content from a number of classes

- Divide class into groups of 4-5 students and ask them to sit near each other

- Ask each group member to number themselves off (e.g., either a 1, 2, 3, 4, or 5) within each group.

- Indicate that all the '1s' in the groups have the whiteboard/paper first and are the only ones for the first round that can write the answer

- Read the question and only the person with the pen/whiteboard can write the answer and everyone else is unable to speak

- The rest of the group can only do 'charades/acting' to try and get their group member to write down the correct answer. In this way, someone else in the group (who knows the answer) doesn't dominate and shout it out (and accidentally shares it with a group nearby)

- The whole class should be relatively quiet with group members doing charades (without any sounds and without writing on the board/paper) to figure out the correct answer

- Once a short period of time has passed (e.g., a minute), ask to see the answers by having students hold up their boards/paper high above their head. Award points to the groups who have the correct answer. Keep track so students are motivated to play

- Pen/whiteboard now moves to the number '2s' in the group. Continue as before until time is up or all the questions are asked

- Optional: have a fun reward for the group who had the most points

9. Ticket Out the Door

A ticket out the door is simply a sheet of paper on which students respond to questions and hand in before they leave class. The tickets are anonymous and provide instructors with a quick overview of what students are learning and where there are gaps.

- Near the end of class, ask students to get out half a scrap sheet of paper or photocopy a sheet with 'blank ticket' images on them and cut the paper in half

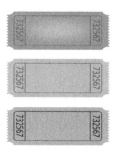

- Post two to three questions about the class you have just conducted

- You could ask both a lower thinking question that simply asks them to show they were listening and ask a higher thinking question that would require a few sentences to explain based on what was taught

- You want them to spend about 2- 5 minutes answering a couple of short questions

10. Conference

A conference is an out-of-class individual or small group meeting to ascertain how students are doing and provide feedback. Depending on your schedule and the number of students, organizing them into small groups (2-4) is an efficient way to meet many in shorter time periods.

- Ask students to sign up for a time

- Post a few questions you are going to ask the students; this gives them a heads-up on what to expect

- A conference provides a time to clarify points, to see if students are grasping concepts, and allows students to ask any questions

- Conferences could last 15 minutes and take place at any time throughout the course

- Students will appreciate the time you spend with them and your personalized feedback

- If you held conferences during the first half of the course, students would know where your office is and feel more comfortable to approach you for help

F. Ten Evaluation Ideas: Obtaining Formal Results

The following section outlines the methods you could use to formally assess students for grades and reporting. As we come to understand the students of this millennium, we need to provide many formats for them to demonstrate their learning. With that in mind, tests and exams are included, but are at the end of the list. Other evaluation ideas are presented first.

1. Artistic, Dramatic, Video/Audio, Musical or Web Composition

By providing students with the opportunity to compose something is a wonderful way to support the development of creativity and allow for a more open-ended demonstration of learning objectives. Give students specific components you want included in their composition and consider an easy way for them to submit their final product for marking. Examples:

- Web page summarizing key concepts

- Video production with interviews or reenactments

- Dramatic presentation video taped

- Digital photo collage expressing major points of learning

2. Model / Diagram / Sketch / Map

You may feel that building a model belongs in another discipline like architecture—but not so. Ask students to design or draw a visual representation of their learning by hand or using computer software. This is an evaluation format that students enjoy! Examples:

- Sketch layouts, in a computer program, of how a set of desks and chairs should be arranged for three types of student performances

- Using modeling software, design the look of a business office for a specific client

- Using dolls as models, design costumes for a specific historical event or period of time

- Make a map of the key concepts learned in a course

3. Prototype / Working Example

Students can design a prototype of how something works to demonstrate higher levels of thinking. They could work alone or in groups to construct a miniature version of a working product. Examples:
- Create a working windmill to show the generation of electrical current

- Design an ergonomic business product that will help people who work in cubicles

- Grow a small habitat in a bottle that has all the elements of an ecosystem

- Create an animation that demonstrates the working parts of the water cycle

4. Problem-Based Project

Problem-based learning is a way of teaching which involves students solving authentic problems. A small twist on this concept is to allow for the creation of projects that revolve around real-world problems. Students have to use content and knowledge from the class to plan the steps, gather the information, and propose a solution to the problem. Students will appreciate this type of assignment because it will be so easy to see the relevance and importance. Examples:

- In order to keep up to the demand for education, a new school for training professionals in your field is required within the next year. What would the curriculum look like, who would teach it, what would be the focus, etc.?

- Recycling is still not happening in all households. What would be a solution to get another 10-20% of the population recycling?

- A book of short stories has just been written and the author wants to publish it. A sample of some of the stories is supplied but you need to figure out if the stories are worth publishing and how might you edit them to be publishable.

5. Demonstration / Experiment

A very easy way to see if students can apply their learning is to have them do a demonstration or conduct an experiment where they have to use specific materials and resources. Allow students to sign up for a specific day to conduct their demonstrations and you then evaluate a specific set of skills. Examples:

- Demonstrate how to clean the teeth of a young girl

- Show how you would give a needle and then properly dispose of it

- Conduct a series of small experiments to explain and identify the properties of a mystery substance—along with making an educated guess as to the substance

6. Learning Log / Blog / Digital Portfolio

Learning logs are a good evaluation method if you are looking to see progress over time, how time was used, and what activities were undertaken. A web learning log (or blog) is a way for students to use the digital medium to share their learning more easily and in an ongoing fashion throughout the term. Free online blogging sites are available for students to set up. Digital portfolios are more structured web sites that include pages each dedicated to a certain topic. Examples:

- Create a portfolio of photos and explanations outlining skill acquisition in a sport

- Keep a learning log of thoughts, hypotheses and outcomes as a set of experiments are conducted throughout the term

7. Case Study

Popular in the business world, case studies have now become great evaluation formats in a variety of disciplines. Case studies ask students to find solutions for various problems within a case. Students like case studies because they relate to real-world situations. Examples:

- Scenario of a patient and ailments requiring a diagnosis

- An urbanization plan is causing city council deliberations to be halted – it now requires a thorough analysis and recommendations to city council

8. Presentation

Presentations are often over-used because students tend to take the slideshow approach and jam as much content on each slide as possible. When it comes time to present, you will often see students reading from slides and including unnecessary use of the software's bells and whistles to impress the audience. When you provide a more specific set of criteria that is more focused on synthesizing information and presenting it in an engaging manner, student presentations become more useful. Examples:

- Presentation that teaches something new to the class

- Video-enhanced presentation that includes video clips along with graphics

- Group presentation where each person is responsible for a distinct section

9. Essay / Research Paper / Report / Wiki

The essay, research paper, or report involves students planning, developing, and writing a number of pages on a topic. It is a common evaluation method. Instructors are encouraged to offer alternative formats for expression of thought. The use of a wiki allows classmates to contribute to various sections and make available their learning to the whole class.   Examples:

- Research paper on global warming: background, problems and solutions

- Group wiki outlining new advances in use of simulation software to teach nursing

10. Quiz, Test, and Exam Questions

The most popular form of evaluation is likely quiz, test, or exam questions. See Chapter 13 to learn about writing proper test questions including multiple choice, true/false, matching, and long and short answer types. Examples:

- Matching question: Diagram of the human body and bank of terms to match up

- Long Answer/Essay Question: Persuasive argument for or against a current topic in media

G. Recording Tools

a. Quizzes, Tests, and Exams

Written quizzes, tests, and exams are the most popular form of recording learning as is the use of machine-marked cards. They need no explanation in this handbook. However, next time try giving short online quizzes to students throughout the term or allow for open-book tests and exams which prevent memorization and promote problem solving and application of learning. Students will appreciate smaller tests and more frequent feedback on how they are doing in your course. Often, online learning management systems have built in quiz functions which immediately mark and return to the student the final marks along with an explanation of the correct answers.

b. Rating Scales

Rating scales include criteria that are rated on a sliding scale (0-5 or 0-7) and allow an instructor to quickly indicate achievement. They are very useful for grading presentations, demonstrations, and experiments. Here is an example of a rating scale used for an in class presentation where one student was speaking for a minute or two about a certain topic.

1. Demonstrated **appropriate volume of spoken words** (e.g., you could hear all words and volume was appropriate to room).

    (poor) 1   2   3   4   5 (outstanding)

2. Demonstrated **clear** and **understandable articulation** and **pronunciation** of spoken words (e.g., good clarity of words/sentences).

    (poor) 1   2   3   4   5 (outstanding)

3. Used effective and appropriate **non-verbal communication** (e.g. eye contact, facial expressions, comfort in front of group).

    (poor) 1   2   3   4   5 (outstanding)

C. Checklists

Checklists are handy for evaluating student work when you are quickly looking for an indication of whether certain criteria have been included. You could give one mark if the item is evident and no marks if the item is missing. Use a checklist for items where you are not concerned about quality, but rather just checking to see if they are included. Here is an example for evaluating a web site to ensure it has the basic components.

No.	Criteria	Included (1 mk)	Missing (0 mks)
1	Head content includes title of page		
2	Head content includes student name		
3	All menu links work		
4	Link to institution at bottom of page		

d. Rubrics

A rubric is a popular tool for outlining criteria and for assessing and evaluating student achievement. A rubric is often presented in a table/matrix with 3-4 levels and descriptions of criteria per each level. Once developed, a good rubric can be used for years. The following pages include two sample rubrics. The first one is a rubric all about the components in constructing a quality rubric. The second one is a sample science rubric. Here are some simple steps for creating a rubric.

Suggested Steps in Creating Rubrics

1. Clearly identify the **learning expectations**, **objectives of task**, **performance**, or **final product** to be evaluated.

2. Brainstorm possible **criteria** of student **performance, product, or process**
   - Include criteria that reflect a broad range of knowledge and skills (i.e., knowledge and understanding; application and analysis; creativity) as appropriate for the particular performance, product, or process

3. From the brainstormed list, identify key **specific, observable,** and **measurable** criteria that best reflect the learning to be assessed
   - Select only the top **5-7 criteria** (any more and it takes too long to mark)
   - Do not make the mistake of having a lengthy and unusable rubric with too many criteria

4. **Create** a **table** of 5 columns wide X 10 rows. Using a word processing program is easiest. You can adjust column/row width as needed later on. An effective rubric includes four levels/four steps in the learning continuum that spans 0-100% for grading.

5. Phrase the criteria **explicitly** so there is no confusion about what is being assessed and put each of the criteria in the first column rows under each other
   - Check to ensure the criteria helps the student know what to do
   - Often the criteria column has examples of what to expect to guide students in knowing exactly what is expected/not expected

6. Brainstorm characteristics that describe each criterion and create a **continuum of learning** through 4 levels of each particular criterion using clear **descriptions**
   - Ensure **criteria are consistently addressed** at each level using suitable descriptions (e.g., address the same elements in each level)
   - Descriptions should distinguish differences between levels by addressing **frequency** (e.g., accuracy—seldom, sometimes, usually, always) or **intensity** (e.g., relevance or clarity—slightly, moderately, mainly, extremely) **amount** (e.g., quantity— few, some, most, all) or **quality** (e.g., choice of examples – poor, satisfactory, good, high)
   - Ensure language is **measurable** *(the less vague the better!)*

7. **Add in marks per each level.** This can be changed according to your emphasis per assignment or course. Just ensure they match the percentages per column.

8. **Reflect and revise** rubric as needed (often 2-3 revisions are required)

Logo

Institution and Department Information

Student Name: _____

Instructor:

Course: Course Name

Note to Students: Please attach this rubric to your assignment so it can be marked.

Rubric for Quality Rubrics

Description of Task: You are an instructor who needs a rubric for a 'performance task' (such as a lab, project, model, presentation, etc). You know that by properly constructing a good (and detailed enough) rubric (with added marks) you'll save yourself a lot of time in marking and you'll provide your students with a good guide to evaluating their ability in this task. You will also be providing your students with a continuum of descriptions that are consistent and measurable. Ensure that you try to phrase your descriptions positively.

The rubric is to be made with a word processing program for one of your term assignments. Use learning objectives from your course to frame the whole rubric. You are to choose 5-7 criteria that you feel will make this an excellent 'performance task'. Choose criteria you feel will come from a variety of skill areas. The criteria need to be fully described with possible examples to give students a clear understanding of what is needed for success. The levelled descriptors should not be vague and should relate to the criteria with qualifiers that are appropriate to that level. Use this rubric as a guide to design your rubric. Good Luck!

Student Comments:

Instructor Comments:

TOTAL MARK **/60**

Rubric for Quality Rubrics - Criteria and Descriptors Per Level

Criteria	Level 1 (0-49%)	Level 2 (50-69%)	Level 3 (70-84%)	Level 4 (85-100%)
Parts of Rubrics				
Basic Identifiers: course/subject/topic, appropriate title of rubric, instructor's name, logo/clipart/image to distinguish rubric, footer with instructor name/year, labels for levels 1-4 and corresponding percentages (can change if wish)	**4 or more** basic identifiers are **not evident** and/or **not** properly **labeled**. 0 - 4.9	**3** basic identifiers are **not evident** and/or **not** properly **labeled**. 5 - 6.9	**2** basic identifiers are **not evident** and/or **not** properly **labeled**. 7 - 8.4	**All (or all but 1)** basic identifiers are **evident** and/or **properly labeled**. 8.5 - 10
Criteria and Descriptions				
Performance Criteria Descriptions are Clear and Detailed: chosen criteria have enough detail to explain what is expected of students, with possible examples/detail to explain any concepts as demonstrated in this rubric on rubrics, chosen criteria are a variety of amount/quantity, frequency and intensity	Description of each criterion is of a **poor quality**, clearly written **none of the time** and is **severely lacking detail** for understanding. 0 - 4.9	Description of each criterion is of a **fair quality**, clearly written **sometimes** and is mostly **lacking detail** for understanding. 5 - 6.9	Description of each criterion is of a **good quality**, clearly written **most times** and has **appropriate detail** for understanding. 7 - 8.4	Description of each criterion is of a **high quality**, **clearly written all times** and has **significant detail** for understanding. 8.5 - 10
Level Descriptions Measurable and Detailed: there is consistent use of non-vague, yet positive language across each of the 4 levels that use descriptors appropriate to the task that allow for ease in understanding what is expected from students; descriptions ensure that the same criteria is discussed across all the levels	Description of each of 4 levels is written in **unclear and non-measureable** terms, with frequent **inconsistent** and **negative language** and **does not address** the **same** components across all levels. 0 - 4.9	Description of each of 4 levels is written in **somewhat clear** and measureable terms, with **frequent inconsistent** and negative language and **often does not address** the **same** components across all levels. 5 - 6.9	Description of each of 4 levels is written in **mostly clear** and measureable terms, with **mostly consistent** and **mostly positive** language and **usually addresses** the **same** components across all levels. 7 - 8.4	Description of each of 4 levels is written in **extremely clear** and measureable terms, with **consistent** and **positive language** and **always addresses** the **same** components across all levels. 8.5 - 10

Visual and Text of Rubric				
Performance Task Description + Overall Written Expression: 6-8 sentences for a performance task description is well written with proper spelling/grammar, overview of the task, enough detail to know what is to be accomplished with some specific details, overall rubric is well written in terms of grammar and spelling	**Little** written work contains proper sentence structures, grammar and spelling. Performance task **barely outlines** the task with **missing details** for understanding.	**Some** written work contains proper sentence structures, grammar and spelling. Performance task **somewhat outlines** the task with **some missing** details for understanding.	**Most** written work contains proper sentence structures, grammar and spelling. Performance task **generally outlines** the task with **appropriate details** for understanding.	**All** written work contains **proper sentence structures**, grammar and spelling (with possible 1-2 minor errors). Performance task **clearly outlines** the task with **significant details** for understanding.
	0 - 4.9	5 - 6.9	7 - 8.4	8.5 - 10
Layout and Design: entire rubric has been properly laid out and displayed with good design sense to aid in readability; use of appropriate fonts/font sizes/bolding to aid in reading, shading/white space to allow space to circle marks, layout is clean and professional looking	Layout meets **few** design components that are **rarely** executed and with **poor impact** on **professional** look of work.	Layout meets **some** design components that are **somewhat** executed and with **fair impact** on **professional** look of work.	Layout meets **major** design components that are **generally** executed and with **good impact** on **professional** look of work.	Layout meets **all to mostly all** design components that are **always** executed and with **significant impact** on **professional** look of work.
	0 - 4.9	5 - 6.9	7 - 8.4	8.5 - 10
Application of Components				
Applied Elements of Rubric Structure: included learning objectives in description, 5-7 appropriate criteria mark range for each level/criteria evident under each level and total overall mark	Rubric demonstrates an application of **limited** elements of structure and elements done with **little care on details**.	Rubric demonstrates an application of **some** elements of structure and elements done with **some care on details**.	Rubric demonstrates an application of **most** elements of structure and elements done with **considerable care on details**.	Rubric demonstrates an application of **all** elements of structure and elements done with **thoroughness and care on details**.
	0 - 4.9	5 - 6.9	7 - 8.4	8.5 - 10

Sample School

Student Name: **Sample Science Rubric**
Date:
Instructor: Sample Instructor
Course: Sample Biology

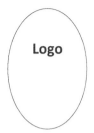

Logo

111555 Sample School Road

Performance Task Description: Model of Mitosis and Meiosis

Mitosis is the process in which a eukaryotic cell separates the chromosomes in its cell nucleus, into two identical sets in two daughter nuclei. Meiosis is a process of reductional division in which the number of chromosomes per cell is halved. To help remember and better understand mitosis and meiosis you will design and build a model depicting the various structures and functions involved in these processes.

Your model can represent your choice of either mitosis or meiosis II. You will build this model using common household and craft products like sponges, pipe cleaners, straws and construction paper. The model must use appropriate materials that logically represent the actual structures. For example, using pipe-cleaners to represent phospholipids would be an appropriate selection of materials. The model must be visually appealing, such that the model captures the attention of the audience and is engaging. The model must also aid in the learning of the concepts with clear and distinct structures. The structure and the function of the model must represent concepts accurately.

In addition to the model you must create a poster or brochure describing the stages of **mitosis and meiosis**, the main differences and similarities between them as well as one real life application. The brochure should be concise and describe concepts accurately. Due Date: _____

Learning Objectives

1   explain the phases in the process of meiosis in terms of cell division, the movement of chromosomes, and crossing over of genetic material

2   investigate the process of meiosis, by using biological diagrams and models to help explain the main phases in the process

Instructor Comments:

Marks	
Total Mark	/60

Sample Biology Rubric: Mitosis and Meiosis

Criteria	Level 1 (0-49%)	Level 2 (50-69%)	Level 3 (70-84%)	Level 4 (85-100%)
Knowledge of Concepts				
Demonstrate an understanding of the **structure** and **function** of mitotic/meiotic cells **accurately**. (e.g., use suitable terminology; use appropriate materials; label and design relevant structures; represent mitotic/meiotic phases)	Demonstrates a **limited** understanding of the structure and function of mitotic/meiotic cells that are **consistently** inaccurate 0 - 4.9	Demonstrates **some** understanding of the structure and function of mitotic/meiotic cells that are **mostly** accurate 5 - 6.9	Demonstrates a **considerable** understanding of the structure and function of mitotic/meiotic cells that are **sometimes** accurate 7 - 8.4	Demonstrates a **thorough** understanding of the structure and function of mitotic/meiotic cells that are **seldom** inaccurate 8.5 - 10
Describe how all relevant cell components carry out various cell processes during mitosis/meiosis (e.g., include descriptions of all major organelles; indicate the function of each organelle; describe the major phases)	Description of each process **rarely** contains **few** of the expected cell components and cell processes 0 - 4.9	Description of each process **often** contains **some** of the expected cell components and cell processes 5 - 6.9	Description of each process **regularly** contains **most** of the expected cell components and cell processes 7 - 8.4	Description of each process **consistently** contains **almost all** of the expected cell components and cell processes 8.5 - 10
Analysis and Evidence				
Analyze concepts appropriately providing details in relation to mitosis/meiosis (e.g., discuss the relevance of mitosis/meiosis in relation to Mendelian genetics; structure is designed to convey relevant details)	Analysis of concepts provides **little evidence** of supporting details that are **slightly** relevant 0 - 4.9	Analysis of concepts provides **satisfactory evidence** of supporting details that are **moderately** relevant 5 - 6.9	Analysis of concepts provides **appropriate evidence** of supporting details that are **mainly** relevant 7 - 8.4	Analysis of concepts provides **extensive evidence** of supporting details that are **extremely** relevant 8.5 - 10

Communication and Terminology

Communicate the process and importance of mitosis or meiosis **clearly and effectively in the model and brochure** (e.g., structures are apparent; phases are presented in a step-wise manner; comprehensible explanation of processes)	The information communicated in the model and brochure is **slightly** clear with **limited** effectiveness. 0 - 4.9	The information communicated in the model and brochure is **moderately** clear with **some** effectiveness. 5 - 6.9	The information communicated in the model and brochure is **mainly** clear with **considerable** effectiveness. 7 - 8.4	The information communicated in the model and brochure is **extremely** clear with **excellent** effectiveness. 8.5 - 10
Use correct terminology when discussing cellular biology with depth and accuracy (e.g., include all necessary and proper vocabulary pertaining to the phases, chromosome stage, chromosome number, structures and functions; proper spelling and grammar)	**Few** appropriate terms are included with **considerable** spelling/grammatical errors (10-12 errors) 0 - 4.9	**Some** appropriate terms are included with **several** spelling/ grammatical errors (7-9 errors) 5 - 6.9	**Most** appropriate terms are included with **some** spelling/ grammatical errors (4-6 errors) 7 - 8.4	**All** appropriate terms are included with **few** spelling/ grammatical errors (1-3 errors) 8.5 - 10

Comparison

Use knowledge of mitosis and meiosis to **make a comparison between the different types of cell divisions** (include all relevant comparisons of structure, function, purpose and chromosome #)	Comparisons are made using **very few** examples that are **slightly** relevant 0 - 4.9	Comparisons are made using **some** examples that are **moderately** relevant 5 - 6.9	Comparisons are made using **most** examples that are **mainly** relevant 7 - 8.4	Comparisons are made using **almost all** examples that are **extremely** relevant 8.5 - 10

H. Assessment: Match Them Up

This activity is a summary of the key components of this chapter. Column A has 7 terms. Column B has 10 definitions. There are 3 extra definitions that are not needed. Write the LETTER of the definition in the box beside the corresponding term. See answer key along the left side of the page.

Column A

1. Assessment

2. Evaluation Method

3. Validity

4. Rating Scale

5. Evaluation

6. Rubric

7. Assessment Method

Column B

A. Popular tool for outlining criteria on student achievement often displayed through a table/matrix with 3-4 levels with descriptions of criteria per each level

B. Is a type of question on an exam, test or quiz that asks students to make a choice between possible answers

C. Criteria that are rated on a sliding scale (0-5 or 0-7) and allow an instructor to quickly indicate achievement

D. Allowing students to demonstrate the use of a piece of gymnastics equipment in a safe manner

E. Informal method of gathering data for feedback to students about their learning

F. Giving students an opportunity to share where they are grasping concepts through an informal set of questions answered in class.

G. Is the ability of an assessment or evaluation instrument to be used in various classes with various students and achieve similar results

H. What you expect of students to be able to do, know, value or demonstrate by the end of the course

I. Formal method of gathering data to assign values and grades to student achievement

J. Is the ability of the assessment or evaluation instrument measuring what it is intended to measure

Answers: 1 – E; 2 – D; 3 – J; 4 – C; 5 – I; 6 – A; 7 – F

Top Ten Takeaways

1. **Consider Assessment and Evaluation Methods Immediately:** After goals and learning objectives have been solidified, ensure you now link those objectives to the assessment and evaluation methods, and not after the course is planned or started.

2. **Alignment:** Each learning objective should be aligned with an assessment or evaluation method.

3. **Definition of Assessment:** Assessment is the informal gathering of information about student achievement. Assessment benefits the students in knowing how they are progressing and benefits you in more effectively planning your classes. There are no marks associated with assessment.

4. **Definition of Evaluation:** Evaluation is the formal grading of student work for reporting and promotion purposes. Evaluation is when there is a 'value' (e.g., number, letter, level, category, mark) placed on student learning.

5. **Ensure Validity and Reliability:** Validity refers to how well the evaluation is matched with the requirements of the learning objective. Reliability refers to how well the evaluation tool is able to be replicated to achieve similar results.

6. **Assessment is Invaluable:** Assessment activities take a short amount of class time but provide valuable learning opportunities to students. A small assessment activity should be included in each class.

7. **Consider a Variety of Evaluation Methods:** Evaluation activities are more formal and usually happen at specific times. Try to consider activities (such as models, presentations, web pages, stories etc.) other than tests and papers.

8. **Recording Tools:** Checklists and rating scales are simple recording tools for evaluation.

9. **Rubrics:** Rubrics are helpful recording tools for giving students clear expectations for achievement.

10. **Rubrics Have Worth:** Rubrics take a while to create but once done they are useful for many years to come. Many instructors use well-designed rubrics with great success.

Next Steps

1. Review your learning objectives and assessment/evaluation methods you have been using. Check if they are properly aligned and are directly connected to the learning outcomes.

2. Try one new assessment and one new evaluation idea in one of your classes this term.

3. If you have not used a rubric before, consider trying one. Look up rubrics on the Internet for a vast collection of examples. Check with a colleague to see if they have any ideas.

4. Review your evaluation methods. Look over exams, tests and quizzes. Re-read assignment details and project descriptions. Check to see if you could be clearer in your evaluation of student learning.

References and Resources

Angelo, T. A. & Cross, K. P. (1993). *Classroom assessment techniques: A handbook for college teachers*. San Francisco, CA: Jossey-Bass.

Petrauskis, V. (2009). *Sample Biology Rubric*.

Wiggins, G. and McTighe, J (2005). *Understanding by design*. Alexandria, VA: Association for Supervision and Curriculum Development.

Chapter 4: Developing Course Content & Structure

Chapter Overview

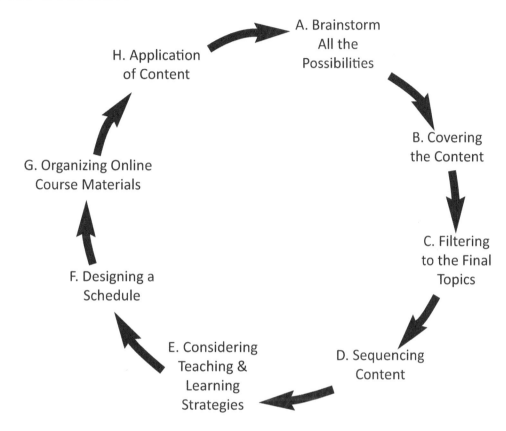

Planning your course content and schedule is best done once you have your learning objectives aligned with your assessment and evaluation methods. In this way, you can now look at the content you wish to teach and start considering how it fits within the objectives and how you will get students to the point where they can be successful. This chapter outlines each of the steps below and gives you a quick overview of things to consider along the way. The process could be outlined as follows:

Brainstorming – What are all the topics you could include in this course?

Choosing Content – What is absolutely essential for students to learn and what is nice to know?

Filtering Topics – What does your revised topic list look like?

Choosing a Sequencing Scheme – What is the best way to organize the course?

Teaching/Learning Strategies – How might you structure the learning?

Designing a Schedule – How will your week-by-week schedule look?

Organizing Online Environment – How will the online environment be organized for optimal teaching and learning?

A. Brainstorm All the Possibilities

Your first step is to brainstorm all the possible topics and sub-topics you wish to include in this course. Try using a concept map format as shown in the example below. A concept map helps you see all the possible topics and all at the same time. It is also a good idea to browse through past syllabi, the textbook, and the Internet along with canvassing colleagues about possible topics. Also, consider new research, innovative technologies, and current issues related to the course that may have changed since the last time the course was taught. Always include sub-topic ideas to help flesh out the full range of the topic.

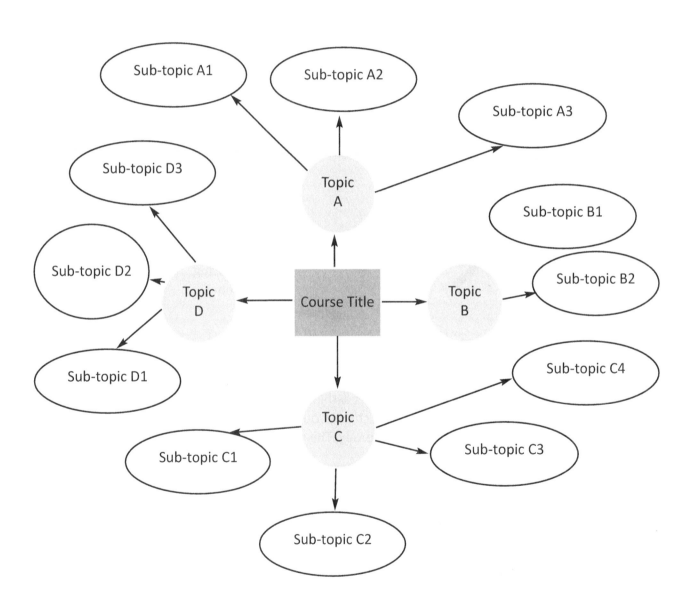

B. Covering the Content

The next step involves whittling down the list of topics to a collection that is manageable and will provide time for student learning.

All instructors generally want their students to accomplish **two things** in their course:

1. **Fully grasp course content**

2. **Learn how to use the content in some way**

Many instructors devote a great deal of time to the first point (course content) and tend to give the second point (learning to use the content) short shrift (Woolvard and Anderson, 1998).

Missing out on point two is not intentional on the part of the instructors. They just want to give students a thorough overview of the course content and provide a complete course. Instructors often feel pressure to cover content or feel a course would be incomplete without including a wide array of content. Voices in the faculty lounge might be overhead saying the following:

- The profession requires us to cover this large amount of content. If I didn't cover it, I would be passing students without complete knowledge.

- I inherited this course and I was told to follow the syllabus and cover all the content on it. If I didn't cover the material I would not be doing my job.

- I use a textbook to fashion my course and there are so many good topics in it that I feel I owe it to the students to make their textbook purchase worthwhile.

- I just can't teach this course without ensuring I cover all the necessary information. I can't go into too much depth as it would take too much time.

- This course is a pre-requisite to other advanced courses. I must cover all the content in order to prepare them. Other instructors are counting on me.

Covering too much content...

- means students are not learning content (Wiggins and McTighe, 2005; Biggs, 2007)

- means students are not able to remember content the next week or next month

- means students are denied opportunities for applying what they are learning and internalizing the content for future use

- results in students becoming overwhelmed with pages of notes, downloaded slide presentations and endless pages of textbook readings

- forces students to resort to memorization for tests as they are unable to make sense of it all and have to use short term memory to make it through tests and exams

- more often than not results in a lot of surface learning rather than deep, meaningful learning

Students need time in and out of class to apply their learning, to work through problems, to understand various angles of a concept, and to ask questions and ensure they are developing a deeper learning experience. If student learning is our prime responsibility as an instructor, then we need to look at the amount of content we are covering and aim for a balanced approach.

C. Filtering to the Final Topics

In order to create more time in the course for higher level thinking opportunities to optimize learning, you need to take some time to filter all the topics.

Looking at your brainstormed chart, group topics into one of three categories:

Nice to Include
- not related to learning objectives
- nice to know information
- course would not suffer if cut out

Possible to Include
- indirectly related to learning objectives
- may include if there is room
- carefully consider purpose

Must Include
- directly related to learning objectives
- essential content for course
- is a core topic for students

Consider the following while you categorize:

1. What amount of control do you have over adding and deleting content in your course? If you have a good deal of control then you should be filtering!

2. What expectations does your program, department or faculty have of this course? If there is content that you know are non-negotiable and are required by your institution, then ensure you include it in the "must include" category.

3. What are the absolutely essential topics you must include in this course? In your professional opinion, what are the core concepts that you need to have students learn before they leave the course?

4. What are the topics you have wanted to remove for some time? Get rid of them now!

The **ESSENTIAL CONTENT** needs to filter to the bottom!
What matters the most for learning?

D. Sequencing Content

At this point you need to take your essential and core content/concepts and consider how they will flow. Courses can take on a variety of organization schemes, but generally flow from a beginning part to a more integrative and complex part. Here are a few examples. Would any of them suit your course?

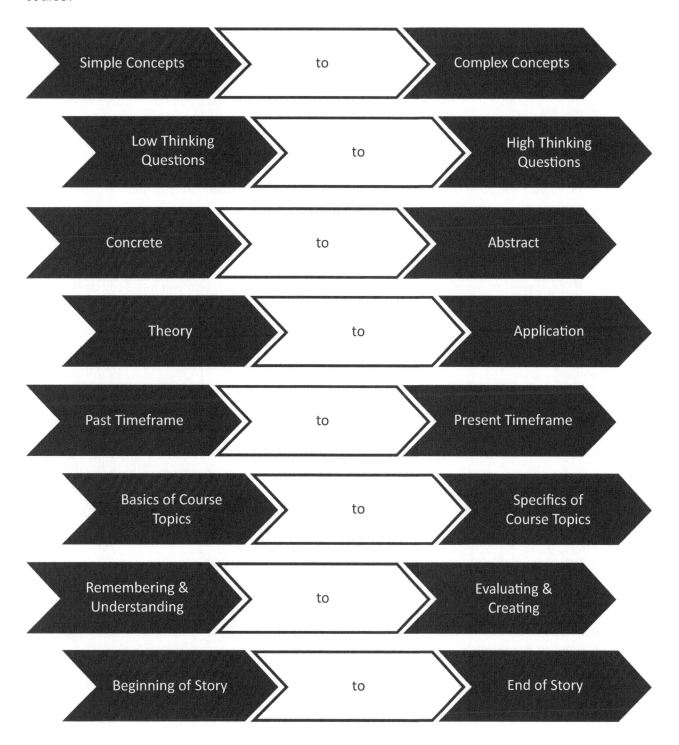

Simple Concepts	to	Complex Concepts
Low Thinking Questions	to	High Thinking Questions
Concrete	to	Abstract
Theory	to	Application
Past Timeframe	to	Present Timeframe
Basics of Course Topics	to	Specifics of Course Topics
Remembering & Understanding	to	Evaluating & Creating
Beginning of Story	to	End of Story

E. Considering Teaching and Learning Strategies

Before you can start plotting your course schedule, you need to consider some broad teaching and learning strategies. This is not about the details of each class. This is more about the overall strategies you want to use throughout the course. Take some time right now to consider what learning opportunities you will create for students. This will allow you to plan enough time in your schedule. See Chapter 7 on Teaching and Learning Strategies for more detail.

Go back to the learning objectives: **what do you want students to be able to accomplish by the time they leave your course?** (e.g., create a product with various tools, debate the pros and cons of climate change solutions, plan a lesson for a science class, write a blog about your reactions to current literature, etc.)

For example:

- If you are going to include a number or experiments or demonstrations in your class time, you will have to allow time to do the experiments and connect them to the class topics.

- If you are going to use group discussion time to explore topics and engage students in solving real-life scenarios, then you will need to plan time for this to happen.

- If you have a mid-term exam scheduled for your class time, you will need to consider using the whole time in a shorter class or half the time of a longer class for the exam.

Ask yourself these questions:

How are you going to get students to be successful with the learning objectives?

How can you arrange the activities so that learning will be supported and students will take steps to completing the learning objectives?

In addition to lecturing, what other instructional strategies do you already use or want to try? Need help with more ideas? See chapter 7!

What activities will you create for students to engage in to acquire the skills and knowledge required for success in your class?

Are there specific instructional strategies that are more suited for practicing and applying content?

What skills and knowledge will students need to accomplish the objectives and be successful in achieving deeper learning in the course?

Have you heard about another way of conducting your class you'd like to try out this term that you feel might better suit students and their learning?

F. Designing a Schedule

➤ Get out the calendar. Jot down the dates and times of your course.

➤ Start mapping out each week topic-by-topic considering the time constraints of your course (do you have one 3-hour class or three 50-minute classes?) How will you work around the days and times?

➤ Are there religious holidays and campus events you need to plan around?

➤ Do you still have too much content? What can you trim off that is not essential?

➤ What assessment and evaluation methods will you use? How long will they take?

➤ When will you explain assignments and when will they be due? How long will it take you to mark them and give them back before the end of course? Set realistic timelines for marking.

➤ What overall instructional strategies will you be using in this course?

➤ What will be the balance of time given to content delivery versus student application?

➤ Do you have some unplanned time to deal with topics or activities that may take longer?

At this point, make some sort of chart to plot out your course week by week. This is an example:

Date	Content and Teaching/Learning Strategies (3 hour class 1X per week)	Assessment and Evaluation Methods
Sept 16	**Week 1: Overview of Course & First Day Activities** • Get-to-know-you Activities: Name Tags, Small Group Introductions, Instructor Intro Slideshow (50 mins) • Course Overview & Syllabus Review (50 mins) • Topic 1 Introduction (1 hour)….	Pre-Assessment of Concepts/Content Quiz
Sept 23	**Week 2: Topic 1** • Video presentation of topic • Group discussion of problem associated with topic….	Online survey about first 2 classes – highs/lows
Sept 30	**Week 3: Topic 1 for first half – then Topic 2** • Scenario case study for small group on topic 1 – take up • Topic 2 basics – lecture….	Ticket out the Door Small online quiz on basic content so far
Oct 7	**Week 4: Topic 2** • Slideshow on application activities with topic 2 • Small group problem solving + take up….	Assignment 1 Due In the Fog About…
Oct 14	**Week 5: Topic 3** • Discuss readings on topic 3 • Note from 20 min lecture on topic….	Ticket out the Door
Oct 21	**Week 6: Topic 4 + Review Session** • Jigsaw on Topic 4 • Instructor explanation of key concepts • Review– Whiteboard Charades Game….	Whiteboard Charades Game
Oct 28	**Week 7: In class mid-term exam** • Instructions (10 mins.), mid-term (1.5 hours)	Mid-term exam

G. Organizing Online Course Materials

Almost all instructors have either a course/learning management system (e.g., Blackboard, Moodle, Desire2Learn, etc.) or have the ability to host a course web site. If you do not have an online environment for learning yet, you likely will soon enough! Having a digital counterpart to a face-to-face course is becoming, more and more, a standard component of post-secondary education. Fully online courses already have a learning management system environment, as do hybrid courses (courses that are part online and part face-to-face). After you have your topics and order fairly down-pat, it is time to work on your online environment. Students appreciate seeing course content (or at least the syllabus and the course topics/assignments) online prior to the start of a course.

How content and resources are organized is a huge component to consider when looking at maximizing student learning. Instructionally designing online learning environments takes a bit of time and some training to properly enhance students' learning experiences. It is clear that students want the content in an online learning management system to be well organized and clearly focused. Here are some of their thoughts on the topic:

My instructor has material all over the place. I find it hard to locate important dates and announcements as they are buried within pages!

My online course is so full of content. It is in so many different formats. Nothing is really organized or easy to locate. I waste a lot of time just searching for things and it drives me nuts!

I have a hard time keeping track of what we need to do online. The instructor puts up new notices, discussion topics, quizzes and homework assignments in various spots. I spend an hour a day just visiting all the areas to see if anything is new.

Some instructors tell us that it is our responsibility to check the course daily. I have no problem with that. But when you have to conduct a challenging scavenger hunt every time – I have an issue with this.

1. Sample Course Layout of Content: "Before"

Sample Course

📄 Week 1 Materials and Content	📄 Week 2 Materials and Content	📄 Week 3 Materials and Content
📄 Week 4 Materials and Content	📄 Week 5 Materials and Content	📄 Week 6 Materials and Content
📄 Week 7 Materials and Content	📄 Week 8 Materials and Content	📄 Week 9 Materials and Content
📄 Week 10 Materials and Content	📄 Week 11 Materials and Content	📄 Week 12 Materials and Content
📄 Week 13 Materials and Content	🖱 Resources and URLs	🖱 Content Website
ⓘ Syllabus	✏ Planning Question Summaries	✏ Assignment # 3 Planning
🖱 Study Help Links	✏ Planning Question Summaries	☑ October 2 Class Quiz A

The main difference between these two sample course online screens is the look and organization of the icons/content items. The message here is keep it simple. While there is more work that could be done on the "after" version, the intent is to show a starting point for a clean format for student learning.

2. Sample Course Layout of Content: "After"

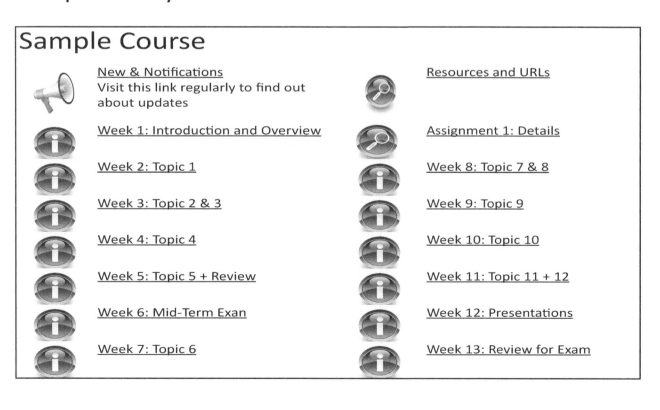

Sample Course

📢 New & Notifications — Visit this link regularly to find out about updates	🔍 Resources and URLs
ⓘ Week 1: Introduction and Overview	🔍 Assignment 1: Details
ⓘ Week 2: Topic 1	ⓘ Week 8: Topic 7 & 8
ⓘ Week 3: Topic 2 & 3	ⓘ Week 9: Topic 9
ⓘ Week 4: Topic 4	ⓘ Week 10: Topic 10
ⓘ Week 5: Topic 5 + Review	ⓘ Week 11: Topic 11 + 12
ⓘ Week 6: Mid-Term Exan	ⓘ Week 12: Presentations
ⓘ Week 7: Topic 6	ⓘ Week 13: Review for Exam

3. Solutions for Improved Organization

Good design principles come into play when designing the online components of a course. Often, many instructors receive assistance only with the mechanics of how to create a course online, not how to design it. Rather than forcing students to take part in a scavenger hunt every time they enter your course, try some of these solutions to allow students more time to focus on learning.

Put all announcements about course, new content uploaded, new discussion topics, homework, etc., in ONE spot. For example, create one page with the date and brief description of the new item and where to find it.

Group all assignments under one icon/area. Put due dates, assignment explanations and resources in this spot so students don't have to search through course material to find details.

Create a page that is a collection of ongoing resources (URLs, books, articles, videos, blogs, wikis) that will help students with course material. Ask students to contribute too.

Embed as much as you can. Rather than sending students out to another web site to watch videos or slide presentaions, if you can, use the code to embed documents right within the online learning environment.

Keep the look and feel of the online course pages clean and simple. Group similar content pages and resources to keep the pages organized.

Use icons/images that are consistent and relevant to the material and do not clutter the pages.

White space – ensure you have as much as you can afford to allow for a clean and visual viewing experience. Do not use busy backgrounds that ruin the positive effect of white space.

Ask students for suggestions on how to improve the layout and design of your course materials. They often have great ideas!

4. Formatting Web Pages to Optimize Learning

Another element to consider when putting together the online portion of your course is interactivity and making sure you include content that engages the students and allows them to apply their learning. At this stage in the planning process, this means considering how you will use the online environment to get your students involved and how you will create learning opportunities for them.

If you look at most online course pages, you will find instructors typically including:

- **Syllabus**
- PowerPoint/Keynote Slide **Presentations**
- **URLs** to web sites with relevant course material
- **Course content** in the form of notes or handouts
- **Textbook-imported content** (e.g., quizzes, summaries, presentations)
- **Email** to communicate with instructor and each other
- **Discussion Board** area to openly post responses to questions (sometimes with breakout chat rooms for group discussions)
- **Drop Box** for assignments to be handed in
- **Grades Area** for instructors to release grades after marking
- **Link to a Web-Conferencing system** (often including web, audio, video, and social networking opportunities for your class)

The main use of online web pages is therefore focused on content. Often in text form (or in presentation slide format with text), students access the online portion of a course to read items, write posts, and access content links. Consider creating and adding the following items to your online course environment which will move students beyond just reading and writing and being more active than passive with content:

- **Informal quizzes** on content (short, variety of questions, marked as students submit, immediate feedback for learning)
- **Concept maps** (which show relationships between content items or provide overview of course)
- **Mini-clips** explaining a concept or solving a problem (done with a screen capture program, audio narration) – students can replay over and over for enhanced learning
- **Assignment explanations** and samples (done with screen capture program, audio narration) – students will appreciate hearing you explain the assignment in your own words, focusing on the marking scheme and possible samples from previous years
- **Videos** presenting course content (e.g., done with iMovie, Picasa, Photostory) where the instructor uses graphics and text phrases to summarize or introduce course material
- **Flash-based interactive** learning objects are created to explain or extend a concept – allows the students to review on their own and play easily with low download time

- **PDF documents** (with bookmarks and active links) – allows for sharing information with easy-to-access bookmarks and active links to reinforce concepts

- **Podcasts** – focus on short 2-3 minute podcasts which explain a concept, review a class, or introduce a new topic so students can listen a few times to grasp all the important parts

- **Wikis and Blogs** – create spots for students to contribute their own knowledge (wiki) or allow students to create a post in a blog about the course

H. Application of Content: True or False?

Let's see how you are doing with the content and application of it from this chapter. After each statement, circle True or False. Answers are at the bottom of the page on the left side.

#	Statement	True	False
1	Covering too much content without time for students to apply and extend concepts can result in surface learning.	True	False
2	Before you make a schedule of classes, instructors should revisit learning objectives and consider some broad instructional approaches they wish to use in the course.	True	False
3	When instructors are filtering content, they should aim to include all the 'must' and 'possible' topics if they can.	True	False
4	One way to sequence course content is chronologically.	True	False
5	All instructors want their students to accomplish two things in their course, yet often fail on the first one. 1. Fully grasp course content 2. Learn how to use the content in some way	True	False
6	Research indicates that it doesn't matter the instructional strategies used, students will get similar results on tests.	True	False
7	Instructors need to consider the length of the class, religious holidays, due dates for assignments, time for marking and returning work and scheduling of in-class exams when scheduling the course material.	True	False

Answers: 1-T; 2-T; 3-F; 4-T; 5-F; 6-F; 7-T

Top Ten Takeaways

1. **Course Content into a Schedule:** Arranging the course content into a schedule involves a few simple steps such as brainstorming, choosing content, filtering topics, choosing a sequence structure, and considering teaching strategies.

2. **Brainstorming:** Generating a collection all possible topics and content for your course is a good place to start. Consider new research, innovative technologies, and current issues related to your course. Using a concept map approach is one way to visually represent all your topics.

3. **Covering Content:** When an instructor 'covers' content, it does not mean that students have truly learned. Instructors need to carefully consider how much content becomes part of a course and plan for activities and strategies to allow students to apply and use their knowledge in new and meaningful ways.

4. **Too Much Content:** Jamming too much content into a course results in surface learning and forces students to resort to memorization of facts, being overwhelmed with pages of notes, and unable to make sense of the course.

5. **Filter Content:** Whittle down content to end up with the essential concepts and key information required for learning. Label all content in one of three ways: "Nice to Include," "Possible to Include," and "Must Include." Focus on the "Must Include" content for your course.

6. **Include Necessary Content:** Consider the important concepts to include in the course that are absolutely necessary for learning. You may have uncontrollable factors such as department expectations and accreditation standards that may alter course content.

7. **Sequencing Content:** This involves choosing a format to structure the organization of your content. Some examples involve progressing from theory to application or from simple concepts to more complex concepts.

8. **Strategies:** Consider broad teaching and learning strategies that align with your learning objectives. Think about how you want to create learning opportunities for students. Some instructors may vary lecturing with discussion, small group exercises, video presentations and solving problems. Aim to change up the class experience with a variety of strategies.

9. **Calendar/Chart Use:** When you design your schedule consider using a chart or calendar. Think about assessment and evaluation methods you want to use throughout the term, jot down instructional strategies you might use, and plan adequate time to distribute course content.

10. **Holidays & Special Dates:** Instructors need to consider the length of the class, religious holidays, due dates for assignments, time for marking and returning work, and the scheduling of in-class exams when organizing the course material.

Next Steps

1. Locate and use a concept mapping program like Smart Ideas or Inspiration to complete your brainstorming. Use color and arrows to visually present your topics.

2. Take a look at the content that has been part of this course (or content that you feel belongs in this course). Check off all the topics that represent the core of the learning required to meet the learning objectives.

3. Chat with a colleague about the course and get another opinion on what constitutes the essential components of the course.

4. Spend some time on the Internet looking at similar courses. Observe what content and teaching and learning strategies are used.

5. Investigate your course topics looking for new information, new ideas, and current research that might need to be included for keeping the course relevant and fresh.

References and Resources

Biggs, J. & Tang, C. (2007). *Teaching for quality learning at university*. Maidenhead, UK: Open University Press.

Carnegie Mellon University. (n.d.). *Plan your course content and schedule*. Retrieved November 27, 2009, from http://www.cmu.edu/teaching/designteach/design/contentschedule.html

Wiggins, G. & McTighe, J. (2005). *Understanding by design*. Alexandria, VA: Association for Supervision and Curriculum Development.

Woolvard, B. E. & Anderson, V. J. (1998). *Effective grading: A tool for learning and assessment*. San Francisco, CA: Jossey-Bass.

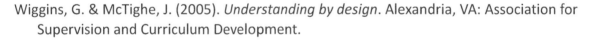

Chapter 5: Preparing Your Useful Syllabus

Chapter Overview

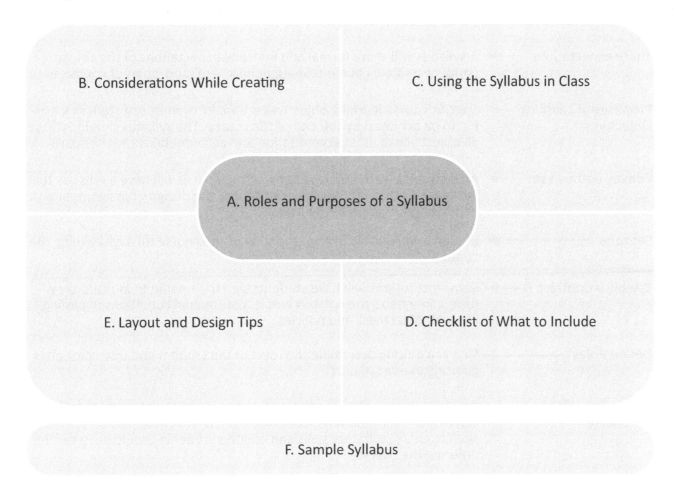

Writing a syllabus (also called a course outline) is a common activity for instructors when planning to teach any course.

Usually instructors inherit a syllabus if it is the first time they are teaching the course. Alternatively, instructors may also resurrect the syllabus used the year prior and update it for current use.

Much has been written on what to include and how to use a syllabus in the classroom (Grunet O'Brien, Mills, & Cohen, 2008; Nilson, 2007). Instructors are now designing more visually informative syllabi, including more much information about policies and student success strategies, and ensuring they have clear expectations of student achievement.

The information presented in this chapter entails the basics you need to know to either start a new syllabus or resurrect an older one. A sample syllabus is included, at the end of this chapter, to help you get started.

A. Roles and Purposes of a Syllabus

The syllabus can serve many roles within your course. Sometimes we take the syllabus for granted and not give it due credit for what it can accomplish. Here is a short overview of some roles and purposes:

Share expectations   ⟶   A syllabus will share formal and informal expectations of the course (student-related, course-related, behavior-related, goals of course, etc.)

Promises of Learning Objectives   ⟶   Specific course learning objectives are really promises of student learning to be achieved by the end of the course. The syllabus should include all objectives to meet accreditation and accountability requirements.

Convey enthusiasm   ⟶   An instructor who is excited to teach the course will have a syllabus that conveys this through the choice of topics, the design of assignments, and the organization of the course.

Set tone   ⟶   Students will quickly pick up the tone of the course through reading the content of the syllabus.

Establish Contract   ⟶   Some institutions will have students sign their name to indicate they have understood the syllabus and its contractual conditions regarding content, objectives, and policies.

Define Roles   ⟶   One can quickly determine the roles of the student and instructor after glancing over a syllabus.

Assess Readiness for Course   ⟶   A good syllabus will give enough detail on course content that students can assess their readiness for taking the course. There may be prerequisite courses required or skills and abilities students should have before entering the course.

Outline Workload   ⟶   By far the most important component of the syllabus for students is how much work there will be! The workload should be clearly outlined.

Explain Policies and Procedures   ⟶   There will always be a standard set of statements and references to policies and procedures that are part of a syllabus. It helps ensure everyone is exposed to the academic expectations of taking the course and the boundaries they must adhere to.

Relay Resource Details   ⟶   Textbooks, workbooks, clickers, specialized materials, safety equipment, and so on, are some of the items students need for a course. The syllabus is the place where this information is found.

Big Picture   ⟶   The syllabus often will share how the course fits within department programs or institutional certificates, degrees or diplomas. You should share the big picture of how the course works within the grander scheme of the profession/discipline.

Learning Tool   ⟶   Well-detailed syllabi are excellent learning tools. They help students design study notes and follow along from week to week.

B. Considerations While Creating

A syllabus is not written overnight! It takes a number of weeks to properly create. Even when you inherit a syllabus from another instructor, you often spend time revising and making it your own. The process of creating a syllabus is also an exercise in refining and organizing course content, choosing teaching and learning strategies, and detailing assessment/evaluation methods. The thought process that goes into creating a useful syllabus also aids in creating a thoughtful course geared for student success. Consider some of these questions that arise from student concerns when they look over your syllabus:

How can I present the content in an interesting way for students?

Is my language conveying who I am? Could I revise some statements?

Do my assignments and tests have a clear breakdown in marks and due dates?

Given students' busy lives and other expectations, does my course workload seem reasonable for their learning?

Have I clearly indicated the importance of taking this course and the benefits students will gain?

Have I shared the topics and content in a way that makes sense and possibly is graphically displayed?

Does the syllabus reflect that I welcome their questions, have times set aside to help them and appreciate feedback?

Do I indicate what type of instructor I am? Do I share information about class format, peer involvement, and resources used?

Does my evaluation match my objectives – is there a valid match? (e.g., if I want higher levels of thinking and synthesizing concepts, should I have all multiple choice question tests?)

C. Using the Syllabus In Class

So you spend a few solid days working on your syllabus. You get it uploaded to your course web site and plan your activities for the first class. Will you read over the syllabus with your students? Will you ask students to read it over? What parts will you cover in class? How long will you spend on explaining the syllabus? After you make it through your first class you likely know that most students never consult the syllabus again. Why did you go through all that work? Was it just for the department or to share with students at the beginning of your first class? Instructors are now using the syllabus as a learning tool and frequently access it throughout the term with their students. Here are some ideas to consider:

Post the Syllabus Online Early

- As soon as you can, post the syllabus on your course web site

- Send students a welcoming message and indicate that the syllabus is up for their perusal

- Post the syllabus in a prominent spot that makes it easy to access all term (e.g., on main page)

Highlight Important Points for Students

- In the first class, you definitely want to bring students' attention to the important points.

- You may wish to have students indicate what they find most important (due dates, workload, assignments, etc.) and, once you hear their concerns, you might inquire about other parts

Provide a Tear-Out Calendar of Assignment, Reading, and Test Dates

- Create a page in your syllabus that looks more like a calendar that only includes due dates for all assignments, readings, and tests. You could create an online version and update it if changes occur.

- Suggest students pull it out and paste it in their notebook/textbook.

- Students will appreciate you creating this for them as they often spend countless hours pulling that information out of poorly-written syllabi—this demonstrates to students how to organize their time around course expectations.

Use Syllabus as Class Starter

- It is one thing to reference the syllabus: "oh, that you'll find in the syllabus;" and quite another to actually make students find it, open it up, and look at it

- Make a point of looking at the syllabus at least every other class with a purpose to point out relationships among content, to refresh due dates, and to re-explain policies and procedures.

- Use as a graphical representation of topics to begin classes and show the big picture of course

Update Syllabus and Post Revised Editions

- If you need to alter the syllabus or revise content due to pre-assessment information you receive from students the first week, ensure you update your syllabus and post it online.

- This will indicate to students that the syllabus is an important document and that it can be changed to reflect student feedback.

Syllabus Quiz or Syllabus Scavenger Hunt

- Create a short online or paper quiz on the key components of the quiz, especially department policies and academic misconduct regulations

- Allow students to work in groups to find answers to quiz and hand in as a group

- Create a scavenger hunt for students to find answers to key questions!

D. Checklist of What to Include

Here is a checklist of the most common elements included in syllabi. The trend in education is to provide as detailed a syllabus as you can and avoid the short 1-2 pagers of the past. If you use your syllabus in your class and reference it frequently, the information below will serve as a strong basis to have a successful course and alleviate many student questions. Use this as a checklist.

✓ Basic Course Information

In as concise a fashion as possible, you need to list the following basics about a course. Students will frequently access this information when needed. With respect to contact information, many instructors do not give out home phone and email information. It is best to just release work contact details for your privacy and protection.

- ☐ **Institution Info** (Institution Name, Department/Faculty, Logo)

- ☐ **Course Title** (Full Course Title, Course Number, Credit Hours, Year and Semester)

- ☐ **Days and Times** (Day of Week, Start and End times for classes, Start week and End week date, days class is not held due to holidays or religious observances)

- ☐ **Class Location** (Building, Room Number)

- ☐ **URL** of Course Web site OR location within course management system

- ☐ **Instructor Details** (Name, Title, Office Location, Phone, Email, Office Hours, Preferred Method of Communication, Appointments or Drop In Requirements, Address, Other Contact Info)

- ☐ **Labs/Tutorials** (Location, Times, Teaching Assistants/Grad Assistants Leading)

- ☐ **Teaching Assistants/Graduate Assistants** (Name, Office Locations, Phone, Email, Office Hours)

✓ Course Description

Students always want to have a big picture overview of what the course is about—beyond what is written in the formal course listing. Ensure you include examples of how you will teach the course and the anticipated workload for students. Learning objectives are a key part of this section.

- ☐ **Prerequisites** (Courses, Skills, Permissions, Signatures)

- ☐ **Overview of Course** (Key concepts/topics, how course fits within program, ideal audience for course, rationale/benefits of taking course)

- ☐ **Learning Objectives** (List all objectives outlining what students should be able to know, do, demonstrate after this course)

- ☐ **Teaching/Learning Strategies** (list of strategies used in course e.g., lectures, group activities, questions, debates, videos, podcasts, to give students a sense of how the class will run)

- ☐ **Workload** (Estimated amount of time you expect students to prepare for class, working on assignments etc. Students appreciate an honest approximation of your expectations)

✓ Assessment and Evaluation Details

This is the first section most students access when they are handed the syllabus. They are very keen to see how you will assessing and evaluating them. Including in-class assessment activity ideas will let them know you will be seeking feedback on learning and how the course is going. Evaluation details will help them see where they will be demonstrating their knowledge.

- ☐ **Term Tests and Quizzes** (how many, total marks/percentage, online or in-class, open/closed book, short/long answer, multiple choice/diagrams/matching, low, medium or high thinking, dates scheduled, length of time, items can bring such as calculator, measuring instruments)

- ☐ **Exam** (total marks/percentage of final grade, date, length of time, in-class or exam timetable, number of questions, types of questions)

- ☐ **In-class Assessment Activities** (what to expect as far as informal gathering of information for student feedback, purpose and use within class, examples such as ticket out door, etc.)

- ☐ **Evaluation Methods** (types e.g., projects, presentations, demonstrations, essays – how many, due dates, marking info, total marks/percentage of final grade, submission format – online or hard copy, indication if they are any opportunities to improve grades through redoing)

✓ Required Course Materials

Be sure to list all course materials from the standard textbook to any web sites or online resources. The most important component in this section is to indicate if it is 'required' or 'recommended' as students will surely ask you this!

- ☐ **Textbook** (author, title, ISBN, edition number, costs, where to purchase, availability of online notes or password access to publisher site for materials, use in course)

- ☐ **Readings** (other than textbook, individual readings students will need to access, URLs, PDF copies on course web site or description of where to purchase/copy)

- ☐ **Course pack** (collection of readings printed and bound, cost, where to purchase, rationale)

- ☐ **Library Reserve** (is a copy of the textbook or other readings on reserve, how long can take out on reserve/or in library use only, name, library number)

☐ **Specific Course Tools** (special calculators, safety equipment, medical supplies, art and photography materials, paper, clothing, software)

✓ Course Schedule of Topics/Content

This does not need to be a detailed explanation of the course content, nor does it need to make you feel tied to dates and topics each week. Students just want to have a general idea of the topics that will be covered in the course and the general progression of them throughout the term.

☐ **Tentative Schedule of Topics** (week by week, graphic representation by whole session, room for flexibility/change, could be a calendar)

☐ **Special Dates/Missed Classes** (religious holidays, special events and times when the class does not meet, off-campus field trips, special performances, last day to withdraw from class)

☐ **Quiz, Test, and Exam Dates** (included in schedule)

✓ Policies and Procedures

Try to phrase policies in a positive and friendly format so it does not sound like you are thinking the worst of students and are out to punish them. If you explain the reasoning behind policies, you are more likely to gain students' cooperation. Additionally, allow for students to ask questions to clarify any policies they are not entirely clear about. You might even get some student feedback on smaller points such as using cell phones, texting, and eating in class.

☐ **Attendance** (lateness, missed classes, penalties, make-up procedures, reporting illness and personal/family emergencies, contact expected with instructor/TAs/GAs)

☐ **Assignments** (format for handing in, lateness penalties, extensions, missed, penalties)

☐ **Academic Misconduct/Dishonesty** (plagiarism, cheating, copying, signing permission form for submitting papers to online plagiarism sites like Turn It In, penalties for infractions)

☐ **Grading** (weighting of components, incomplete, pass/fail explanations, grade appeals, requirements for passing course, completion of all components)

☐ **Tests and Exams** (what to do if late or missed, penalties, procedures)

☐ **Participation** (expectations around class participation, involvement in group activities etc.)

☐ **Decorum/Professionalism** (what and how you expect students to behave in your class, disrupting students/class, use of cell phones, inappropriate use of laptops, other situations which may result in students' learning being affected, etc.)

☐ **Safety** (procedures for lab safety, health issues, proper attire, safety equipment needed, what to do in case of a earthquake, tornado, fire, hazardous spill, bomb threat, violent intruder, or other emergencies that threaten the safety of students in your class; notification procedures for inclement weather/impassable roads – radio, institution web site)

☐ **Respect** (include a statement about your expectations around listening and respecting the points of view of their peers, about how to handle any controversial course content and how to manage their feelings and words when they encounter different attitudes, opinions and information)

✓ Learning Resources

This is not a common section in most syllabi but it is nice to include if you have some suggestions or tips to pass onto students. Students will be very appreciative of any ideas you have from previous students or offerings of the course in terms of misconceptions, areas where students get confused, and what works in terms of studying for exams and completing assignments.

- ☐ **Tips for Success** (different approaches to success in course, time management tips, common course misconceptions, sample test questions, topics that might cause confusion etc.)

- ☐ **Glossary** (technical terms, specialized info to help in studying)

- ☐ **URLs** (to previous exam questions, student assignments, style manuals, web-based resources to podcasts/video/and support material)

✓ Accommodations for Students

Your department or faculty might have a standard statement about accommodating students. You may also wish to approach the student learning/support centre at your institution for any further details on workshops, consultations, and information they provide for students of all needs.

- ☐ **Disabilities** (a statement about inviting students with physical, medical, mental, or learning disabilities to approach instructor for any accommodations required for success in course)

- ☐ **Learning Support** (location, times, offerings of learner support centre/student support area at your institution, possibly invite a representative to your class to speak for a few minutes about resources and people there to help)

- ☐ **Missed Classes** (a statement about accommodating students who need to miss your class due to religious beliefs, observations and practice, athletic/sports team participation, job/admission interviews, family/personal emergencies, and circumstances out of their control)

✓ Rights and Responsibilities of Students

- ☐ Many institutions are developing rights and responsibility statements with both instructor and student bodies. Here are some examples that are showing up in syllabi:

  - ► Right of students to have class meet on required days throughout term; instructors have right to expect students to show up on time for learning

  - ► Right of students to have an instructor organized and prepared class; instructors have right to similarly expect students to be prepared and ready for learning each class

  - ► Right of students to expect instructors to grade and return assignments and tests within a reasonable time frame; instructors have right to expect students to hand in assignments on time

✓ Disclaimer

- ☐ It is wise to include a statement about the subject of change. Guest speakers, length of time to cover a topic, a field trip, or even some class formats may change due to a variety of reasons. Try not to change assignment and test dates. If there are any changes, inform the students both in writing and orally in class. Provide an updated syllabus on your course web site.

E. Layout and Design Tips

Many instructors think that a shorter syllabus is better, but students do appreciate a comprehensive syllabus that covers most of the sections listed on the previous pages. It will ease their anxieties about the course, answer their questions and, most of all, provide them with a helpful guide about what to expect throughout the term. Once you have all the components for your syllabus, you need to take a few minutes and format it to ensure it is useful, informative, and formatted for best readability. Sometimes, you may be expected to use departmental or institutional templates for formatting, but most often it is up to you. Here are some tips.

Bold / Increase Font Size of Headings and Important Information

Don't make font size too small or jam too much on a page.

White space will help with making it more readable.

Try representing your content through a flowchart, timeline, concept map or a way of visually showing connections between topics.

S	M	T	W	T	F	S

Create a calendar or simple listing of all due dates and tests.

- Use bullets
- Use short phrases
- Use headings and sub-titles to break up information

Course Title

Topic

Topic   Topic   Topic

F. Sample Syllabus

Most instructors design their syllabi in a word processing program with a standard font and text flowing from the left to the right margin. There may be bulleted information, but there is a great deal of prose and sentences within the syllabus and few, if any, visuals. There often is some bolding, underlining, or italicizing to add emphasis and draw the students' attention to important parts. A quick search on the web will result in hundreds of syllabi looking fairly similar in terms of layout and formatting. Research on effectively using visuals and text in learning materials (Mayer, 2005) consistently points out the huge benefits of visually formatting content for improved student comprehension.

It is not a bad thing to create a syllabus in a word processing program or have it looking fairly generic. By all accounts students tend to view them the first class and then toss them aside for other notes and papers from the class. But if you took a few more minutes to consider a different layout, adding some graphics, or including a calendar or chart to outline course content, you would be providing students with a better tool for accessing course information and possibly accessing it more frequently throughout the term.

Take a look at the following 7 pages. They are based on a fake Communications course at a fake education institution. The content shared in the previous part of this chapter is laid out in a different manner through the use of a desktop publishing program to create newsletters (e.g., Microsoft Publisher). This format involved the use of fewer pages and content was more visually displayed to aid in quick referencing and future use of the syllabus. See what you think!

COMMUNICATION 1000

NEW SCHOOL
DEPARTMENT OF COMMUNICATION

Comm 1000, Winter Term, 3 credits

Course Highlights

- *Speaking, writing and digital communication —an interactive class!*
- *2 hours of preparation per week for 7 in–class quizzes (5% each) and 5 in–class assignments (5% each)*
- *2 individual presentations (10% each) will take about 3-4 hours each to prepare—given in class*
- *Final 2 hour exam (20%) based on 4 case scenarios on situations with poor communication*

COURSE INFORMATION

Days & Times:
Tuesdays and Thursdays
2:00—3:30 p.m.

Dates:
January 4—April 5th
Reading Week: Feb 14-18

Class Location:
Madison Arts Building
Room 210 (Computer Lab)

URL: http://www.new.edu/deptcomm/comm101

Instructor Contact Info:

Name: Dr. Kate Morgan

Office: # 519, Peterson Bldg

Hours: Mondays and Fridays 9:30 a.m.—12:00 p.m. (drop in, no appointment needed)

E: kate.morgan@new.edu

P: 999.555.1234

Preference: Email is answered within 24-48 hours

Address: New School, 2000 Academic Drive, Newton, New State

My background is in effective communication practices for the business and education sectors with an emphasis on proper use of technological communication tools.

There aren't any labs or tutorials associated with this course. If you have any questions, please feel free to drop in during office hours or send me an email to arrange another time that is mutually agreeable.

I am here to help you learn!

COURSE DESCRIPTION

Prerequisites
This is an introductory course. Any student can take it. It also is a core course for anyone taking the Communication Stream and must be taken prior to taking COMM 2000.

Course Overview
This course looks at the basics of good communication in the oral, written and digital media. It introduces you to current practices, socially acceptable etiquette and proper form and function of various communica-

tion methods. The course aims to give you an overview of this field, yet at the same time give you time to practice and hone your communication skills through activities, presentations and creative assignments.

Teaching and Learning Strategies
There will be a lot of interaction and participation expected. It is a communication course—so we must communicate! There will be short readings to do prior to class, a number of small in-

class quizzes and then opportunities for you to practice your skills through assignments and in-class presentations. Sometimes I will give you partial notes; sometimes you will create your own. It will be a fun class in that we'll talk lots, write lots and produce exciting digital communication pieces.

Workload
I expect you to do about 2 hours of preparation for the class each week (for quizzes and in-class work). The 2 presentations will take about 3 hours each to prepare.

COMMUNICATION 1000

Course Content by Topics

Introduction to Communication—Jan 4

Importance of Communication in Today's World

Communication Processes

Verbal Communication

Non-Verbal Communication

Public Speaking

Listening

Presentation # 1: Personal Story Public Speaking—Feb 3

Digital Communication

Slideshow Presentations

Presenting with Props and Slides

Web 2.0 Tools for Communication

Web Page Design

Written Communication

Formats and Types

Word Processing and Desktop Publishing

Presentation # 2: Blog, Wiki or Web Page Demonstration—Mar 29

Review of Communication—April 5

Learning Objectives

By the end of the course students will be able to:
- Explain five major roles communication plays in today's world
- Identify 3 communication processes

By the end of the course students will be able to:
- Give a 2-3 minute public presentation using verbal and non-verbal skills for effective story telling
- Apply understanding of verbal and non-verbal skills in advising others how to improve their speaking skills

By the end of the course, students will be able to:
- Create a slideshow presentation utilizing current and proper communication techniques for clearly and professionally conveying messages and information
- Make valid suggestions for improvement of digital communication products
- Identify 10 main points to consider when presenting with props or slides
- Choose appropriate Web 2.0 communication tools for varying situations
- Explain what makes a good web page in terms of communication and design

By the end of the course, students will be able to:
- Create a wiki, blog or web page using appropriate web tools or software
- Apply conventions and mechanics of proper writing to various forms of written communication

ASSESSMENT AND EVALUATION DETAILS

In-class Quizzes (5% each)

- **7** in-class quizzes
- Online and individually completed
- 10 minutes to complete
- Based on the textbook, other readings and activities we have done in class
- **Dates:** Jan 18, 25, Feb 1, 8, Mar 1, 8, 22 (Tuesdays)
- Multiple choice, matching, true/false, matching and short answer

Total: **35% of final mark**

In-class Assignments (5% each)

- **5** in-class assignments
- Digital and individually completed
- 30—60 minutes to complete
- Based on activities in class, application of knowledge and skills, often done on the computer and handed in digitally
- **Dates:** Jan 13, 27, Feb 24, Mar 3, 17 (Thursdays)
- Creating, designing, writing, manipulating digital compositions

Total: **25% of final mark**

Presentation 1: Public Speaking

- In-class presentation
- 2-3 minutes in length
- Application of verbal and non-verbal skills to tell a personal story to class
- Peer assessment for informal feedback
- Date: Feb 3

Total: **10% of final mark**

Presentation 2: Blog, Wiki or Web Page Demonstration

- In-class presentation
- 2-3 minutes in length
- Application of practices in digital format to demonstrate a blog, wiki or web page you created
- Peer assessment for feedback
- Date: Mar 29

Total: **10% of final mark**

Final Exam

- April 24
- 2 hours
- 4 case study scenarios revolving around communication problems—written answers
- Each case should take about half an hour to answer

Total: **20 % of final mark**

In-class Assessment Activities: Every now and then I will ask you to participate in a short activity which will allow me to hear how you are feeling about the course, where you are having problems and where I can help you.

COURSE MATERIALS

Textbook: Communication Basics by Rodney Teather, 2011 4th Edition by New Books Inc. ISBN: 99-9999-9999-09 (Bookstore - $ 89.00)

Readings: Each week I will provide you with readings to supplement the text book. You will be provided with URLs to the PDF documents or web pages. You will see these listed on the course web site.

Library Reserve: 2 copies of textbook on reserve (3 hours only library use), under my name at front desk

Course Tools: You can work in the computer lab or work at home. You will need a computer that has good access to the Internet if you are working from home.

COMMUNICATION 1000

January

Sun	Mon	Tue	Wed	Thu	Fri	Sat
						1
2	3	4 First Class	5	6	7	8
9	10	11	12	13 In-class Assignment (5%)	14	15
16	17	18 Quiz (5%)	19	20	21	22
23	24	25 Quiz (5%)	26	27 In-class Assignment (5%)	28	29
30	31					

February

Sun	Mon	Tue	Wed	Thu	Fri	Sat
		1 Quiz (5%)	2	3 Presentation # 1 (10%)	4	5
6	7	8 Quiz (5%)	9	10	11	12
13	14 Reading Week	15 Reading Week (No class)	16 Reading Week	17 Reading Week (No class)	18 Reading Week	19
20	21	22	23	24 In-class Assignment (5%)	25	26
27	28					

March

Sun	Mon	Tue	Wed	Thu	Fri	Sat
		1 Quiz (5%)	2	3 In-class Assignment (5%)	4	5
6	7	8 Quiz (5%)	9	10	11	12
13	14	15	16	17 In-class Assignment (5%)	18	19
20	21	22 Quiz (5%)	23	24	25	26
27	28	29 Presentation # 2 (10%)	30	31		

April

Sun	Mon	Tue	Wed	Thu	Fri	Sat
					1	2
3	4	5 Last Day of Class	6	7	8	9
10	11	12	13	14	15	16
17	18	19	20	21 Final Exam	22	23
24	25	26	27	28	29	30

COMMUNICATION 1000

POLICIES AND PROCEDURES

Attendance and Assignments

It is important to attend class. There are 7 in-class quizzes and 5 in-class assignments. There are also 2 presentations required to be performed in front of the class. If you are unable to make it to class, please send me a short email at least an hour prior to class start. If you have an appointment or personal situation you know of ahead of time, please also let me know as soon as possible. We will work together to ensure you have an opportunity to make up a missed quiz (by taking another version online at a later date) or complete a similar assignment you miss. Presentations will have to be scheduled in another class or in my office. If you fail to email me or miss more than 1 quiz or more than 1 assignment, there will be no opportunities for making up missed work. You must take the final exam. If you miss the final exam, you will have to take a make-up exam at a later date.

Academic Integrity

It is required that students be informed of the university policy that any act of academic dishonesty is a serious offence. Plagiarism (the unacknowledged use of another writer's work) may be dealt with by the instructor giving a "0" (zero) on any assignment containing plagiarism in the course. A final grade of "0" (zero) may be awarded to the student guilty of academic dishonesty regardless of how well the student is doing in the course at the time. Please refer to the academic policy in the Academic Calendar.

"The problem with communication ... is the illusion that it has been accomplished."

George Bernard Shaw

Grading

All in-class quizzes are worth 5% and all in-class assignments are worth 5% of the final mark. The two presentations are worth 10% each of the final mark. The final exam will be worth 20% of your final mark and is mandatory you take it regardless of your mark in the course. Grades will be calculated and submitted on April 30th with final marks being available to see May 1. If there are any questions with your final grade, please make an appointment. Information on grade appeals appears in the academic calendar.

Participation

This is a highly participative course. Each class we will be doing activities, having discussions and interacting with each other. It is expected you will participate in as many ways as possible.

Professionalism

It is expected that you act professionally at all times in your written and oral communication both online and in the classroom. Any devices or activities which disrupt the learning of others will not be tolerated and you will be asked to stop (e.g., watching videos on laptop, texting on phone, talking to someone while others are speaking, writing an email etc.). If you are found disrupting the class more than once, you will be asked to see me.

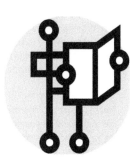

Safety

If there is a lockdown initiated (e.g., harmful individual or bomb threat) or a natural disaster (e.g., tornado or earthquake) please follow my directions. Please listen to the local radio stations for any notice on school closures due to weather or campus incidents. Be safe at all times coming to and from school.

Respect

There may be different points of view raised in this course. It is hoped that you will respect everyone's point of view and give people the time to speak and be heard. We'll do the same for you when you speak. After the two presentations, it is expected you will give useful and positive feedback to your classmates.

A Practical Handbook for Educators

LEARNING RESOURCES

Tips for Success

Here are some suggestions for success in this course that have helped former students.

1. Attend class—it is simply the best way to grasp content and practice applying it.

2. Discuss the readings with a friend before the quiz. It helps solidify concepts and details.

3. Choose a story for your public speaking presentation that means something to you—it will be easier to talk about it.

4. Work on your second presentation well ahead of the due date. It isn't something you can complete the night before.

5. Paste the calendars (included in the syllabus) in the front of your textbook or binder to remind you about all the quizzes and assignments.

6. Buy the textbook—it is worth the cost and will help you with future communication courses. The readings from it are quite interesting.

7. See the instructor if you are confused or not sure about something.

Access URLs and resources I provide you in the course web site. They are all helpful in supporting you in this course.

"To listen well is as powerful a means of communication and influence as to talk well."
John Marshall

ACCOMMODATIONS

To ensure that disability-related concerns are properly addressed during this course, students with documented disabilities and who may require assistance to participate in this class are encouraged to speak with me as soon as possible.

Students who suspect they may have a disability that may affect their participation in this course are advised to go to the Centre for Students with Disabilities or see your Academic Advisor.

Please feel free to approach me should you be encountering any academic problems.

There is a Learner Support Centre on campus which helps students in a variety of areas such as studying, writing papers and time management.

PRIVACY WHEN USING SOCIAL MEDIA WEB TOOLS

When you use social media web tools, your privacy is always at risk. Ensure you read the privacy guidelines for any media or tool you use and keep the settings set at the highest level to protect your identity and personal information.

- This course asks you to create a web page, wiki or blog.
- The social media web tool (e.g., Blogger, WordPress) you may choose to complete the assignment may store your information on a server housed outside of our educational institution—often in another country. Laws in other countries may make it possible for your information to be accessed from the server without your consent.
- Any information you put on the web often is difficult to erase. Please be careful what you write, link to or upload to any social media or web-based tool environment.
- If you are uncomfortable with the privacy risks you may encounter, please see me and I'll provide you with an alternative format for completing your assignment. Be safe online!

DISCLAIMER

The items presented in this syllabus (assignments, dates, policies, procedures and topics) are subject to change in the event of unforeseen circumstances, but only by mutual agreement of the students and instructor. This would be done with the goal of supporting your success in this course.

One of the basic causes for all the trouble in the world today is that people talk too much and think too little. They act impulsively without thinking. I always try to think before I talk.

Margaret Chase Smith

There is more than a verbal tie between the words common, community, and communication.... Try the experiment of communicating, with fullness and accuracy, some experience to another, especially if it be somewhat complicated, and you will find your own attitude toward your experience changing. John Dewey

Top Ten Takeaways

1. **Syllabus Creation:** Writing a syllabus is common task for every instructor.

2. **Purposes:** Syllabi serve many purposes such as sharing expectations, setting the tone for the course, outlining workload, and explaining procedures and policies.

3. **Student Questions:** When creating a syllabus, consider the questions students might be asking when they read through it. Questions about workload, evaluation, topics, and teaching and learning strategies used.

4. **Online Accessibility:** Post your syllabus online as soon as it is complete. Students will appreciate an early look at the course and can prepare questions prior to class.

5. **Address in Class Time:** Take time during the first class and subsequent classes to address the syllabus, go through important parts, and explain key information pieces. Using the syllabus frequently will signal to students that this is an important document to understand.

6. **Checklist of Components:** There are many required components to your average syllabus. Use the checklist of sections included in this chapter.

7. **Group Content:** Try to group syllabus content within appropriately titled sections. This will help students find materials quickly.

8. **Layout and Design:** Consider the layout and design of your syllabus. It might take only half an hour more to format sections or add some graphics or include a chart, but it will be worth the time to present your syllabus in a more readable manner.

9. **Visual Representation of Topics:** Try representing your content/topics in a format other than a list of week-by-week events. Is there a visual layout (hierarchical chart, circles, Gant chart, concept map) that might help students see the connections between topics or progression of learning throughout the semester?

10. **Desktop Publishing:** Using a word processing program with text flowing from the left to right margins is a common format for creating a syllabus. To possibly reduce pages and allow for ease in chunking content, try a desktop publishing program (e.g., Microsoft Publisher) and a newsletter template to quickly produce a syllabus that is a bit different!

Next Steps

1. Ask your department head, supervisor or colleagues if there is a standard template or format for the syllabus at your institution. Even if you have been teaching the course for a while, new changes might have come into effect. Ascertain what you are able to change and what must be worded or formatted a certain way.

2. Do an Internet search for syllabi. You will find many different formats available for a quick scan. Consider what you like and don't like in what you are finding.

3. Look over your current syllabus (yours or one you inherited). If you were a student looking at it, what questions might you have about the course? Can you find that information quickly and is it explained clearly? Students mainly want to know about workload, assignments, tests, and what the course is about.

4. Look at your content/topic outline and what you'll do each week. Research indicates that visually presenting content in a graphic format will aid students in understanding and will more clearly present the big picture of the course. Is there a layout (flowchart, mind map, hierarchical chart, circle, etc.) that would work for displaying the basic topics of your course and the relationship they have to each other?

5. Constructing a useful syllabus takes time. Set aside a day or so to begin considering the checklist in this chapter. Start checking off what you have already and what you need to include.

References and Resources

Carnegie Mellon University (n.d.). *Write the syllabus*. Retrieved November 30, 2009, from http://www.cmu.edu/teaching/designteach/design/syllabus/index.html

Davis, B. G. (2009). *Tools for Teaching*. San Francisco, CA: Jossey-Bass.

Grunet O'Brien, J., Mills, B. J. & Cohen, M W. (2008). *The Course Syllabus: A learning-centered approach*. San Francisco, CA: Jossey-Bass.

Mayer, R. E. (2005). *The Cambridge Handbook of Multimedia Learning*. New York, NY: Cambridge University Press.

Nilson, L. B. (2007). *The Graphic Syllabus and the Outcomes Map: Communicating Your Course*. San Francisco, CA: Jossey-Bass.

Section II: Creating and Designing Learning Opportunities and Experiences

Chapter 6: Making Learning Accessible

Chapter Overview

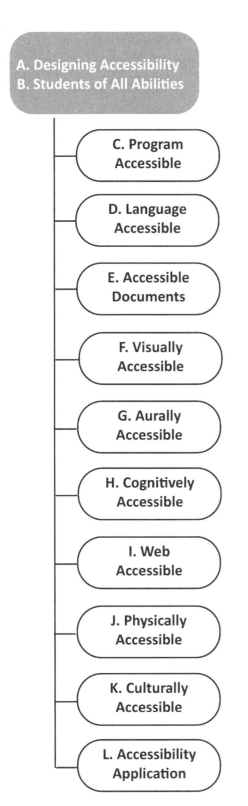

A. Designing Accessibility
B. Students of All Abilities

C. Program Accessible

D. Language Accessible

E. Accessible Documents

F. Visually Accessible

G. Aurally Accessible

H. Cognitively Accessible

I. Web Accessible

J. Physically Accessible

K. Culturally Accessible

L. Accessibility Application

When you plan to modify resources, lectures, class activities, web-based content and communication methods for students with disabilities, you end up making learning MORE accessible to ALL students.

This statement is the premise of this chapter. Making learning accessible is a responsibility of instructors to ensure that there are fair opportunities for anyone who wants to learn. Internationally, governments have implemented, or are soon to implement, laws and requirements for buildings, communication, resources, and learning to be more accessible to people of all abilities and disabilities.

This chapter outlines a lot of generic suggestions that are not hard to implement and will make learning more accessible for all students. If nothing else, the information will make you more aware of how to modify your teaching and learning strategies to meet students' needs.

There are some suggestions that will take a bit more time to implement or reconfigure for meeting accessibility standards. Do not fear! Taking small steps and working on one course component at a time is a good way to go. After a while, you will begin to see through a new set of lenses; those that immediately consider a few small tweaks that could increase the accessibility of learning by all!

Take a look at some ideas in this chapter—you may be doing them already!

If you are creating a course for the first time, it is wise to consider making it as accessible as possible from the beginning. Take the time now to ensure the course makes learning accessible to all students. Get it right from the start!

A. Designing Accessibility

This section introduces you to the 'universal design' movements afoot in many countries and the resulting principles that are being applied to all levels of education. This section will help set the context for the sub-sections within this chapter. With more students taking on post-secondary studies than ever before, educators are seeing more and more students with disabilities who require modifications or accommodations for academic success. Instructors are finding it challenging to respond to student requests for alternative formats for content, while they are planning classes. Does the following scenario resonate in some way with you?

Dr. Jones arrived at her first class of the semester. She went through the syllabus, ensured she covered all the course topics and clearly explained the evaluation methods. She then let students know about the faculty policy about students with disabilities or those who required modifications within the course. She let her students know it was their responsibility to disclose to the instructor any information about disabilities. She also sent around a pamphlet from the Centre for Disabilities with information on the steps to undertake for documenting disabilities, the paperwork required and the length of time it would take to get everything done. About two weeks into the semester three students in her class came to her office to disclose their learning disabilities. A week later the students returned with a form from the Centre for Disabilities indicating the changes she would need to make to accommodate these students. Dr. Jones sat in her office one day looking at these forms and wondered how different things might be had she planned her course with these sorts of students in mind. These were her students:

- *Tom had low vision. He wore glasses and could see things at a distance but had a hard time with small print and small fonts on PowerPoint presentations. He required most of the content to be digital and uploaded before class so he could use his laptop to enlarge the print. He also needed PowerPoint presentations to have the font at least 18-20 point in size on every screen and the ability to have the presentation on his computer at the same time for taking notes. He also appreciated auditory explanations of assignments, or the chance to talk to the professor in her office to discuss evaluation particulars.*

- *Jasbir was learning English for the first time. He was fairly good with understanding the spoken form but struggled with the written form. He needed a bit more time to write tests, to understand questions and appreciated the opportunity to discuss the course with his peers. He also didn't completely understand plagiarism and how to write by citing authors and giving credit to their work. This was all new to him and he needed a bit more help with understanding special terms, jargon, and acronyms which were used a lot in class.*

- *Neela had a learning disability. She was unable to process material quickly and could not take notes and listen to a professor at the same time. She needed to have content given to her in a few different ways (e.g., video of professor talking, audio clip of presentations, presentations, questions to ponder, etc.) as the textbook was not a useful learning tool for her.*

Dr. Jones realized these were just three students, but their learning required quite a bit of work on her part to modify content she already had, create some different versions of other content, and change the teaching and learning strategies she had planned to use in the class. She overhead some of her colleagues returning from a session on "Universal Design" at the Teaching and Learning Center; might they have some thoughts on how she could rework her course to meet these students' needs and maybe others too?

Universal Design is a solution geared at producing buildings, environments, products, and communication that are accessible by any person. The architecturally-based concept was originated by Ronald Mace in the early 1970s. He founded the Center for Universal Design at North Carolina State University (Scott, McGuire & Shaw, 2003).

> *The intent of universal design is to simplify life for everyone by making products, communications, and the built environment more usable by as many people as possible at little or no extra cost. Universal design benefits people of all ages and abilities.*
> Center for Universal Design, College of Design, North Carolina State University, 2008

Universal design is not just for those with disabilities. The focus is to make our world more accessible to as many people as possible. Some people have embraced the universal design movement and provided helpful tools, processes, and places where access is barrier-free, especially recognizing our aging population. You have seen examples of universal design in your world:

- Curbs being cut so that there is a smooth transition from the sidewalk to the street

- Busses have a lowered floor for ease in getting on and off

- Door handles are designed as levers for pushing down on rather than having to turn a knob

- Counters and water fountains are installed at various heights

- Wider doorways give more room for moving around in smaller spaces

- Light switch panels are flat allowing people to press rather than having to lift a small toggle switch

Out of the universal design movement evolved the Universal Design for Instruction (UDI) framework and the Universal Design for Learning (UDL) framework which both took a lot of similar concepts that Mace proposed and adapted them to education (McGuire, Scott & Shaw, 2006). While there are a number of other frameworks and models built upon the universal design movement, it is worthy to consider the principles of these two frameworks.

These frameworks do not propose accessibility by 'all' or the need to abandon student support services. Rather, they give educators examples of how they can begin to make courses and programs available to a greater number of students. The word 'universal' in the universal design world does not mean that it is 'generic' or 'one-size-fits-all' in terms of teaching and learning. The notion of 'universal design' is that students would need to rely less on the services of support people, be more seamlessly integrated into the classroom, require fewer demands on instructors for modifications and create less disruptions to the class. Student learning would be a key focus in the design or refinement of courses and programs—all the while benefiting the greatest number of students (Silver, Bourke, & Strehorn, 1998).

The Universal Design for Instruction (UDI) framework focuses on teaching processes (creation, design, and implementation of classroom instruction) that meet the needs of students in a barrier-free environment and that do not require the need for specialized design. The main work on this framework is done at the Center for Postsecondary Education and Disability (CPED) at the University of Connecticut. Their focus is to find ways to develop resources that university and college faculty can use to ensure access for students with cognitive and learning disabilities (McGuire, Scott & Shaw, 2006).

The Principles of Universal Design for Instruction © designed by Scott, McGuire and Shaw (2006) outline 9 components to consider when planning your course.

1. **Equitable Use:** This means the design of instructional materials is accessible to all students. For example: a web learning tool can be used by students who are blind and using screen readers to convert text and images into speech, as well as by other students.

2. **Flexibility in Use:** This means the design allows students to have a variety of ways of approaching the material depending on their abilities, choice, and preference for learning. For example, a lesson on new math concepts can be learned through taking notes during a presentation and asking questions or through an online video clip of the professor demonstrating the concept and providing a few examples to complete independently.

3. **Simple and intuitive use:** This means the design is easy to understand and doesn't require a specialized set of knowledge, skills, or experience. For example, the web environment used to upload assignments to a digital drop box is easy to follow, has simple instructions and buttons that make sense and the user does not get confused. Students are confident their assisgnments have been successfully submitted to the instructor.

4. **Perceptible information:** This means the design communicates information and works in conditions where there are distractions or the inability of the student to hear or see. For example, a guest speaker comes with a PowerPoint presentation and a handout capturing the key concepts to supplement the verbal explanations he gives of video clips and pictures.

5. **Tolerance for error:** This means the design does not allow students to run into too many problems when they conduct an action. For example, the undo button in software programs allows students to undo their mistakes or wrong actions.

6. **Low physical effort**: This means the design results in minimal exertion or exhaustion by the student. For example, allow students to create an audio file of their reflections rather than having to type or write out a paper. Talking into a microphone might be less tiring than writing for some students.

7. **Size and space for approach and use:** This means the design has adequate space and size for students to reach, use, manipulate, turn and move around in regardless of body size, posture, or mobility. For example, the tutorial room has enough room for the student in a wheelchair to enter, turn around, and have a desk in front of them. There is also enough room to present and to work alone or in groups.

8. **A community of learners:** This means the design of learning involves students and instructors communicating and working together. For example: an instructor has virtual office hours and puts up a digital discussion board for students to share thoughts and ideas about topics as they come up in class.

9. **Instructional climate:** This means the design of the learning environment is purposely supportive, non-threatening and comforting. For example, an instructor asks for student feedback about how the class is going, responds to needs, and creates a warm and caring environment for learning.

Take a look at your course. Does it meet some or all of these nine principles? With some effort, could you modify your course to be responsive to these principles of design?

Sharing some similarities to Universal Design for Instruction (UDI), is the Universal Design for Learning (UDL) framework attributed to research done by the Center for Applied Special Technology (CAST), the Council for Exceptional Children (CEC) and other schools, states, and individuals. Based on the work of researchers in neuroscience and social constructivism, along with the adaptive technology tools and digital media, this framework has three main principles in terms of designing curricula, assessment, and evaluation and teaching strategies. As educators, we want courses and curricula to be flexible in that they provide alternative ways for students to access learning regardless of their ability or disability (Rose & Meyer, 2002). These principles are a bit different than the nine previously listed, but they do share many similarities. Could you design a course providing examples of these three principles?

Principle 1: Provide Multiple Means of Representation

- ☐ Give students a variety of entrance points to approach content by presenting content and concepts in a variety of formats (e.g., text, video, audio, concept map, diagram, etc.)

- ☐ Provide numerous examples of the content and concepts

- ☐ Highlight important skills and knowledge (e.g., point out critical components, use your voice to emphasize items, summarize key points at end of class)

- ☐ Use digital media (and all the variations it affords) to represent information for students

- ☐ Connect new learning with already acquired knowledge and skills (e.g., use a web page to provide links to previously learned material, to background knowledge, and to review pages)

Principle 2: Provide Multiple Ways for Students' Action and Expression

❏ Create and design learning opportunities in a variety of formats to get students actively engaged in learning (e.g., use a collection of teaching strategies—small group, individual, large group, etc.)

❏ Provide teaching and learning strategies that allow students to apply their learning through arts-based activities, group activities, problem-solving activities, or brainstorming activities.

❏ Scaffold and sequence the learning of complex components (e.g., provide a video of steps to follow and explain and give an example of each step)

❏ Give students lots of opportunities to practice and get feedback on how they are doing

❏ Allow students choice in how they demonstrate their learning (e.g., written paper, presentation, speech, design a model, solve a case study, create a software program, model a 3D image etc.)

Principle 3: Provide Multiple Methods to Engage Students Through Motivation and Interest

❏ Develop a variety of hooks to engage students in a class, a new topic, a project (e.g., making topic relevant to real world situation/problem, connecting to a career path, demonstrating a phenomena/experiment that connects learning, etc.)

❏ Give students choice in terms of the tools they use during learning experiences (e.g., clickers, video simulations, online surveys, multimedia authoring programs, etc.)

❏ Provide suitable levels of challenge and stimulation (e.g., variety of problems to solve getting increasingly more difficult, progressing through levels in a simulation software program, varying assignments from beginning of term to end of term that become more challenging)

❏ Offer choice of environment required for learning (e.g., quiet individual work, small group discussion, music available in background while class works, discussion on a topic, headphones on listening to a podcast or video presentation, etc.) (Rose & Meyer, 2002)

B. Students of All Abilities

Today we are more aware than ever before of the diversity of students we have in our classrooms. As instructors, we cannot ignore the urgent need to ensure our programs, courses, and classes are accessible. We have so many different students. The following list is not meant to overwhelm you, but merely point out the diversity that exists in today's classes. We have students with/who have/who:

➤ Anxiety disorders (e.g., obsessive-compulsive)
➤ Are unable to hold a book or paper
➤ Arthritis
➤ Autism

➤ Autism Spectrum Disorders
➤ Brain Injuries
➤ Communication disorder
➤ Deaf (e.g., with a profound hearing loss)
➤ Deaf and does not talk

- ➤ Developmental disabilities
- ➤ Difficulty accessing information on the Internet
- ➤ Down Syndrome
- ➤ Epilepsy
- ➤ Financial obstacles
- ➤ Geographical challenges for attending face-to-face classes
- ➤ Hard-of-Hearing
- ➤ Intellectual disabilities
- ➤ Lack of interest or engagement
- ➤ Learning a new language
- ➤ Learning disability
- ➤ Mental illnesses
- ➤ Mood disorders (e.g., depression)
- ➤ Muscle Spasms
- ➤ Non-visible disabilities
- ➤ Physical disabilities
- ➤ Seizures
- ➤ Sensory and physical disabilities
- ➤ Slow bandwidth for Internet access
- ➤ Stutters
- ➤ Use walkers, mobility aids
- ➤ Use wheelchairs
- ➤ Vision loss

This chapter gives you some easy tips for creating accessible learning environments for students that take into account the principles of universal design.

You do not have to invest a lot of time or energy into changing your courses or creating new resources; some simple tips will make a course more accessible. Over time, create new resources with accessibility suggestions in mind from the beginning.

Do not be overwhelmed by the many sub-sections of this chapter. Accessibility is a diverse topic and you could only read the sections that apply to the students you have, or will have, in your class.

Many of the suggestions are just 'good teaching and learning' practices; you may be doing many of them already. Check them out!

C. Program Accessible

Definition: What Does Program Accessible Mean?

An accessible program is a flexible program that provides choices, options, and support in program information, design, and delivery.

Audience: Who Are The Students That Need Accessible Programs?

- • student working to finance his/her academic study
- • student working to support self and family
- • student who is managing family commitments and problems
- • student with learning disabilities
- • student who is geographically at a distance from institution
- • student without a disability

Student Point of View

"I want to get into a program that will allow me to take some short breaks to get in my required hospital visits, but will still allow me the flexibility to catch up on missed material."

"I would like to get into a program that has a hybrid learning environment. I am able to attend classes some of the time, but I like the ability to have some of my program online so I can stay at home more with my newborn child and family members who need my care."

Suggestions: How Do You Make A Program Accessible?

Clarity

- ☐ Make clear what knowledge, skills, and experience students need to have to take your program.

- ☐ Ensure all potential students are able to find program information prior to applying.

Support

- ☐ Provide academic advisors students can talk to prior to and during the program.

- ☐ Outline academic resources for students to access prior to and once in program (e.g., assistive technology, learner support areas, centre for students with disabilities, English as a Second Language assistance, peer mentoring programs, writing and research workshops, interpreters, library help, etc.).

Choice and Variety

- ☐ Design ways for the program to be studied in different formats (e.g., hybrid, fully online, part-time). A flexible program always accommodates more students.

- ☐ Provide choice in the program (e.g., courses, method of delivery, time classes are offered, location of classes, methods of evaluation, places to access information, instructors, etc.)

- ☐ Try to have more than one instructor capable of delivering a course. A student might find a different instructor easier to listen to, read lips, understand language, etc.

- ☐ If a student were to miss some classes, have reasonable ways to allow the student to get caught up. Possibly have a program or department statement on this topic.

Clear Expectations Upfront

- ☐ Ensure students entering your program understand what is expected of them. Be clear on what the program looks like, how many courses are involved, strategies required for success in the classroom, typical class/lab/tutorial activities, costs of textbooks and resources, the length of time to complete the program, graduate-job rate, possible careers, etc. When students are clear on the program components, they are more likely to make wise decisions regarding application and being proactive about any requirements for flexibility in learning. You can do this through web site videos, list of tips from former students, or host a 'Jump Start' day a few months prior to the start of a program.

❑ Provide clear information on program/discipline to dispel any misconceptions or misunderstandings. Ask instructors to be clear in the first class about course expectations and strategies required for success in the course. In this way, everyone will be on the same page about what is required.

D. Language Accessible

Definition: What Does Language Accessible Mean?

Language accessible refers to ensuring students, whose first language is not the language used in the course/program, are supported and understood. Additionally, students who have a language disability are given accommodations so that they can be successful in a course/program that requires a lot of speaking.

Audience: Who Are The Students That Need Accessible Programs?

- student who does not have English as a first language
- student who is new to the country and is just learning the native language
- student who has a learning disability
- student with a communication disorder
- student who stutters
- student without a disability

Student Point of View

"English is not my first language but I do okay with it. I have an instructor who talks so fast it makes it impossible to follow."

"The instructor makes me really nervous when he just randomly calls on students to speak in class. I have a hard time formulating good sentences and then clearly speaking on the spot because I stutter and can't think that fast."

"I had an instructor who used to talk down to me like a child when I asked a question. She spoke louder and in a voice that wasn't natural. I felt very embarrassed and won't ask questions again."

"My professor reads from the PowerPoint very fast. I have a hard time writing and listening at the same time. He references pages in the textbook and quickly mentions web sites we should visit, but I am completely lost as the information flies by so fast. I would appreciate the page numbers and web links to be on the PowerPoint too."

Suggestions: How Do You Make A Class Language Accessible?

Speaking and Questioning

- ☐ Avoid use of jargon, slang, and colloquial expressions.

- ☐ Speak with a clear and distinct voice. Avoiding mumbling or speaking fast.

- ☐ Speak slowly and clearly while facing the class.

- ☐ Take pauses when speaking so that the language can be processed by students.

- ☐ Use visual elements (images, video, drawings) to more clearly communicate your points.

- ☐ Have numbers, specialized terms, longer phrases, and key terminology outlined on digital slides or write on the board.

- ☐ Use your voice to emphasize important points (e.g., pausing on the point, be stronger in voice).

- ☐ Ask open-ended questions that allow students to more freely express their thoughts, as opposed to yes/no questions, short answer questions, etc.

Course Content

- ☐ Create an agenda and post online prior to class and show during class. It will help students follow and take better notes. Reference your agenda when you move to another topic or activity.

- ☐ Provide two formats for some class content and assignments (e.g., explain an assignment in class and also on an audio file that is linked to your course web site). Students will appreciate the alternate format to help them with processing.

- ☐ Have a glossary of key words and expressions used in your course. The definitions will be very helpful for students who are struggling with language. This could be done as a wiki where students can contribute new words and more language-proficient students can provide the definitions.

- ☐ Create an environment where students of all abilities feel comfortable to ask questions and clarify points. Be supportive of any answer, give students enough time to respond, and allow for students to ask questions in a variety of ways (e.g., anonymous slip of paper, online survey, etc.)

- ☐ Have lots of small group discussions where you assemble the class in a variety of ways. Smaller group settings afford new language students to participate more, formulate thoughts and ideas easier, and get informal feedback from their peers.

E. Accessible Documents

Definition: What Does It Mean to Have Accessible Documents?

Accessible documents allow all students to access, read, (or have screen readers read for students who are deaf or having some extent of hearing impairment), and obtain information easily from digital and paper-based materials containing text and images.

Audience: Who Are The Students That Need Documents to Be Accessible?

- Every student

Student Point of View

"I sometimes have difficulty downloading or opening a file I find on the Internet. I like to be able to click on it, have it download, and easily open for me."

"My screen reader has difficulty with a large number of documents in my courses. I rely on the screen reader to read a document to me so that I can learn."

Suggestions: How Do You Make A Document Accessible?

Overall Design Considerations

☐ Provide the greatest contrast between the text and the background. For example, black text on a white background produces a high contrast level for ease in reading. Colored fonts on colored backgrounds often produce much lower contrast levels, especially if the background has an image or design, and decreases readability. This mainly applies to PowerPoint presentations, but ensure paper-based handouts have clean backgrounds without busy designs.

☐ Use sans serif fonts as they are easier to read by a greater number of people, especially in web-based formats. Sans serif fonts and those without the curls/ticks that are at the top and bottom of each letter. Sans serif fonts = Calibri, Arial, Helvetica

☐ If you have video or pictures in your document, ensure you have descriptive text so that screen readers can read them. (For photos this is called the alt tag, for videos this is called closed captioning or captioned).

☐ Charts, diagrams, and columns provide a challenge for screen readers. Ensure you have captions to describe them. Just a few sentences will be helpful!

Word Processing Documents

☐ Use style sheets in word processing documents. Define and use a style sheet when you are creating a new word processing document (e.g., Microsoft Word) so that the document is properly organized, has consistent fonts, font sizes, titles, and spacing to allow any student and screen readers to 'read' through a document. Style sheets really are a great way to make any word processing document professional and easy to read.

☐ If you use a style sheet, saving to an accessible PDF document is even easier. If you are using Microsoft Office 2007 or higher, you need Adobe Acrobat (free program) already installed on your computer OR the Microsoft PDF Add-in installed. In your program (e.g., Microsoft Word), go to Save As Adobe PDF, once the dialog box comes up for naming the file note the "Options" button in bottom right corner. Make sure a green check mark is in the box beside "Create Accessible (Tagged) PDF File". Consult the Internet for instructions on how to make an already created PDF accessible.

PowerPoint Presentations

☐ Avoid too much text in any presentation. PowerPoint is not a teleprompter or a screen to be read line by line. Unfortunately, typing text on a slide is easy to do when trying to quickly prepare a class. However, PowerPoint is best at depicting images, video, animations, and other visual elements (supplemented by a little bit of text such as a title, phrase, quote, etc.) to enhance learning. If you have a lot of text you need to share with students, consider making a handout and posting online. Much research in the area of good design suggests that digital slides full of text that students copy is not resulting in good engagement or learning in the class.

☐ If possible, consider uploading your PowerPoint show to a server site so you can embed the presentation right into your web page and allow people easier access than having to download or view the presentation in the browser. Another preferred format is to PDF your PowerPoint.

F. Visually Accessible

Definition: What Does Visually Accessible Mean?

When something is visually accessible, someone has considered **layout** (columns, page orientation, spacing); **organization** (chunks, numbering, amount of content); **design** (font type, size and style, white space, colors); **readability** (language, amount of content, clarity, contrast of font and background); **format** (PDF, web, word processing document); and use of **visual images** (type, size, photos vs. vector-based, scalability) to maximize availability of visual information (text, images, captions, diagrams, charts) to students who rely on vision as their primary source of learning.

Audience: Who Are The Students That Need Visual Accessibility?

* student who has partial vision loss

* student who is deaf

* student who has some hearing loss

* student with a learning disability

* student who has intellectual or development learning disabilities

* student without a disability

Student Point of View

"I have low vision. I sometimes need a magnifying glass to read the computer screen but I can see fairly well beyond that. I appreciate it when instructors make materials in digital format that I can also use the screen enlargement tool or software that magnifies the font."

"I became deaf in my teenage years. I rely on my two interpreters to sign for me in most of my classes but I also appreciate oral material being captioned or at least a summary of what it is. I essentially learn in a visual manner."

Suggestions: How Do You Make Information Visually Accessible?

Organization and Layout of Material

☐ Carefully choose what content/material you really need available to students. Remove excess or unnecessary information as it clutters up the screen/page and makes learning more challenging.

☐ Use line spacing and white space well. Use 1.5 or double spacing between lines for improved readability and ensure space between sections and margins is large enough to make information clear.

☐ Use left justification with a ragged right edge for greatest ability to read. Do not full justify your text (like a newspaper) as this makes it harder to read.

Font Type, Style and Size

☐ Use digital versions of any material so that it can be enlarged (with screen magnifiers) and viewed on larger resolution screens.

☐ Provide materials with large font (16-20 points or larger).

☐ Use a sans serif font (e.g., Arial, Calibri) for ease in reading. Refrain from using specialty fonts or script fonts which are hard to read.

☐ Avoid the use of italics, bolding, and underlining of content. They all contribute to making any text more difficult to read.

☐ Use PowerPoint slides for projecting key content on a screen so that it is as large as possible for viewing. Additionally, students can download slides for viewing on their own laptops and manipulate the size of items.

Images

☐ Ensure charts, graphs, and diagrams are clear and easy to understand.

☐ Try to use a similar type of image throughout a document (e.g., use all photographs or all line drawings) to keep things consistent and easier to visually access.

❏ Choose images, particularly photographs, carefully to ensure that the correct meaning is evident when 'reading' the photo. Try to look for clean and large photos that do not have busy backgrounds, are distorted, or are out of date. If photocopying, ensure the photo copies well.

Video and Visual Presence in Class

❏ If students are lip-readers, ensure your face is visible (e.g., try to face the class as much as possible, do not cover your face with your hands when talking, try to not to mumble, put on a spotlight if you are teaching in darker room).

❏ Capture your class/lecture as a video. Many post-secondary institutions have the ability to capture direct to a computer server and host the video for linking to a course web site.

❏ If shooting video for on screen use, consider closer shots rather than long and wide shots. In this way, the video will show better and be more visible in smaller windows in which video is often viewed.

❏ Captioning is a process of translating audio in a video into subtitles or captions that usually appear at the bottom of the screen.

G. Aurally Accessible

Definition: What does Aurally Accessible Mean?

When something is aurally accessible, someone has considered **sound quality** (speaking clearly, low to no background noise, clearest sound recording as possible, use of microphone to ensure quality is heard by all); **ability to change volume levels** (use of a microphone when speaking, putting sound control on digital formats, or indicating to users how to vary sound on computer); and **format** (digital sound recordings are in various formats for playback, on as wide a range of computers as possible, easy to download, not too large in file size) to **maximize availability of oral information** (sound on video, podcast, person speaking) to students who primarily rely on using hearing for learning.

Audience: Who Are The Students That Need Aural Accessibility?

- student who is blind
- student who has some vision loss
- student who has some hearing impairment
- student with a learning disability
- student who has intellectual or development learning disabilities
- student without a learning disability

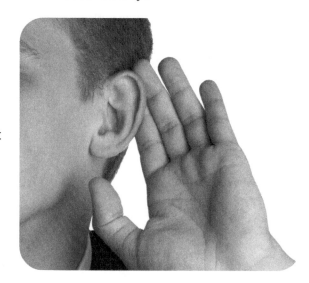

Student Point of View

"I am blind and rely 100% on my hearing to learn. I've done quite well so far in my education and I hope this can continue. I just need my instructor to speak clearly and explain anything that is a chart, diagram or a video."

"I have a hearing loss in one ear, but can hear very well from the other ear. I appreciate when my instructors in large lecture halls use a microphone.

Suggestions: How Do You Make Information Aurally Accessible?

Presentation Pointers

- ☐ Speak at a speed and volume that will benefit all students. Ask your class about your speed and volume. Students who are mainly relying on listening to an instructor need to have time to comprehend and process what is being said.

- ☐ Avoid use of jargon or complex language. Define any subject-specific jargon, acronyms, etc.

- ☐ Wear a wireless microphone (if available) to amplify your voice in larger classes.

- ☐ Avoid the use of any sound effects or noises embedded in PowerPoint presentations that are distracting or would not provide any relevance to the learning required. This will just confuse someone who is trying to listen to the professor.

- ☐ Share with your class the need to keep distracting noises, whispering, and talking to a minimum when there are classmates talking or the instructor is delivering material.

- ☐ Students who are deaf or hard of hearing may have sign language interpreters with them for all their classes. Ensure there is a spot the interpreter can sit to face the student. Before the class, if you can provide the interpreter with any jargon or unique terminology this will help them in more accurately signing. Share with the class how they can support their peers during small group work where the interpreters will provide translation of sign language.

Audio Formats

- ☐ Consider providing an audio format for some information (e.g., narrated description of photos/video, audio explanation of an assignment, podcast summary of key concepts from a class, etc.). Use the built-in recording tool on your computer and post the file to your course web site. Students will appreciate the opportunity to play it over a few times to ensure they got it all.

- ☐ Allow students to record your lectures/classes with a digital recorder. Be aware that transcribing taped classes takes a long time and students may benefit more from class notes from a few students or an instructor summary of the class.

- ☐ If a student is going to use a screen reader, ensure content is clearly written and organized. A screen reader is software that converts text from a computer monitor to voice or to Braille.

- ☐ Look for any resources your textbook publisher has that are in an audio format for students to listen to content.

H. Cognitively Accessible

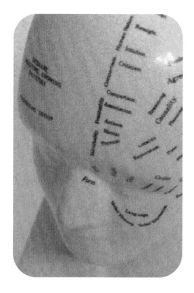

Definition: What Does Cognitively Accessible Mean?

When something is cognitively accessible, someone has considered **how the brain works to process and encode information and that the content being produced meets the age/development level** to maximize availability of information to students.

Audience: Who Are The Students That Need Cognitive Accessibility?

- student who has a learning disability

- student who has an intellectual or developmental disability

- student without a disability

Student Point of View

"We are being marked on how much we can memorize and not what we have actually learned. I don't have a photographic memory and it is challenging to memorize ten chapters in the textbook."

"I find note-taking challenging when I can't process everything at once. My brain isn't able to handle the instructor speaking at the same time as the PowerPoint slides showing different content in long blocks of text along with pictures. I just wish there was time to stop and process everything!"

Suggestions: How Do You Make Information Cognitively Accessible?

Class Components

- ☐ Provide an agenda so students know what to expect and how the class will progress.

- ☐ Allow time for students to ask questions in small or large groups. Try having small group opportunities for discussion before a large group discussion. You may find more participation from students if they have had a chance to think and process a question with their peers.

- ☐ Use humor sparingly. Humor can be confused and may offend some students.

- ☐ Ensure you consolidate and summarize the content of a class before the class is over. This reinforces key concepts that were learned and provides feedback to you and the students as to where more work is needed and what was learned.

- ☐ Provide a glossary of terms found in the course (or provide a link/reference to one already created) so students can understand special terms and language used in the course.

Availability

- ☐ Have both face-to-face and virtual office hours so students can approach you in a number of formats. Some professors have a time each week they are available online for discussions, instant messaging, answering email, or talking in a VOIP (voice over internet protocol) provider (e.g., Skype)

Content and Organization

- ☐ Have an organized course with topics and assignments clearly laid out from the course beginning.

- ☐ Ensure material is chunked into smaller sections that are more digestible for optimal learning.

- ☐ Use short sentences (or charts, tables etc.) to present information that is easiest to understand.

- ☐ Post learning materials a day or two prior to class. This will allow students to look it over, process it, and take their time to be prepared for class.

- ☐ Present information in a variety of formats so that students can approach their learning from a variety of angles.

Flexibility and Choice

- ☐ Give extra time to complete work, take notes, write tests and exams, etc.

- ☐ Provide flexible assignment and test dates. Describe both in writing and orally.

- ☐ Consider oral examinations as an alternative to a paper-based test or exam.

- ☐ Give students choice in some aspects of the course (e.g., choice about topics for an assignment, choice about a due date, etc.)

- ☐ Have note-takers or people scribe notes for someone unable to process both listening and writing.

Digital Slides and Text

- ☐ Avoid using semicolons, colons, and lots of commas in written text. It makes it more challenging to read. Additionally, try not to break up words with hyphens at the end of a line of text.

- ☐ Tests and exams should have a nice balance of both reading (multiple choice, matching, true/false) and writing answers to questions (open-ended, short answer, essay).

- ☐ Have as few slides as possible in your PowerPoint presentations.

- ☐ Slides should have high contrast between the background color and the text color (e.g., black text on a white/light background).

I. Web Accessible

Definition: What does Web Accessible Mean?

When something is web accessible it means that students with disabilities can use the Web in terms of understanding, navigating, interacting, viewing, accessing, contributing, searching, and learning from the Web with effective speeds of uploading and downloading capabilities. A web site that is deemed accessible (by standards and guidelines published by the Web Accessibility Initiative of the World Wide Web Consortium, W3C) allows for all students, with different situations and needs, to access the information regardless of ability/disability and to use assistive and adaptive technology (e.g., screen readers) with success.

Audience: Who Are The Students That Need Web Accessibility?

- student who has no access to high-speed Internet
- student who has difficulty reading or writing on a screen
- student who is not comfortable or experienced with computer technology
- student with a temporary disability such as a broken arm
- student without a disability

Student Point of View

"My online course has information in so many different places. It is hard to navigate to find the deadline dates and assignment descriptions. I wish it was easier to find things in this course!"

"I am not a savvy computer student. I am pretty good with software on my laptop, but I am not so good at downloading and uploading files and information. I need clear instructions and a good web site to be able to do things well."

Suggestions: How Do You Make Information Web Accessible?

Navigation

- ❑ Ensure a student can navigate your web site with ease (e.g., menu items have good titles, menu is clear to read, you can make your way back to the home page with ease etc.).

- ❑ Try to ensure your web site can be navigated by the use of the keyboard (arrow keys or shortcut keys) as some people do not have the use of a mouse.

- ❑ Provide ways for your students to be able to find content within your website. That might mean a clean 'site map' outlining the key topics, a search engine using keywords, or a help feature to allow users to find out how to use the site.

Readability of Text

- ❑ Text must be readable. That means font size, style, and type are all suitable for viewing on a monitor. This also means that backgrounds, animations, and other visual elements are not distracting for someone trying to read the material.

☐ Make sure the contrast between the text and background is fairly high. This will ensure people can more easily read material off the web.

Printing and Screen Readers

☐ Provide the capability for the student to print web pages. This means that a print command and associated button are included on each page and also might include the ability to remove any images, advertising, or extraneous information from being included on the printed page.

☐ Have content be able to be read by a screen reader. Use style sheets, mark up language, and current web accessibility tools to make your web site clean and easy to be scanned by screen reader software.

☐ Create portable file documents (PDF) with accessibility features turned on. A PDF is much easier to access for more students than word processing documents or spreadsheet files, which can be saved in so many different formats.

Video and Audio Content

☐ Give users enough time to view or listen to material that appears for a definite time. For example, provide controls to stop/start/pause content, allow a sequence of rotating pictures to be viewed again, etc.

☐ When you have video, graphic, or audio content ensure you have provided an alternative way to access that information (e.g., put captions on graphics through the use of the alt tag, provide summaries of videos, and give text equivalents of any audio content).

☐ Watch the size of your files (especially video and audio ones if not streamed from a server). A large file does not download quickly on slow connections and, as a result, learning time can be compromised.

Web Pages

☐ Design clean and well organized web sites to optimize the accessibility of your content. This means being consistent with the look of it from fonts, colors, and the organization of items.

☐ Describe all images (charts, graphs, photos, diagrams) with "alt" tags which is essentially a short description of the image that appears when you roll over your mouse on the image.

☐ Make moving around (navigation) your web site very simple and intuitive. Always have a 'home' button/link on every page. Do not bury items deep within many sub-sections.

☐ If you have video or audio playing, ensure there are visible controls. Students should be able to have control to stop and start media.

☐ If you create a web page from a word document, use style sheets. Save the document and then choose Save As. Where the dialog box says "Save as type" choose "Web Page, Filtered" as the type. This will allow a screen reader to read the web page much easier directly off the web. This small step in saving your document before uploading to your course web site or learning management system will help with accessibility.

J. Physically Accessible

Definition: What does Physically Accessible Mean?

When something is physically accessible, there are considerations about **a providing safe and spacious access to gain entrance to and exits from buildings, classrooms, and lecture halls as well as alternative access points (e.g., elevator, ramp)** to maximize availability of physically supporting students.

- student who uses a wheelchair
- student who uses a cane, walker, or a mobility aid
- student with arthritis
- student who has materials that may take up space or require room for movement
- student without a disability

Audience: Who Are The Students That Need Physical Accessibility?
Student Point of View

"I find navigating in and out of small or tight classrooms a challenge with my backpack on wheels. I carry a lot of stuff with me and it is hard to lift it and move it around when chairs and desks are tightly arranged."

"I find it best to sit in a row seat so I can easily get in and out. I like it when instructors understand my needs and accommodate me during group work or when we are moving around the class."

Suggestions: How Do You Make Environments Physically Accessible?

Class Space

☐ If you know you have student(s) who will be using a wheelchair or have challenges with mobility, ensure your assigned lecture hall/classroom is going to work.

☐ Ensure the classroom has enough space for wheelchairs, those on crutches, or those who need extra space to bring in materials (e.g., bag on wheels).

☐ Arrive at class at bit earlier to ensure desks and chairs (or other class equipment) are properly located so your class can arrive without any obstacles.

Class Movement

☐ When moving students into different groups, be sure to take into account those who need a physically accessible environment. Possibly leave them in the same spot and have the group form around them or ask the student what would work best for them.

Other Class Locations

☐ If you are taking your class on a field trip or moving to another location on campus, ensure all students will be able to have no barriers for access. Provide sufficient time for students to move to the new location.

K. Culturally Accessible

Definition: What Does Culturally Accessible Mean?

When something is culturally accessible, there is consideration **of all genders, all ethnicities, all cultures, and all sexual orientations** to maximize learning environment for all students.

Audience: Who Are The Students That Need Cultural Accessibility?

- student from a different culture, country, language
- student who is of a different sexual orientation
- every student

Student Point of View

"I like a professor who realizes that there is diversity in the classroom by using correct terminology when referring to groups of people or cultures."

"I come from a culture where learning involves copying the work (or producing similar work) of the noted authors in a field of study. I am not that good at paraphrasing, since English is not my first language. So I have been told I am plagiarizing and I am not entirely sure what that means or how to fix my work. It was all just a mistake – I didn't intentionally do it."

"I feel very uncomfortable in a class where the instructor isn't open and understanding of the different people who make up a class these days. Even if it is part of humor, I can sense people feeling ostracized."

Suggestions: How Do You Make Information Culturally Accessible?

Language and Presentation

- ☐ Treat each student as an individual. Set the same expectations for high quality learning from all of your students. Avoid making assumptions or conclusions about students.

- ☐ Use inclusive language. Become aware of the terminology used to describe groups of people. Ask if you are not sure. Terminology changes over time so ensure you are using the most current terms.

- ☐ Speak slowly and clearly.

- ☐ Pronounce students' names correctly. Ask students how their name is pronounced and make a note of it.

- ☐ Always strive to be as clear as you can. Give examples. Show visuals. Explain things in different ways. Ask students to explain something for determining comprehension.

- ☐ Ask students to let you know if you are not providing an inclusive and culturally accessible class. Let them know you are trying, but would appreciate any feedback (anonymously).

- ☐ Be aware of your body language both in the classroom and in office meetings. For example, students from various cultures may get mixed messages or miscommunication from their interpretation of crossed arms, leaning too far forward, or over-smiling.

Content

- ☐ Try to use content that is free of cultural stereotypes, uses current terminology, and is gender-neutral. This may involve doing some minor edits to existing content.

- ☐ Provide examples from various cultures, genders, people, and groups during your course.

- ☐ Use photographs and other visual images that show people of all genders, all ethnicities, all groups, all cultures, etc.

- ☐ Consider current issues and cultural events and see if your course content can include some relevant examples, field trips, or videos.

- ☐ Skim through your course material to ensure you are using inclusive language, respecting diversity, and including examples and images that are fair and inclusive.

- ☐ Chunk content into 15-20 minute segments. Allow students time to digest an activity or look over their notes between segments.

- ☐ Provide examples of assignments so students are clear on expectations.

Space and Proximity

- ☐ Be aware of how the distance between you and a student is interpreted through various cultures. Some students may immediately not look you in the eye. Some students may appreciate a desk between you and them when you are having a meeting or discussing the class. Some students may stand at a distance when they are speaking to you or stand up when giving an answer. Be kind and patient with students. Ask them any questions to help you understand their preferences for communication.

- ☐ Some students may not engage in a conversation with you, yet rather come to your office to just get advice or suggestions about how to improve their work. When in doubt, ask the student about any cultural norms that you could learn about to help facilitate a good academic relationship in the class.

Academic Dishonesty

- ☐ Plagiarism may be interpreted differently by students from different cultures. Often not intentional, students may fail to reference authors of other works because they have been schooled to believe it is acceptable to use their work without required citations. Ensure you look into whether the work was deliberately or unintentionally copied or improperly referenced.

- ☐ Clearly communicate to all of your students what plagiarism is and how to properly cite academic references with accompanying examples explained both in words and in print. A lesson on the topic of plagiarism (by the instructor or an expert at the institution) might be beneficial to all.

- ☐ Provide a link to a useful web site and also give examples as they pertain to your class and discipline as to how you wish work to be written, referenced, and acknowledged.

L. Accessibility Application

Determine the best choice for each question. Consult the chapter. See answer key along left side.

1. Jenny has approached you with a note from the Disability Office. She has a cognitive processing difficulty, which means she is challenged when there is a lot of content and she has to think through it and create responses and answers. Which of the following course modifications might best benefit Jenny?

    A. Tell Jenny she should get notes from one of her classmates and to just not worry about participating in class.

    B. Provide Jenny, and the rest of the class, with partial handouts of class content and give all students time to work in small groups to discuss application questions.

    C. Allow Jenny extra time to take tests as this will give her time to think through all the questions and write her answers.

    D. Provide Jenny with your notes of the class and tell her to spend some time out of class discussing them with a peer to help her understand.

2. Abduhl has approached you with a request for supporting his learning. He has not been diagnosed with a learning disability, but he is a new immigrant, is slowly learning the native language, and does often struggle with his academic studies. He has some strategies that instructors have often complied with in the past and this has allowed Abduhl to be successful. Which of the following strategies do you think Abduhl suggested to you? Circle all that apply.

    A. Explain terminology, speak clearly and slowly and refrain from using jargon.

    B. When possible provide a text version of any spoken content.

    C. Check for understanding in a variety of ways: ask students questions, have short comprehension activities in class and allow students to email you with questions.

    D. Include small group opportunities for students to discuss concepts and share their understanding with each other.

3. Suzanne and Nathan have come to speak to you about some struggles they are having in class. They are both slow readers but also take a while to process a lot of information. They had lots of positive things to say about your class but they are struggling with documents (handouts, web pages, PowerPoints) that are "jammed full of stuff" that they are having trouble reading and processing. What TWO modifications might work for them?

    A. Tell them to take your documents and print them out and highlight just the important materials. Then they will be able to see the key concepts and study more easily.

    B. Make your documents less "busy" by including more space, larger margins, sub-headings of key concepts and trimming back some of the extra content.

    C. Make your documents a bit more glitzy and interesting so that students will be interested in reading them. Add in transitions, animations and some cartoons for fun.

    D. Add a few more useful graphics (charts, photographs, images) to your documents to explain concepts and break up all the text.

Answers: 1 – B; 2 – A, B, C & D; 3 – B, D

Top Ten Takeaways

1. **Universal Design (UD):** Concept originated in the early 1970s through the field of architecture and applied to buildings, walkways, and environments to enable people to have access that was barrier-free. Now the concept has been extended to education with the goal of making learning accessible to as many people as possible.

2. **Universal Design for Instruction (UDI) and Universal Design for Learning (UDL):** UDI has nine guiding principles and UDL has three guiding principles that focus on making teaching, learning, and learning environments accessible to the greatest number of students possible. These principles set the framework for the rest of the chapter which delves into specific modifications an instructor can make for different groups of students. Much research has been conducted to support the movement for enhancing learning in higher education.

3. **Higher Numbers of Students with Disabilities:** Today's post-secondary classes include more and more students who have a range of disabilities and abilities. With more students attending post-secondary environments, there is a greater need to provide learning experiences and opportunities that try to meet as many of their needs as possible.

4. **Language Accessible:** For those who do not speak the native language or who struggle with language in general, ensure you speak slowly, avoid the use of jargon, include the use of visuals to explain concepts, and provide small group opportunities for students to discuss.

5. **Documents That Are Accessible:** Use sans serif fonts, the greatest contrast possible between text and background, style sheets, and consider less bullets and text in PowerPoint presentations.

6. **Visually Accessible:** Use large fonts and well-produced graphs and charts, face your students so lip readers can see your mouth and consider captioning video or providing a text summary of visual elements used.

7. **Aurally Accessible:** Speak slowly and clearly, be aware of distracting noises during classes, wear a wireless microphone and possibly provide a podcast of lectures or assignment descriptions.

8. **Web Accessible:** Design web pages with appropriate font types and sizes, cleanly designed layouts, easy-to-follow navigation, and the use of style sheets.

9. **Physically Accessible:** Ensure the learning environments allow students to easily enter and exit, be part of the class, take part in activities, and not experience any barriers to participation.

10. **Culturally Accessible:** Consider proper terminology to describe groups of people, use a variety of examples and images in class content, be sensitive to how you respond to students, and ask students how they would like you to interact with them.

Next Steps

1. Think about your course. Are there any parts of your course that may not be accessible to most students? Think about content, delivery format, assignments, evaluation methods, etc.

2. Jot down a short list of the types of students you have encountered in your teaching to date. Consider all students with all abilities and disabilities. Do you remember how you accommodated or modified your class or teaching to meet their needs?

3. Discuss with a few colleagues what types of students they have had in their classes? How do they accommodate and modify their course, classes, or activities to meet their needs? It would be interesting to compare what your colleagues do with what you have been doing.

4. Go through each of the sub-sections in this chapter and check off what you are doing already in your course and teaching with respect to making learning accessible.

5. Make a list of a few things you can do to make your upcoming courses more accessible for a greater number of students. Just focus on a few things to begin with, and then work toward a few more the next time. Before you know it, you could have a fully accessible course!

References and Resources

Center for Universal Design, College of Design, North Carolina State University (2008). *About UD.* Retrieved March 27, 2010, from http://www.ncsu.edu/www/ncsu/design/sod5/cud/about_ud/about_ud.htm

Council for Exceptional Children. (2005). *Universal design for learning: A guide for teachers and education professionals.* Arlington, VA: The Council for Exceptional Children.

Kortering, L. J., McClannon, T. W., & Braziel, P. M. (2008). Universal design for learning: A look at what algebra and biology students with and without high incidence conditions are saying. *Remedial and Special Education, 29* (6), 352-363.

Innovation Centre. (n.d.). *Making your documents accessible.* Retrieved March 22, 2010, from http://x.dc-uoit.ca/accessibledocs/

McGuire, J. M., Scott, S. S., & Shaw, S. F. (2006). Universal design and its applications in educational environments. *Remedial and Special Education, 27*(3), 166-175.

Ministry of Community and Social Services, Province of Ontario. (2009, January 28). *Making information accessible.* Retrieved March 20, 2010, from http://www.mcss.gov.on.ca/en/accesson/tools/making_information_accessible.aspx

Ministry of Community and Social Services, Province of Ontario. (2009, January 28). *Talk about disabilities: Choose the right word.* Retrieved March 20, 2010, from http://www.mcss.gov.on.ca/en/accesson/understandingDisabilities/right_word.aspx

Newcastle University (2009, May 26). *Making learning more accessible for dyslexic students.* Retrieved March 16, 2010, from http://www.ncl.ac.uk/students/wellbeing/information/dyslexia/accessible.htm

Pisha, B. & Coyne P. (2001). Smart from the start: The promise of universal design for learning. *Remedial and Special Education, 22*(4), 197-203.

Rose, D. H. & Meyer, A. (2002). *Teaching every student in the digital age: Universal design for learning.* Alexandria, VA: Association for Supervision and Curriculum Development.

Sarpong, J. & Patel, N. (2008). *Teaching the ESL learner.* Retrieved March 22, 2010, from http://x.dc-uoit.ca/esllearner/

Scott, S. S., McGuire, J. M., & Shaw, S. F. (2003). Universal design for instruction: A new paradigm for adult instruction in postsecondary education. *Remedial and Special Education, 24*(6), 369-379.

Silver, P., Bourke, A., & Strehorn, K. C. (1998). Universal instruction design in higher education: An approach for inclusion. *Equity & Excellence in Education, 31*(2), 47-51.

Social Care Institute for Excellence. (2005, June). *How to produce information in an accessible way.* Retrieved March 14, 2010, from http://www.scie.org.uk/publications/misc/accessguidelinespublications.pdf

The University of Strathclyde. (2000). *Teachability project: Creating an accessible curriculum for students with disabilities.* Retrieved March 14, 2010, from http://www.teachability.strath.ac.uk/teachabilityintro.html

World Wide Web Consortium (W3C) (2010). *Web accessibility initiative.* Retrieved, April 4, 2010, from http://www.w3.org/WAI/

Chapter 7: Choosing Teaching & Learning Strategies

Chapter Overview

Choosing a teaching and learning strategy is not an easy task. This chapter opens with some thoughts on a common strategy, the lecture, and some small ways it can be revamped to improve student learning.

The chapter then provides short synopses of nearly 40 different strategies for creating learning opportunities in your class. Many of the strategies are very easy to implement or modify for your discipline. Some of the strategies do take some time and effort to set up, but they are worth it! Some of the strategies show how technology can support learning. Some of the strategies are tried-and-true classics with a current update or twist. The strategies are all applicable to most class sizes, most disciplines, and most content.

More than anything, the strategies will contribute to enhanced student learning. The research is quite clear: anytime students are actively engaged in learning, exploring new ideas, and grasping the conceptual nature of the discipline, they are learning in a deeper and more meaningful way to apply that knowledge and those skills to other parts of their lives.

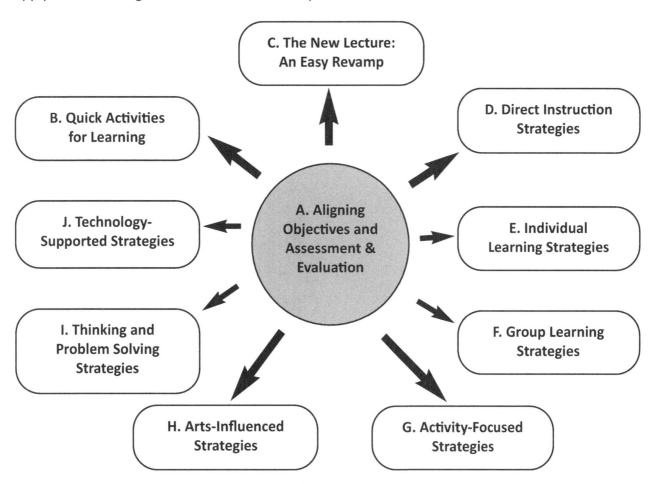

A. Aligning Objectives and Evaluation

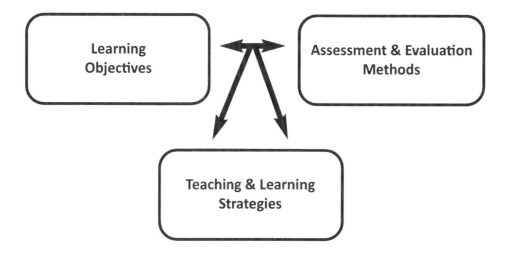

Do not even consider what teaching and learning strategies you want to use in your classes until you are firm on your learning objectives and their relationships to the assessment and evaluation methods you have chosen. This is a common mistake by many instructors. Take the time to ensure your learning objectives and assessment and evaluation methods are lined up, make sense, and are firm for the course. Then you can begin to consider the ways in which you will create learning opportunities for students to achieve those objectives.

For example:

Learning Objective: By the end of this Communications 101 course, students will be able to demonstrate five key principles of effective public speaking by giving a final talk on a subject of their choice.

Assessment Methods: Ongoing instructor and peer feedback on practice speeches; peer feedback on the final product

Evaluation Methods: Rubric outlining the details of final talk, what is expected, what the student needs to demonstrate, what will be handed in (e.g., outline and notes used in planning)

Given the above, students need to

1. Have knowledge about key principles of effective public speaking

2. See what these principles look like and then practice them

3. Receive feedback and ongoing suggestions for improvements

4. Design, research and outline a final talk on a topic

When the instructor chooses which teaching and learning strategies to use, the four points above need to be considered. Here are some possible teaching and learning strategies:

Teaching and Learning Strategies:

1. **Demonstration:** The instructor could demonstrate some of the key principles in class (or show a video of a similar demonstration) and then ask students to work together to see if they can identify the principles. This allows for modeling to happen and for students to get a clear idea of what is expected.

2. **Small Group Discussion:** The students could work in small groups on activities geared at understanding the basics of a good public speech. By giving them questions, they can consider and report back to the whole class.

3. **A Date with a Debate:** The students could engage in a debate to practice their public speaking skills along with demonstrating their ability to outline and defend arguments and rebuttals. By debriefing the debate, students could outline the strong and weak points about the talks.

B. Quick Activities for Learning

The following eight activities are easy to prepare and conduct with your class. Try out one or two with your students and observe their reactions.

1. Fast-Write

Before starting a new topic, have students jot down their own thoughts. This short activity allows students to begin writing about a topic. Students do not stop writing until the instructor tells them to do so (1 – 5 minutes). The quick writing activity allows the students to start formulating thoughts and piecing together what they already know in a free-flowing manner. It also helps stimulate critical thinking. Ensure you conduct a brief follow up to this activity by having students share in small groups or contribute to a discussion.

2. Think - Pair - Share

This is a strategy that begins with students thinking alone for a couple of minutes in response to a question posed by the instructor. Then have students pair up and share their responses with a partner. Finally, students share in a larger group or with the whole class. This strategy works well with any class size. It gives students time to think about a question or topic before being asked to participate.

3. Snowball

This is a strategy where students write something on a piece of paper, crumple it up, and toss it across the room. Students then pick up one of the crumpled balls of paper ("snowballs"), read them individually and then share with the class. The paper may contain students' initial thoughts on a new topic, opinions on current news items or answers to a homework question. This is a fast way of allowing students to express their thoughts and having other students (anonymously) share those responses. It also allows students to have a brief physical activity.

4. Gallery Gander

This activity involves students posting work on the walls of the classroom and then walking around quietly to view all the work. It is akin to walking through an art gallery in a quiet and thoughtful manner taking note of the work on the walls. The work can be from in-class or out-of-class activities (e.g., concept map, diagram, artwork, flowchart, spreadsheet, short writing activity etc.). The point of the gallery walk is to have students spend a bit of time reflecting on the work of their peers and share their insights in a small or large group discussion. This strategy is useful for obtaining informal feedback from peers on a draft of an assignment or to showcase results of a class learning activity.

5. KWL Chart

Before a new topic or unit, have students create three columns on a piece of paper. In the first column, labeled with a "K", students write what they already **Know** about the topic. In the second column, labeled with a "W", students write what they **Want** to know about the topic. They can keep this list or hand in to the instructor. At the end of the topic or unit, students complete the last column, labeled with an "L", which stands for what they have **Learned.** A short discussion about the benefit of this chart might be helpful to connect what students learned from the three columns.

6. Mix and Mingle

Pose a question or statement to students. Ask them to get up from their seats and gather in the aisles or the front of the class. Then ask them to find one other person to strike up a conversation about the question or statement. After a few minutes, stop the students and ask them to find another partner to have a conversation about the topic. After a few more minutes, ask one pair of students to find another pair (now making a group of 4) and ask the group to continue discussing. After a short period of time has elapsed, ask students to sit down. This activity allows students to get out of their seats, chat with different peers, and also to start formulating thoughts about a topic.

7. Four Corners

Before class begins, post four signs each in the four corners of the room, namely: Strongly Agree, Strongly Disagree, Agree But May Be Convinced Otherwise, Disagree But May Be Convinced Otherwise. Post a statement on the board (or a slide) that all students can easily view. The statement has to be a topic that could have differing (and possibly quite polarizing) opinions from students. It could be a statement about a current news item, about a well-known issue, or something taken from a recent class discussion. Ask students to consider the statement for a minute to determine whether they agree or disagree with the statement. Point out the four signs in the four corners of the room. When instructed, ask the students to move to the corner that best represents their thoughts on the statement. Encourage students to talk with other students at each station and explain why they are there, what their thoughts are, and what evidence/reasons might support the position they have taken. After a few minutes, ask some members of the "Strongly Agree" group to swap spots with a few members of the "Strongly Disagree" group and so forth with the other two groups. By mixing up the other groups, you will foster a rich discussion. This is a great activity to get students thinking about a topic and takes very little time to organize.

8. Group Formation Ideas

Here are some ideas for getting students to form groups so they are not always working with the same people or choosing their friends:

- Hand out colored recipe cards to students on their way in the class (students with the same colored card make a group) – put a R (for recorder) and a P (for presenter) on two of the cards per each color and these would automatically assign roles to two students per group.

- Have students choose colored candies from a bowl. Those with similar colored candies (or similar type of candy) form a group.

- Ask students with birthdays in similar months to form groups.

- Make up a number of group formations prior to the start of the year. For each group activity, show students the combination you have chosen for that class. Possibly, share with students the day prior so students will know where to sit the next day.

- Number students as you go around the room. For example, if you need 6 groups, number everyone from 1 through 6.

- Have students stand up tallest to shortest and then number students for groups.

- If students sit at tables, appoint a few students to move to the next table and so forth before they get their materials set up. Rotate the students in different directions each class.

C. The New Lecture: An Easy Revamp

According to surveys of instructors in higher education, 55 – 80% of faculty report that they use the lecture method as the predominant form of teaching (Brown & Race, 2002; Blackburn et al., 1980; Lammers & Murphy, 2002; Thielens, 1987; Higher Education Research Institute, 1999) and males are more likely to lecture than females (Lammers & Murphy, 2002; Thielens, 1987). Lecturing is a comfort zone for many instructors and need not be eliminated, however there is a definite need to revamp it and consider variations to allow for greater student learning.

By lecturing, what do we mean?

Lecturing often means the instructor:

- Transmits information to students and most often verbally

- May use the blackboard/whiteboard to write content for students to copy while adding in more details from his/her talk

- May use overhead transparency sheets or digital slides (PowerPoint, Keynote) with pre-written content for students to copy while adding in more details from his/her talk

- May show a video clip or visual images to relate to the content

- Most often is the main speaker in the room

- May ask some questions to solicit responses

In summary, the instructor is the focal point and/or the content he/she is transmitting. Transmission of content means that students listen and write notes based on the information they are hearing. In a lecture, students often do not participate in small group activities or other forms of engagement.

Lecturing is thought to have **positive benefits because** the instructor is able to:

- Get through a vast amount of information in the time period

- Be most effective when having to teach large classes of 100's of students

- Maintain control over the class as students are fixed and focused on taking notes and listening

- Prepare and deliver a lecture with relative ease and planning as the focus is on the content and the slides or overheads that go along with the content

- Reuse lectures from year to year if the content and course format do not change

Lecturing is a teaching/learning strategy mainly employed in higher education. Although it has been in existence for centuries and a large percentage of instructors still use it, lecturing has been shown to not support deeper learning experiences.

- Students need to be more engaged and active in their learning during class time

- More opportunities are required for deep learning to emerge in non-lecture teaching activities

- Lecturing is seen as a passive form of learning that wanes after 15-20 minutes of attention

- Students need more variety during class time to approach material from a few angles

- Students prefer small group work activities and opportunities for choice and flexibility in learning

- Learning opportunities should be created to fit the discipline and topic under study

Since it isn't easy to adopt new strategies or make major changes to courses, here are some ideas for taking the 'old lecture' and updating it with some easy-to-implement ideas for making it a 'new lecture' format.

Before The Class: Small Revamping Ideas

☐ **Sharing the Big Picture**

- Consider using a diagram or chart to show how a class relates to the whole course. Students need to see how the content connects to what they've learned already and are still to learn

☐ **Chunking the content into small sections**

- Try breaking up the content into smaller sub-sections and titling them appropriately. Students will be more engaged and make better notes if the class is presented as small chunks

- Organizing the class as if it were mini-lectures of 10-15 minutes each helps students learn

☐ **Creating questions based on content**

- Try designing 2-3 questions per each 'chunk' and have them written on a slide or on paper for students to see

- Questions should make students think, apply, or evaluate to properly answer the question

☐ **Finding real-life/relevant examples of content**

- Finding a small video, or a short story or a diagram that is relevant to the content helps students make valuable connections in their learning

- Plan to show the example near the end of the 10-15 minute chunk

☐ **Designing a short hook to grab students' attention**

- Try designing a question you can ask students to ponder during the beginning of class (students could talk amongst themselves, vote on answer by raising hands, or share a few thoughts about answer through a brief discussion)

- Showing a short video clip, cartoon, or something that relates to your topic helps grab students' attention and makes connections to the content

☐ **Creating an agenda**

- On a slide (or on the board) try presenting all the sub-sections of the class

- Sharing online before class starts aids students so they can anticipate class and have notes ready

---

Activity:

1. Look at the list of suggestions for revamping a lecture. Put a checkmark in the boxes that correspond with components you do already.

2. What else do you do to change-up your lectures other than what has been listed above? Jot your ideas below.

   - _____

   - _____

   - _____

3. Have you ever been able to watch someone in your department/faculty teach a class?
   a. If so – what did you observe when you watched him/her?

   b. If not – could you arrange to watch a lecture/class sometime this term? It is a valuable

A Sample 50 Minute Class—Revamped!

1. Sharing the **agenda.**
   - Read through the agenda, explaining each sub-section title and what students can expect

2. Briefly **reviewing key points** from last class.
   - Reminding students of what they did last class will help them see the connection to this class.

3. Doing a topic **hook.**
   - Get students interested in the topic for this class by hooking them into learning.

4. Showing or explaining to students how this class fits into the **big picture.**
   - Show a framework, diagram, or explain where the topic fits into the course.

5. Indicating that you are going to **talk and share content for 10-15 minutes on a sub-topic.**
   - Communicating with excitement, speaking slowly and clearly and using appropriate language.

6. At the end of the 10-15 minutes, asking and **answering any questions** about the content.

7. Asking students to **discuss a question or two** based on the content OR sharing a **relevant example.**

8. Indicating you are going to **talk and share content for 10-15 minutes on another sub-topic.**

9. At the end of the 10-15 minutes, asking and **answering any questions** about the content.

10. Asking students to **discuss a question** or two based on the content OR sharing a **relevant example.**

11. Indicating that you are going to **talk and share content for 10-15 minutes on another sub-topic.**

12. At the end of the 10-15 minutes, asking and **answering any questions** about the content.

13. Posing the following two questions to students to answer in the **last 2-3 minutes**. Have them get out a scrap piece of paper to write the answers and then hand into you on the way out.
    - **What I liked most about this class....**
    - **What I do not understand is....**

With a small amount of effort and time to create some questions and chunk content, you can easily improve your lecture so that learning is enhanced and students have a chance to digest the content.

The rest of this chapter outlines many other ideas for teaching and learning – take a peek!

D. Direct Instruction Strategies

Direct instruction often refers to lecturing or when the instructor spends the majority of the time directing the learning. However, direct instruction has other variations and is especially beneficial in certain situations:

- presenting content so students quickly acquire background or key concepts

- modeling how something is done so students can view the desired outcome

- obtaining information only the instructor knows

- reviewing and connecting prior information in an effective manner

1. Demonstration

The instructor is demonstrating how something works or how something should be done including the steps, safety precautions, materials, and tips for ensuring success.

- demonstrations work best when there is not an opportunity for every student to engage (e.g., not enough supplies, too dangerous an activity, too long to do, etc.), but there is value in watching a demonstration that is narrated by the instructor

- demonstrations may also be done in a digital format; the instructor may video-tape the demonstration for viewing online or the instructor may locate a digital video that best exemplifies the concepts of the demonstration

- demonstrations are often helpful in disciplines where it is valuable to watch a full process conducted by the instructor before students undertake their own attempts

- students could also watch a demonstration and then model the steps and process to a smaller group of students for feedback; the original demonstration is viewed as the model

- Examples: how to cook something, how to conduct a chemistry experiment, how to build something, etc.

2. Within the Framework

The instructor is providing an outline or framework for structuring the whole class. The instructor should frequently refer to the organizer throughout the term.

- instructors create frameworks to allow for greater understanding, relevance, and connections amongst the components of the course

- students use frameworks to focus their note taking, studying, and overall comprehension of how a topic fits within the whole course

- instructor creates a framework of how the course topics look together—showing connections, sub-topics, hierarchies and other relational aspects of the course (may be part of a syllabus, first class or something that is referenced each class)

- frameworks give structure to a course, allow a course to be passed onto another instructor, and also provide clear connections and meaning between content for student learning

3. Guest Speaker

The instructor is inviting a guest speaker into the class to present content, give alternative perspectives on an issue, share different opinions, or tell stories about real-world experiences.

- instructor needs to find suitable speakers and provide enough time for arrangements

- guest speaker should be given details on how the visit fits into the class content

- students should be given preliminary details on the guest speaker so they can prepare questions ahead of time, design presentations for feedback from guest speaker etc.

4. Step Master

The instructor is modeling or presenting a concept or skill in a sequence of steps. At each step the students replicate the concept or skill until they have it mastered. The instructor continues until all steps are demonstrated by students.

- strategy works best for skills and concepts that are complex or are not easily learned independently

- skills and knowledge may be related to a profession that requires mastery of specific tools, processes, equipment, materials, etc. (e.g., operating heavy equipment, conducting a physical examination, putting together a complicated tool, installing plumbing fixtures)

- students may need multiple practice opportunities with repeated modeling to achieve success

E. Individual Learning Strategies

The key concepts of individual learning strategies include

- Some students prefer to learn on their own

- Some students are able to work independently with success

- Group learning is not always possible in some classes or situations

- Works well in online learning courses

- Allows for individual accountability of learning

1. Good Ol' Homework

Students are doing homework outside of class time and handing in.

- homework can take a variety of forms (e.g., completing online quizzes, reading and responding to questions, solving problems, investigating, researching, etc.)

- homework is often smaller in time, effort, and thinking compared to an assignment or test

- homework can be checked in class for completion; can be marked by self, peer, or instructor for accuracy; can be discussed in a group; etc.

- giving small quizzes on homework activities, students are more accountable for completing and comprehending learning

2. In-Class Worksheets

Students are completing worksheets during class time. The worksheets are done individually, but may include the opportunity to discuss or investigate answers with peers.

- students are responsible for completing worksheet within the class timeframe

- worksheets can be in a variety of forms (e.g., using the Internet to find answers, solving problems, demonstrating tasks on the computer, using materials in class to find answers)

- answer key could be provided so students can check their own work as they move through a worksheet, or students could confer with peers once they are done to compare answers

2. Online Discussion Posts

Students are thinking about a question or statement and composing their own thoughts and responses in an online discussion post.

- students appreciate the opportunity to think about a topic, issue, or question before they respond

- online learning management systems (e.g., Blackboard) have discussion-board components where students can post their thoughts and reply to peers, share new knowledge, etc.

- online discussion posts work best when the class is split into smaller groups (10-15) and given a question that isn't simply a rephrasing of textbook material or items from the Internet

- discussion posts work when there is an expectation that students will extend a discussion from class and put some thought into a well-constructed response

4. Self-Paced Learning Activities

Students are completing activities either in class or at home. The activities often build upon on each other to allow the students to master each step along the way.

- students may use a workbook that accompanies a textbook, work on textbook activities or be given instructor-created activities

- self-paced activities could take many forms, such as learning how to use a software program through a variety of mini-activities to master the program's abilities (e.g., photo editing software, keyboarding software, video editing software); learning how to use a tool (cooking, mechanical, carpentry, medical) by working through activities designed to be comfortable with the tool

- self-paced learning activities work well when there are checkpoints along the way for the instructor to assess learning; when there are opportunities to repeat or redo activities when mastery has not been completed; when a lot of instructor feedback happens and quick learners are accommodated with other enriching activities rather than being forced to repeat learning they have mastered

5. What's in Your Portfolio?

Students are designing a collection of required components that demonstrate their understanding of a subject area.

- students may use a paper-based or digitally-created collection to pull together samples of exemplary work, newly formed philosophies, new learning examples, etc.

- portfolios are unique representations of student learning and are built over the duration of a course

- students often work alone in assemblig all the required pieces

- portfolios can be shared in small groups for informal feedback, or shared online

F. Group Learning Strategies

The key concepts of group learning include

- groups collaborating together for a common goal

- each group member making a valuable contribution

- group members assisting each other when needed

- no emphasis on competition

1. More than Just a Number

Small groups work together to solve a problem. Each group member has been assigned a number. When sufficient time has passed to solve the problem, the instructor calls a number and the students in each group assigned that number respond one at a time.

- works well with class sizes up to 75 students

- 4-6 students per group works best; number off such as student 1, student 2, student 3, etc.

- instructor gives a problem (e.g., a math problem, chemistry equation, historical event description to find/formulate, engineering process to explain, poem to interpret, etc.)

- instructor then calls a number and the student with that number in each group responds

- all members of the group are involved in thinking and talking as they work collectively to respond to the question and ensure that each member of the group understands the answer

- this strategy is a great alternative to whole-class discussion/questioning or for reviewing/summarizing content before a final test or exam

2. Peer Instruction

Students are working in small groups to discuss and debate problems that often lead to misunderstanding or misconceptions in the subject matter. Multiple choice questions are often used and are specifically designed to be challenging enough for 30-70% of the class. The process of answering the questions both individually and also after a small group discussion allows students to engage in reasoning and application skills of concepts.

- students read/review topic prior to attending class; class time is spent analyzing specific problems and questions that address misconceptions and challenging concepts required of the discipline

- questions are designed to elicit misunderstandings with material (often are multiple choice format)

- instructor displays question on screen/board; asks students to think about question on their own

- students are given 1-2 minutes to come up with their own answer and make their choice known (either through a clicker/classroom response system or holding up a card with a letter (A, B, C, D, etc.) that corresponds with their answer) in an anonymous fashion

- instructor lets the class know how many people were correct in their choice

- instructor then indicates that in small groups of 3-4 students the question needs to be discussed with the goal of reaching consensus on the correct response; everyone in the group should understand why the group is making the choice, offer their insights into the question, defend their choice, etc.

- instructor asks students to vote again for correct response (again either by card or clicker)

- instructor then discusses the correct answer with the class; if many students did not get the correct answer on the 2nd vote, then a mini-lesson is required to further elaborate the concept

- research has shown dramatic results in increased understanding and a greater number of correct answers once students have time to "peer instruct" each other

- Eric Mazur (Harvard University Professor) is credited with developing this method and the research that attests to its effectiveness (see: http://mazur-www.harvard.edu/research/detailspage.php?rowid=8)

3. Discussion Session

Students are engaging in purposeful talk through discussing good questions. Students communicate with each other to discuss a topic, to probe an issue, or to resolve a problem.

- instructor plans well-designed questions on a topic along with an appropriate structure and time frame for holding a meaningful discussion

- have students think about the topic and related questions before the class, along with small group mini-discussion will help the discussion be more lively and rich in responses

- emphasis is on students talking and listening to each other, as opposed to the teacher giving all the answers. Redirecting the discussion is a key skill to keeping things on task

- questions should be designed beforehand and aimed at eliciting a variety of cognitive responses (from short answer, low-level thinking questions to more complex answers requiring students to synthesize, analyze, and evaluate information)

- see Chapter 12 on Questioning (and how to facilitate discussions) for more ideas

4. Expert Connection

Students are gaining a variety of perspectives and information by participating in a specialized group (often called the 'expert group') and then by sharing what they learned back in their 'home' group (comprised of original group members).

- works well with classes of less than 40 students

- instructor decides how many topics required for the class (a topic per each expert group)

- instructor creates a set of instructions per each topic, along with resources and tasks

- if there are 6 expert groups/topics, then each 'home' group needs 6 people; if there are 5 expert groups/topics, then each 'home' group needs 5 people

- the expert groups work best with 5-10 people

- assemble home groups (let students choose or appoint members); have each student number off according to the expert group numbers (e.g., expert member for group 1, expert member for group 2, etc.)

- the goal is for expert members in each home group to go out and become an expert in a topic and then return to the home group to share/teach others what they have learned

- if there is a quiz or fun summary of the learning, students will be more motivated to become the best experts they can be and the best teachers of that content

- allow 15-30 minutes for expert groups to become comfortable with their content and allow home groups about 2-4 minutes per expert member to share

- the strategy may provide a review of previously learned material or identify questions or problems within an issue or topic

- if students have access to laptops, allow students to use Internet resources in expert groups

5. Team-Based Learning

Team-Based Learning (TBL), a strategy for organizing your class learning, is attributed to Larry Michaelsen, Dee Fink, and Arletta Bauman Knight. It involves an application of course concepts by student teams through set readings and tests, along with lots of class time to practice applying content in team exercises. See http://tblc.camp9.org/ for more information.

- students acquire their initial exposure to the content through specific readings and then are tested on their knowledge through an individual quiz and then again through a group-consensus quiz. Both individual and group quiz marks count.

- students provide input about allocation of percentages for evaluation components

- class time is used to practice applying content through individual and group activities, assignments, and projects that mostly take place within class time

- students are accountable for contributing to the group; peer assessment is used

- instructor has some up-front work for preparing weekly quizzes and group assignments, but the construction of knowledge and learning rests mainly with the students

G. Activity-Focused Strategies

Activity-focused strategies are

- students learning by doing activities

- active learning experiences

- allow students to explore, make choices, solve problems, and interact with others

- engaging, interactive, and fun!

1. Sharing in the Round

Small groups are formed and each one is asked to read, interpret, and summarize course content to share with classmates. During a set class time, half the groups present to other students who rotate through in short time periods. The groups then switch and the other half of the class presents.

- works well with classes of 25-75 students, regardless of seating arrangement

- instructor creates groups of 3-5 students, assigns each group a topic related to the course, gives each group a research article, related reading, portion of a textbook chapter, news article, etc., to read, interpret, and summarize key points

- small groups convene to discuss reading (may meet online or during class time)

- groups discuss guiding questions (given by instructor) and are asked to collectively decide the most important components or concepts to share in a short presentation (5 minutes) during the next class

- instructor produces rotational schedule (have half groups present one day and half another day)

- two students are appointed to be the presenters and remain, while the rest of the group rotates to listen to designated speakers from other groups

- students are encouraged to take notes during each of the rotations

- large group discussion of the whole activity helps solidify notes, clarify points, answer questions

- prevents time-consuming and repetitive reports to the whole class, allows students to take on the role of interpreting information and summarizing key points

2. Experimenting

Experimenting is a strategy whereby students (individually, in pairs, or in small groups) conduct an experiment or activity with a set of instructions and related resources.

- works well with classes under 25 either in a classroom or a lab environment

- instructor may find experiments or lab activities in textbooks and Internet

- gives students a chance to hypothesize what they think might happen, conduct the experiment, and then discuss the results

- can use simple (found objects) or may use discipline-specific resources

- students can create their own variations of an experiment or ask them to design a brand new experiment; allows for higher levels of thinking

- experiments do not have to be scientific in nature; experiments can be done in other disciplines with people, online tools, elements found in nature, observations, etc.

3. A Date with a Debate

Half the class is assigned to argue an issue/topic from the pro side and half are assigned to argue from the con side using a variety of resources to formulate points and rebuttals. Some students could be judges.

- works well with classes of 10-100 students, regardless of seating arrangement (with larger classes have two different debates)

- choose a controversial topic, hot issue, or argumentative statement from your field of study

- introduce topic to the students and assign half to one side and half to the other side of the issue

- give each 'side' class time and resources to build 3 major arguments for their position, 3 rebuttals against the other side's arguments, and an opening and closing statement

- outline the roles students can play e.g., opener, closer, argument # 1, rebuttal # 2, etc.

- some students could play the role of 'judges' to make a decision at the end of the debate. These students would be responsible for researching the topics as well as creating a format/scheme for determining who 'wins' the debate

- put a diagram on the board/slide to show the order of speakers

- debrief the whole experience after sharing positive comments about work done and points made

- debates help strengthen and extend students' understanding of an issue while developing and demonstrating cognitive thinking, research, and communication skills

4. Simulation Situation

A simulation is a situation that closely mirrors real conditions through which students respond as though the situation were real.

- instructor puts students into small groups (5-10) and gives them details about how to create a simulation related to the course content

- students must interpret the details and create a simulated situation (may use props, costumes, software, music, other students, etc.)

- simulations can take a number of forms such as role playing, case studies, enactment of a real event, online environment, etc.

- software applications can create computer models of real-life situations and can be effective in developing and sustaining virtual situations while testing a set of variables

5. Fishbowl Fun

This strategy involves two circles of students. The inner circle is comprised of students sitting on chairs—also known as 'the fishbowl'—who are part of the active discussion. The outer circle of students are standing—looking in at the fish in the bowl—and listening to the discussion. If some-one from the outer circle wishes to be part of the discussion they tap someone on the shoulder and change places.

- this strategy works well with classes of 30 or less. If you have larger classes you can set up two circles or fishbowls and monitor both by moving between

- students are given a topic/issue to discuss that would elicit a rich conversation

- have students research, investigate, and jot down points on paper before activity starts

- arrange approximately 10 chairs in a circle

- ask for volunteers who would like to be the first to sit in the chairs to start the discussion

- arrange other students standing around the circle

- those in the chairs are the only ones allowed to speak

- after a few minutes of discussion, ask if anyone around the outside wants to jump in and join the conversation, if they do, indicate they are to gently tap someone on the shoulder and exchange places

- discussion continues with reminders about moving in and out of the circle (fishbowl)

- debrief the activity once the discussion has reached its peak or time has run out

6. A Game By Any Name

A game can be a challenging activity, simulation, or contest played according to rules. Games engage students, allowing them to work together in a co-operative or competitive spirit.

- games are meant to be fun and played within a protected environment

- games can motivate students, build enthusiasm, and aid in reviewing test concepts

- many game 'templates' can be found online (e.g., Jeopardy, Millionaire) and can easily be modified for discipline-specific questions

- the simplest of games involves two teams competing to answer questions for points

- variation: ask students to create questions for a game (along with answers)

7. Station Nation

The instructor creates tasks for students to do at stations set out around the class. Students rotate through each station, read the instructions, complete the task, and move onto another station.

- works very well with classes of 45 students or less

- instructor has some preparation work in creating each station (about 5-7) and tasks for students, but students benefit from the learning they undertake at each station

- sample station activities might include answering questions on a related reading, summarizing an article, discussing a case study/scenario, working together to create a problem, designing something, proposing solutions to a situation, working with materials to conduct a small experiment, using resources to explore the discipline, etc.

- each station requires a short set of instructions for students, all resources, and links/references (best to include in a large envelope or a plastic bin)

- station-based learning works very well when you have materials or resources which are short in supply for everyone to use at once, but work very well with small groups using them on rotation

- ensure each station task is able to be completed within the rotation time

- provide a tracking sheet for students to check off when they complete the task; this sheet may be handed in at the end of the class or when all stations are complete

- this activity could last one or more classes; ensure you provide time for answering questions, extending the learning at the stations, and debriefing the activity

- consider an 'end product' of station-based learning such as students discussing what they have learned, designing a report on their learning, or taking a quiz etc.?

8. Tripping in the Real World

A field trip happens when an instructor arranges for students to leave the traditional classroom for a visit to an off-campus location to learn more about the discipline.

- instructor sees value in taking the class off campus during a time when all students are able to attend

- instructor often pre-visits the location to scope out all components of field trip

- students are given adequate time to prepare and plan for attending (e.g., may be a weekend trip or a trip during a 2 or 3 hour scheduled class)

- possible locations might be a local museum, art gallery, high tech industry, community service, business, hospital, school, another university/college, native reserve, government office, etc.

H. Arts-Influenced Strategies

Arts-influenced strategies

- help students to develop creative outlets for learning

- increases students' ability to think creatively

- are not just limited to the arts! Many arts-based strategies work very well in sciences, social sciences, technology, etc.

1. Give Me an Oscar!

Students are taking on a role to explore the thoughts, feelings, and actions of another person. The students investigate a discipline-specific situation and create roles, dialogue, and movement around a scene.

- works well with all class sizes; smaller group sizes can be modified (pairs, small or large group)

- role playing could be used to look at the viewpoints of others, improve communication methods etc.

- in any discipline, role playing could examine a historical or current event allowing students to research all aspects of a character, as well as designing an authentic character

- students engage in co-operative, authentic, and engaging learning experiences

2. Modeling Time

Students are creating a representation or model of a concept, process, or component related to the discipline. The creation can be digital or non-digital.

- asking students to design their interpretation of how something works leads to a lot of creativity, problem-solving, and designing skills

- ask students to sketch or design a prototype to get feedback from the instructor/class

- students can make models out of found objects (e.g., toilet paper rolls, garbage), craft materials (Styrofoam balls, toothpicks), modeling software (chemistry molecule software, 3D software), or through animation (Flash or custom animation in PowerPoint)

- allows students to explore concepts in greater depth and explain/present in a simple format

- models can be brought into the class and shared through a rotational format (e.g., Sharing in the Round strategy found under "Activity-Based Strategies"), small groups, or pairs

3. Sketch It Out

Students are visually representing the ideas they hear, read, or think about in pictorial/graphic form during or immediately following a presentation.

- works as a nice complement to concept mapping

- instead of taking written notes, ask students to draw a sketch of their representation of a concept just discussed in class (e.g., a framework diagram, images that come to mind when they are listening, etc.)

- ensure you give students clear instructions about what is expected and that the 'written notes' that accompany the sketch will be created or given to them after

- allow students to share sketches with each other in small groups

- have a large group discussion about this activity and obtain class feedback

- take a digital picture of some sketches (with student permission) to post on class web site

4. Storyboarding or Cartooning

Students are creating a storyboard (or a cartoon strip) that includes a series of quick sketches/diagrams that depict events, dialogue, and character interaction in sequential order. Storyboards show thought and planning, as well understanding of events and activities.

- instructor would ask students to work individually (or in pairs) in class or outside of class time to sketch out a storyboard (or a cartoon strip) for a topic related to the discipline

- each frame consists of scenes or figures with descriptive text so someone else reading the storyboard/cartoon would have enough information to understand the event

- each frame would be a camera shot if this was a television commercial (storyboard) or a frame of a cartoon that progresses the story

- storyboards give students the opportunity to translate ideas or stories into a different mode of expression rather than text

- allow students to use online storyboard/cartooning software to create their frames and tell their story, post links to their work, allow for feedback and interpretation time

- have students swap their storyboard/cartoon with their peers and ask for their interpretation

I. Thinking and Problem Solving Strategies

Thinking and problem solving strategies involve students

- using an organized format to plan a solution

- focused on solving a problem either independently or together

- being forced to use higher levels of thinking abilities

- often working on authentic problems

1. Brainstorming

Small or large groups of students are generating ideas, concepts, solutions, plans, or topics together. The group's goal is to produce as many ideas as possible without judgment or feedback from the group until the process is complete.

- works well with small to large classes (larger classes can brainstorm in small groups)

- the first time, an instructor may wish to model or help facilitate a group brainstorming session before students complete one on their own

- brainstorming works best when the students can immediately see the ideas being generated. Consider using a software program like SmartIdeas or Inspiration to capture ideas that can be later color-coded and organized or use chart paper or overhead transparency

- students need to be reminded not to get off track by arguing about the inclusion/exclusion of ideas, but rather capture all ideas regardless of their relevance or importance

- once a brainstorming session is complete, students should be instructed to consider all that has been gathered and start organizing and assembling the ideas into categories

2. A Case To Solve

A case study is a description of a situation (based on real-life or simulated events) that is examined by students to consider major and minor problems and propose possible solutions.

- instructor may need to write a case study to ensure all components are included for class

- instructor should go through a sample case study with class to demonstrate how to organize, research, investigate, analyze, and synthesize information to make informed solutions

- students may or may not have been exposed to the situation in the case study

- case studies allow for students to conduct rich investigations and research into elements of the case

- small groups work best in solving case studies with students exploring various components of the case

- assumptions have to be made considering not all the information is provided

- students may work independently to come up with their own answers before working in a small group

- can take place during a class period or may take weeks to solve before being presented or evaluated

3. Problem Solving

Studnets are applying critical thinking skills to generate a solution for a proposed problem. Problem solving occurs in all disciplines and often involves workable problems that can be solved within class time or over the course of a few weeks.

- instructor should ensure students understand the problem first

- problem solving is also part of a process where students understand a problem, explore all aspects of the program, select a strategy, make a plan, carry out the plan, solve the problem, check results, and then communicate the results to others in a variety of formats

- the problem solving process may need to be reviewed for students and possibly modeled

- there are a number of problem solving strategies such as drawing a diagram, making a model, looking for a pattern, guessing and checking, simplifying the problem, drawing a chart/matrix, working backwards, using equations or formulas, and using resources such as the Internet, calculator, etc.

4. Concept Mapping

Students are generating items /ideas /information and organizing them around course concepts. As a strategy, concept mapping operates on a much higher thinking scale than brainstorming and forces students to consider relevant connections and relationships amongst content to draw out conceptual elements.

- instructor often demonstrates or models the creation of a concept map

- students are then asked to create a concept map (or build on one already started) using either digital or non-digital means (SmartIdeas and Inspiration are excellent software programs for creating a concept map as they have images, colors, arrows, and other tools to show connectivity between ideas; work can be easily saved and shared with others and printed or uploaded to the web)

- small groups of students share concept maps to draw out different perceptions that they observe

- post concept maps online on a course web site to share with students

5. Problem-Based Learning

Problem-based learning is a strategy whereby the instructor poses an authentic open-ended problem to students and guides and supports them in reaching the solution.

- instructor must set out the expectations and the nature of problem-based learning before starting

- students work in small groups and either work on a similar or different program than other groups

- problem often takes weeks or the whole semester to solve and may have deliverables that are handed in along the way (components of problem, plan, strategies being used, resources found, etc.)

- students are more engaged if the problem is authentic (problems can come from society and may be current and newsworthy) because they see the relevance and meaning in solving the problem (i.e., they may experience this problem in a job or somewhere in life at some point)

- groups must be aware of what information they already know about the problem, what information they need to know to solve the problem, and the strategies to use to solve the problem

- comes from a constructivist approach to learning where students are encouraged to construct/build their own knowledge and reflect on their learning processes and styles

- problem-based learning is heavily used in medical programs, but is gaining popularity in other disciplines

J. Technology-Supported Strategies

Technology tools:

- Not a strategy on their own, but support other teaching, learning, and assessment strategies

- Used to make some strategies more accessible for students

- Used to engage students more

- Often able to extend the life of the in class experience

- Provides multiple ways of approaching content and concepts

1. Interactive White Boards

Interactive white boards are able to display the screen of a desktop or laptop computer and allow for interaction through touch. They are also referred to as a SmartBoard which is the name of a major manufacturer of interactive white boards. They are synchronized with the computer to allow an instructor (and students) to use their fingers or a 'pen' to touch the surface to interact, collaborate, and draw information on the screen. The following are examples of ways to use an interactive whiteboard for supporting learning:

- collaborate on a problem (many students can contribute with different colors of text, lines, and diagrams, and by saving the work and returning to it later) and move to board at various times

- focus attention to particular features (e.g., by drawing, highlighting, or zooming in on items)

- classify and sorting objects/ideas/concepts (e.g., dragging, dropping, hiding, labeling items)

- adapt to individual learner's needs by allowing student to physically move objects, see items up close, have work saved etc.

2. Clickers

Clickers are hand-held devices that remotely respond to a receiver when a response (pushing a key) is initiated. Other names include classroom performance systems, classroom response systems, or personal response systems. Students purchase a clicker for the class (or in smaller classes the instructor may borrow a set for students to use) and use it when the instructor poses questions or statements that require them to 'vote'. The student punches in a required key corresponding to their response and the instructor uses software on a computer to tally the votes and either show or verbally share with students the response totals. The following are examples of ways to use clickers for teaching and learning:

- seek agreement/disagreement with various statements related to topic (use as a pre-assessment method to ascertain what students know/feel about concepts)

- solicit levels of accuracy to problem solving questions (use a teaching method for instructing new content to allow students to practice applying knowledge and getting immediate feedback)

- seek understanding of content learned in class (use as a consolidation method for allowing students and instructor to find out level of comprehension and application of content from a class)

- practise content before an exam or test (use as a review method for allowing students to find out how much they know/don't know about concepts and content prior to a formal evaluation)

3. Web-Based Learning Tools

Web-based learning tools are small software applications that have been designed around one or two main concepts in an interactive manner to allow students to practice their learning. Sometimes called learning objects, learning tools, animations, or interactive learning environments, they are built to be easily accessible on the web, are often used within a browser, and work with a variety of bandwidths for quick interaction and immediate feedback. Here are some ways web-based learning tools can be used for teaching and learning:

- introduce a topic (showing the tool to the whole class at once, asking students to make decisions about how to interact with it, determining what they know already)

- teach new content (having students work individually or in pairs on a laptop or a computer with the tool, possibly having a worksheet to complete)

- consolidate content (showing the tool to the whole class at once, asking students to make decisions about how to interact with it, allowing small group discussion as a response)

- review content (giving students links to the tools to use on their own as practice/review)

4. Digital Video

The best way to use digital video is when it is uploaded and accessible on the Internet. Teacher Tube, You Tube, and educational web sites that host video are some places to look for video. You can also conduct an advanced search through a browser for content that is only in a video format. Here are some ways digital video can be used in teaching and learning:

- ask students to view a video before class and engage students in a discussion

- show a video in class (short or long) and ask students to do an activity based on the video

- have students shoot their own video (most students have phones or cameras that can capture short video segments) and post online as a way of answering a question

- show a video that exemplifies content/concepts being used in a related job or real-world experience

- use video to capture a lecture, demonstration, or experiment you do and wish to share with students so they can view many times and take better notes

5. Digital Audio

The best way to use digital audio is when it is uploaded and accessible on the Internet. You can conduct an advanced search through a browser for content that is only in an audio format. When something is recorded as digital audio and is made available through a feed or posted online for subscription, this is often referred to as a podcast. Here are some ways digital audio can be used in teaching and learning:

- ask students to listen to podcast before class and engage students in a discussion

- have students answer questions via digital audio, post online, and then discuss as a small or large group

- refer students to podcasts created by other instructors to listen to prior to class (e.g., iTunesU podcasts)

- interview a guest/expert and record your phone conversation and post the audio to your course site for students to access (as a resource, as a required course component, etc.)

6. Online Surveys and Self-Marking Quizzes

Online surveys are anonymous feedback mechanisms for students to vote, answer questions, or voice opinions on course content, concepts, and learning. Online surveys are a little different than using clickers to answer questions. An online survey is often created within the online learning management system (e.g., Blackboard has an anonymous survey tool) or a link you provide to a web-based, safe, survey-environment that gathers students responses and produces a report for the instructor. Some survey tools can be structured to give feedback on the accuracy of an answer so that students get immediate feedback on learning. Here are some ways to use online surveys:

- ask students to answer questions about a topic before you begin formal lesson (engages students in becoming curious about course content)

- survey student knowledge and skills after completing readings/homework (gives feedback to students and instructor as to where more time is required for learning)

- obtain student input on class structure, teaching and learning strategies used, and assessment/evaluation methods to meet their needs and refine class instruction

7. Presentation Environments

Instructors have a variety of presentation environments through which to communicate with students. The most popular environment is Microsoft PowerPoint or Apple's Keynote, which often are used in a linear fashion with slides composed of content (text, images, video, audio, etc.). Prezi is another environment that is a large canvas where content (text, images, video, audio, etc.) is placed and the instructor either sets a pre-determined path or zooms/moves the canvas to show and explain content. Here are some ways to use presentation environments:

- share content using gapped slides (main topic headings, some key content); students need to come to class to get rest of content

- use a presentation environment to tell a story with images

- showcase examples of content with audio and video components

8. Software

Software refers to the computer programs that benefit students' learning. The software may be a program you install on the computer or an online software program that works within the browser. There are various categories of software such as productivity software (e.g., word processing, spreadsheets, desktop publishing), concept-mapping software (e.g., SmartIdeas, Inspiration), design-oriented software (e.g., graphics editing, video and audio editing), and discipline-specific software (e.g., modeling, math, statistics, medical). Here are some ways to use software:

- to demonstrate something related to the discipline

- to draw or visually represent something

- to record student ideas to share with class offline

- use productivity software to make agendas, titles, or emphasize content in larger font

9. Screencasting

Screencasting is the process of capturing the sounds and images from your computer screen. Products like Jing, Camtasia Studio, and Pixetell allow users to record audio, visual, and movements of the mouse from the screen of the computer. Using a tablet will allow you to write on the screen where typing and mouse movements are not sufficient for full or clear explanations. Here are some ways to use the software:

- Explaining how a problem is solved

- Showing how to use a piece of software

- Outlining how to search for information on the Internet

10. Web 2.0 Tools

Blogs, wikis, shared documents, social networks, bookmarking, collaborative learning environments, tagging, sharing files, RSS feeds, podcasts, and multi-user virtual environments– these are some of the ways instructors and students can use Web 2.0 tools for learning:

- Instructor uses a blog to share thoughts, insights, new revelations, information

- Instructor uses online sites to share presentations, videos, podcasts, etc.

- Small groups of students use a wiki to build their knowledge and understanding of a course topic

- Students use instant messaging, voice/video communication to work on a project

- Instant sharing of resources happens between students while working on an activity

Top Ten Takeaways

1. **Choose Strategies After Determining Objectives and Assessment/Evaluation Methods**: Choose a teaching and learning strategy only after you have solidified your learning objectives and assessment and evaluation methods.

2. **Create a Variety of Learning Opportunities for Students**: Designing a class involves providing a variety of ways through which students can access learning. Those opportunities need to fit with your discipline and the learning that you expect of your students.

3. **Start with Low Risk Activities**: Try some low risk, quick learning activities in your classroom the next time. Choose one or two from the list of 8 simple ideas.

4. **Revamp The Lecture**: Try to include more questions, shorter chunks of information, and examples related to the content. This will help students be more engaged and learn better.

5. **Active Learning**: Lectures are a common component of any higher education setting but most often lead to passive learning, and low motivation and engagement on the part of students. Trying some other teaching and learning strategies will greatly increase active learning opportunities for deep learning!

6. **Strategy Types**: Consider your personality, your teaching style, and your experience within your discipline. Which teaching and learning strategy category (Activity-Focused, Group Learning, Arts-Based, etc.) works best?

7. **Provide Flexibility, Communication Opportunities, and Variety for Students**: Today's students like discussing with their peers, verifying their thoughts, working in groups, and having choice in the way they learn. They also like being able to have flexibility in their learning environment and have a variety of ways of expressing themselves. Consider this when you are choosing teaching and learning strategies.

8. **Have an Open Mind**: Conduct a short investigation into the teaching and learning strategy through online research or talking to your colleagues. Take a small risk and try something new.

9. **Fairly Low Risk Strategies**: Many of the strategies included in this chapter are low to medium in risk. This means it would take very little of your time to set up and implement with a good majority of your students accepting the different strategy. Even if you implemented one strategy per class, you'd be helping students immensely!

10. **Technology Supports Teaching and Learning**: Technology-supported strategies are other ways to engage students while designing rich learning experiences. Technology can often be used with many of the other teaching and learning strategies.

Next Steps

1. Make a list of all the teaching and learning strategies you used in your teaching. Which strategies do you use the most and which ones do you use least?

2. Talk to your colleagues and ask them about their teaching and learning strategies? Which ones are most frequently cited? Which strategies are not used as frequently? Are there reasons pertaining to the instructor, the faculty, or the discipline that affect which teaching and learning strategies instructors use?

3. After skimming through this chapter, which strategies might interest you? Why are they piquing your interest? Make a short list of the strategies and which ones you might want to start with first.

4. Look over your upcoming courses. Are there any opportunities to try different strategies at certain points in the term? Which strategies would be easy to implement and which strategies might you need a bit of time to set up?

5. Take some time to search the Internet for further details on the strategies included in this chapter. Reading other instructors' accounts or finding a research article outlining the benefits might be an interesting start to modifying your teaching.

Resources and References

Blackburn, R. T., Pellino, G. R., Boberg, A. & O'Connell, C. (1980). Are Instructional Programs Off-Target? *Current Issues in Higher Education, 1*, 32-48.

Brown, S. & Race, P. (2002). *Lecturing: A Practical Guide*. London, UK: Kogan Page.

Higher Education Research Institute (1999). *The American College Teacher: National Norms for the 1998-99 HERI Faculty Survey*. Los Angeles, CA: Higher Education Research Institute, University of California at Los Angeles.

Lammers, W. J. & Murphy, J. J. (2002). A Profile of Teaching Techniques used in the University Classroom: A Descriptive Profile of a US Public University, *Active Learning in Higher Education, 3*(1), 54–67.

Mazur Group. (2010). *Chaos in the classroom*. Retrieved February 21, 2010, from http://mazur-www.harvard.edu/research/detailspage.php?rowid=8

Team-Based Learning. (n.d.). Retrieved February 22, 2010, from http://tblc.camp9.org/

Thielens, Jr., W. (1987). *The Disciplines and Undergraduate Lecturing*. Paper presented at the annual meeting of the American Educational Research Association, Washington, DC.

Chapter 8: Planning Your Classes

Chapter Overview

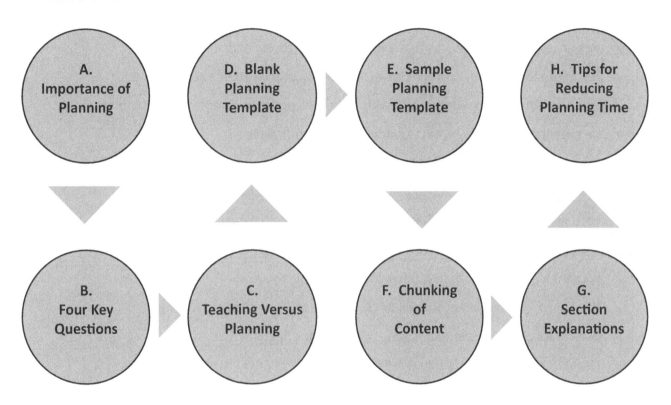

Good instructors create thoughtful teaching plans for their classes. Rarely does a good instructor just walk into a classroom and teach a class 'off the top of his or her head' or with merely an hour of preparation. Teaching a 50 minute, 1.5 hour, or 3 hour class requires time and thought. Teaching is gaining greater attention in the media because students are demanding high quality classes and learning experiences that will benefit them for years to come. Students want to be engaged, they want to have a chance to apply their learning, and they want to find meaning and relevance in the topics studied.

Like a good book, there is a beginning, middle, and end to a successful class and the content is divided into chapters or chunks of learning. From novice to experienced instructors, planning is the glue that holds the class or lecture together. But, planning need not be feared! The time required to plan an effective class will lessen as one gains experience. A great plan will mean a great class!

This chapter gives you a template to help plan a class and aid in the smooth delivery of content and activities.

A. Importance of Planning

When you take time to plan your classes, you and your students will see improvements in teaching and learning experiences. Listed below are the benefits of taking the time to plan a class. Planning allows you to do the following:

- ✓ consider how your class fits within the whole course
- ✓ design learning experiences that will address key topics and content
- ✓ be on the look-out for current stories, videos, or special events related to your topic
- ✓ give students the knowledge and skills to be successful in completing assignments
- ✓ be organized and know what is coming next in your class
- ✓ manage the flow of your class
- ✓ provide varied and interesting learning opportunities for your students
- ✓ accommodate special needs students by considering their requests/needs
- ✓ integrate technology effectively and prepare a back-up plan too
- ✓ present a cohesive class that flows from one topic to another
- ✓ think through possible problems or challenges and be prepared for them
- ✓ pre-create questions and anticipate answers for effective discussions
- ✓ chunk content for your students to learn easier
- ✓ include time for student questions and feedback

Planning is a vital component to being an effective instructor. When you plan more, you will see an improvement in the flow and delivery of your content. Your students will also see a competent instructor who has an organized class and this is something students appreciate! It is important that you take time to lay out a plan for your classes to ensure success for both you and your students.

B. Four Key Questions

1. What shall I teach?
2. How shall I teach?
3. How can I organize it?
4. How can I assess it?

Before planning can begin, consider the four questions listed in the box to the left.

The answers to these questions will help you begin your class planning process.

Refer back to your course syllabus and outline of topics.

Consider how this class fits into your whole course.

Pinpoint the main objectives of the class.

You will need to specify the content students need to know by the end of this class and how will you know they have learned it.

Take a few minutes and think about these important questions.

Activity: Looking at the two flowcharts below, consider the differences between how instructors teach versus how instructors plan.

HOW INSTRUCTORS TEACH

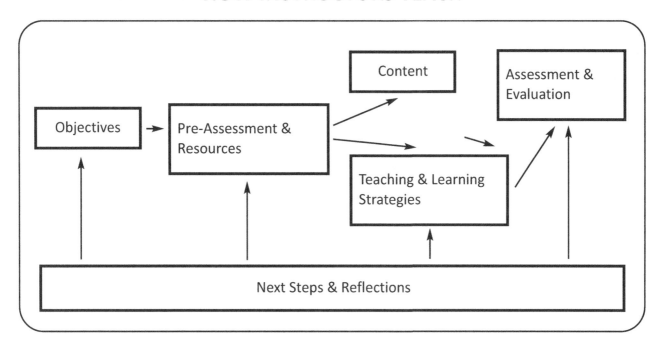

HOW INSTRUCTORS PLAN

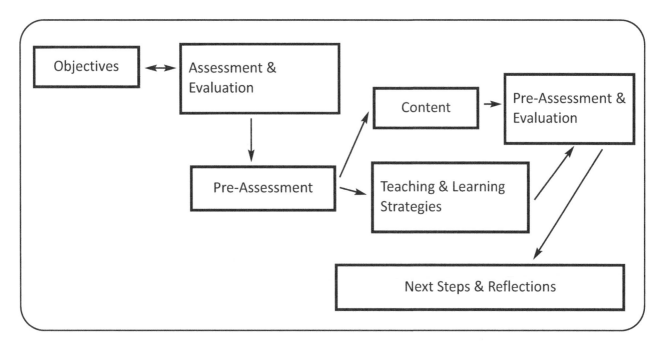

C. How Instructors Teach Versus How Instructors Plan

In the preceding flow charts, did you notice any differences between how instructors teach versus how they plan? There are many. Inexperienced instructors tend to plan in the same order as they teach, but soon learn that this is not an effective method. Here is a brief explanation of how an instructor should consider planning.

Objectives: You should always begin by considering what objectives you wish to cover in your class. These will come from your course syllabus. There should be 1 or 2 objectives that could be reasonably covered within your class time (e.g., 50 minutes or 3 hours)

Assessment & Evaluation: Next consider how the objectives will be met. This is called backwards planning or planning with the end in mind, which basically means you figure out how you will be assessing and evaluating student work in relation to the objectives. It is like thinking about the 'end' first and working backwards to figure out how you will get your students there (Wiggins and McTighe, 2005). You need to consider how your students will demonstrate to you that they have met the objectives.

Relationship between Objectives and Assessment & Evaluation: These first two steps in planning are linked together often with a double-headed arrow. You may go back and forth considering the objectives and deciding on different assessments or evaluations. This step may also take a bit longer. It is like planning a trip. You need to find the destination first and then spend a good chunk of time planning how you will get there.

Pre-Assessment: At this step, you have to think carefully about your class (number of students, students with disabilities, age of students, previous knowledge about the topic, social and behavioral characteristics, etc.) and how this will impact your class. It is a step that involves pre-assessing what you know already about your students and taking that into account when you plan the rest of the class.

Content/ Teaching & Learning Strategies: This step involves brainstorming all the content required for your class and narrowing it down to key concepts. Once you have those key concepts, you should be chunking them into 10-15 minute chunks. How you will deliver the content revolves around the teaching and learning strategies you choose (lecture, small group activity, video, discussion, etc).

Pre-Assessment & Resources: After the class has been developed, it is important for you to go back and ensure that all your students are being considered through the teaching and learning strategies chosen. Are student needs being met? At this point, it is also time to list the resources (web site links, books, videos, stories, handouts, etc.) you will need for the class.

Next Steps & Reflections: After the class is over, ensure you jot down notes for next year and reflect for a short time about the class. Changes, deletions, and additions are key things to consider.

Activity: *What are your planning experiences?*

For the following statements, check off those you do most or all of the time.

- ☐ I like to plan my classes at least a week in advance.

- ☐ I find it helpful to consider ideas found on the Web when planning my classes.

- ☐ I tend to use notes and ideas from previous instructors who taught this course.

- ☐ I build some of my classes around my research interests.

- ☐ I tend to over-plan by considering more items than I normally get through.

- ☐ I write my class plans on cue cards to use when teaching.

- ☐ I often start planning by considering the content I have to cover.

- ☐ I put my abbreviated class plans up on the Web a few days prior to class for students to obtain a preview of the class agenda.

- ☐ I write my lecture on paper.

- ☐ I like to plan my classes with my teaching assistants and/or other instructors teaching other sections of this course.

- ☐ I usually plan very little for my classes.

- ☐ I like to do a skeleton/overview plan of the whole term first.

- ☐ I plan using a template or an organizational format.

How many checkmarks do you have? Everyone has a different way of planning. There is no right or wrong method. It is advisable to plan at least a few days in advance of your class to ensure you are properly organized and prepared. It is also advisable to focus on the objectives of the course and use those to guide class content. A common mistake many instructors make is to deliver too much content and not leave enough time to have students apply their new knowledge and practice with problems and examples. Good instructors pare down a course to the key content components and ensure that there is a lot of discussion and engagement by students. The old adage "less is more" often applies to good teaching. You should focus on the most important concepts and ensure students can understand and apply them.

Class Planning Template

The following class planning template has been created to show one way an you can organize content. This template is only a guide; feel free to modify it as you wish. The template points you in a direction for planning your classes with an organized format. The template allows you to plan ahead, as well as having an outline. A sample class and a more detailed description of each section follow the template.

D. Class Planning Template – With Descriptions

Course Title:	Class Date:	Time:	Room:

1. Class Objectives

- Include only 1-2 objectives as they will be the ones you will assess or evaluate by end of class
- Ensure the objectives are related to class content and are measurable and observable

2. Pre-Assessment

Student Accommodations to Consider: Briefly indicate how you will accommodate students with specific academic needs, learning disabilities etc.

Student Academic Knowledge of Content: Briefly indicate what skills and knowledge your students will have prior to this class

Other:

3. Content / Teaching & Learning Strategies

a) Beginning *(Introduction, Agenda, Hook)*

Item	Description	Timing	4. Assessment & Evaluation
Introduction/Agenda	• Welcome students to class • Post and/or explain agenda (components) of class	Time – Time	*Include strategies here alongside appropriate class components.*
Announcements	• Attend to housekeeping items • Announcements about class or upcoming tests and projects	Time – Time	
Hook to Start Class	• Include a short hook (quick story, video, demonstration) to motivate the students to consider new content and get engaged in the class • Spend no longer than 5-10 minutes on the hook	Time – Time	

b) Main *(Content and Application)*

Item	Description	Timing
Content 1	• Brief points about the content to present • Sample questions and anticipated answers	Time – Time
Application-Content 1	• Activity to apply learning of content	Time – Time
Content 2	• Brief points about the content to present • Sample questions and anticipated answers	Time – Time
Application-Content 2	• Activity to apply learning of content	Time – Time

c) Ending *(Consolidation, Next Steps)*

Item	Description	Timing
Consolidation of Class Content	• Explain class components + relationship to final evaluations • Ask questions about main components	Time – Time
Next Steps/Next Class Information	• Include information about homework, preparing for next class, readings, possible feedback from students on class, etc.	Time – Time

5. Resources & Materials for Class

•

•

6. Reflections & Notes for the Next Year

•

•

E. Class Planning Template – Sample

| Course Title: Course 201 | Class Date: November 21 | Time: 1:00 – 4:00 p.m. | Room: C345 |

1. Class Objectives

- Students will be able to list the five significant concepts in X topic

- Students will apply concepts in a small group activity with summary of key ideas

2. Pre-Assessment

Student Accommodations to Consider:
- student X/learning disability – be sure to meet with them after class to answer questions

Student Academic Knowledge of Content:
- previous required course touched on topic, will know some basics
- 2nd year course – need to ensure students have time to copy notes

Other:
- 75 students, need to organize into groups easily, class happens after lunch and they are often tired

3. Content / Teaching & Learning Strategies

a) Beginning

Item	Description	Timing	4. Assessment & Evaluation
Agenda	• Explain class components + relationship to final exam	1:00 – 1:05	Take note of answers to recap discussion
Previous Class Recap	• Ask questions about main components from previous class	1:05 – 1:10	
Video Clip	• Introduction to class topic and 2 questions – hook for class	1:10 – 1:20	

a) Main

Item	Description	Timing	
Gapped Handout	• Ask students to find their print out from web, extras if needed	1:20	Content is on final exam
Content 1	• Terms and Definitions • Background • Importance	1:20 – 1:30	Observe students who don't bring handouts to class

Item	Description	Timing	
Discussion Content 1	• Put students in groups of 4-5 • Pose questions about content on slide/blackboard • Give each group 7-10 minutes to discuss • Summarize in 5 minutes with group sharing of key points	1:30 – 1:45	Give feedback to group participation as walk around classroom
Content 2	• Theories and background • Relationship to Content 1 • 2-3 sample questions on content 2	1:45 – 2:00	
Application Activity for Content 1 + 2	• Small Group Activity • Summary of Content 1+ 2 • Answer questions	2:00 – 2:25	Give feedback to small groups and to students who summarize for group
	Break - 15 minutes	*2:25 – 2:40*	
Content 3	• Visual slides of images of content • Stories of each slide (approx 4-5 minute story per each of 5 slides) • Notes provided online for students to read along with text later • 2-3 sample questions on content 3	2:40 – 3:00	
Application Activity for Content 3	• Put questions on screen – have students vote for correct answer (raise flash cards/clickers) for answer • Discuss with partner nearby • Vote again on answer after discussion • Take up question • Repeat once more with a second question	3:00 – 3:15	Take note of number of correct answers on first and second vote – feedback on how well students are grasping

c) Ending

Item	Description	Timing	
Content 4	• Students work individually reading a passage you hand out (5 minutes) • Answer questions in notes with partners (5-7 minutes) • Take up questions as a whole class • 3-4 sample questions for whole class after content 4	3:15 – 3.30	Observe students reading and working together
Class Summary Content 1	• Discuss main points of class • Ask students to look over notes to ensure have points • Answer questions • Explain homework/readings for next class	3:30 – 3:45	
Ticket Out The Door	• Ask students to list 2 important things they learned today about X topic and 1 item they are still confused or need more help with • Collect papers as students exit • Say good-bye to them as they leave	3:45 – 3:50	

5. Resources & Materials for Class

- Slides with images
- Laptop/data projector
- Gapped Handout – extra copies
- Questions for discussion
- Activity materials
- Extra scrap paper for ticket out door

6. Reflections & Notes for Next Year

- Need to plan to have more details of stories for slides
- Students seemed to like hands-on activities and time to chat about content
- Chunking of each section seemed to go well with enough detail – need to give students more direction on what their notes should include

F. Chunking of Content

It is highly unlikely any student can sit for three straight hours and take effective notes while listening to a long lecture-focused class. Human brains do not have the capacity to sustain such concentration, understand and make sense of the content during long classes. We often wonder, as instructors, why students are yawning or not interested once we reach the one hour mark. If you have been a student yourself in such a situation, you will know the challenge of teaching in higher education.

A simple answer for making your classes more engaging is to chunk your content and activities into 10 to 15 minute segments. Some segments should contain content and some segments should contain activities for applying the content. Your students need to interact with you and their classmates and should have a change of pace in the class.

Here are some suggestions for breaking down your lecture or class into more manageable pieces. It may change the way you teach and how your students learn.

1. Gather all the content required for your class.

2. Identify sub-sections or sub-topics within the content: consider where appropriate breaks could occur in terms of delivering the content.

3. Pare down each sub-topic into points that would cover approximately 10-15 minutes of either lecturing or some form of direct instruction to students.

4. In a 1 hour class you need about 2-3 sub-topics to fill segments throughout the class; for 3 hour classes you need about 4-5 sub-topics.

5. Between sub-topic segments, include an activity that involves students applying the content you have just taught. These activities could also be 10-15 minutes long and would allow students to interact with the material by having a chance to stop taking notes and engaging with their peers.

6. Examples of learning activities: a small group discussion, watching a small video related to the topic, solving sample problems, using clickers or flash cards to vote on answers to questions, engaging in a debate about the topic, students independently answering questions, reading a passage, teaching a peer, etc.

7. Your class plan should have content interspersed with activities.

8. Allow time for a break (10-15 minutes) within a 2-hour or 3-hour class.

The biggest challenge for most instructors is choosing and knowing how to implement various learning activities to apply content. See Chapter 7 for suggested activities and explanations as to how to implement in your class. As you experiment with this format for your classes, you may wish to adjust how much content and what sorts of activities work best for your students.

G. Class Template: Section Explanations

This section describes each section of the template in the order an instructor should consider when planning a class. See the sample class plan (on previous pages) for additional information and examples.

Objectives

- 1 – 2 taken from course syllabus: keep in forefront of mind when planning class

- Consider these when planning assessment and evaluation

Assessment & Evaluation

- Assessment: Informal feedback to students about how they are doing with respect to the objectives and related course content (e.g., written and oral comments, practice test feedback, discussions, questioning) that do not have marks or grades

- Evaluation: formal grading and marks (e.g., tests, assignments, papers, mid-terms, exams)

- What assessment and/or evaluation strategies do you need to have so you are accountable for students' learning and addressing the course outcomes and objectives?

- What assessment and/or evaluation strategies should you include in your class? (e.g., sample questions, activities, quizzes, tests, homework rubrics, assignments, presentations, etc.)

- Ask yourself these questions:
  - What evidence will you look for to know whether or not your students actually learned what you intended for them to learn?
  - What will the evidence look like?
  - If the students are "applying" their knowledge of the content you just taught, how will you know that they understood those concepts? How will you record this?

Pre-Assessment

Take a few minutes to jot down characteristics of the class, pinpoint certain students you need to keep in mind, and look at the overall needs of your students.

Student Accommodations to Consider:

Remind yourself of students with learning disabilities or those who have been identified as needing some assistance with learning in your class. How will you be able to meet their needs with this class? List any strategies you might use (e.g., checking in with student, giving another example, allowing more time to complete an assignment, etc.). What principles of universal design can you consider in modifying content or providing alternatives for learning?

Student Academic Knowledge of Content:

Briefly list the background knowledge that you expect your students to have of this content (e.g., Were there previous classes where content may have surfaced? What might they know from secondary school or general knowledge?). This will help you set the stage for planning the class. Sometimes instructors conduct short pre-assessment quizzes, which are not marked, to ascertain what students already know. These are called diagnostic tests.

Other Items to Consider:

- Number of students: larger classes may require modifications to class content

- Social and behavioral characteristics of students: year of class (1st year, 4th year, etc.), maturity level, interest in topic, time of day class is held

- Preparedness levels: how prepared are your students for taking notes, doing readings, grasping main ideas of lecture, doing homework? This may affect how you structure your class, the level of assistance you may need to provide, and how slow/fast you can talk

Content/ Teaching & Learning Strategies:

- Brainstorm all content for this class. Lay it all out so you can see scope of content.

- Chunk your content by arranging it into manageable 10-15 minute chunks or segments

- Plan for activities that allow students to apply their learning and intersperse these between the content chunks

- Sequence content and activities in a step-by-step fashion

- Include approximate timing (either in minutes or actual times for the class) to help you decide how much content to include and predict how long class components will take

- Include sample questions you wish to ask with anticipated answers. See Chapter 13 on Questioning for more details. By including questions in your plan, you can easily refer to them, especially for detailed and critical thinking ones.

- Consolidation / Next Steps
    - Be sure to include a wrap up or summary of the content before the class ends as it is crucial for students to be reminded of what you just covered and it helps them finish off their notes with proper emphasis on key points
    - Consider a feedback mechanism (e.g., Minute Paper or Ticket out the Door) to elicit information from students about their learning and the class

- Revisit this section a number of times to refine, provide detail, and ensure it flows

- Agenda/Overview and Introduction – do at the end once you have class organized

Pre-Assessment & Resources:

- Revisit student needs now that sequence of instruction and application is established

- Ensure that pre-assessment information has been taken into account in the class design

- Resources – list key websites, resources, handouts, readings, and books you need for the class

Next Steps & Reflections:

- Make short comments about how the class progressed: what went well, what did not work, what you would change for next year, what took longer or shorter, etc.

- Indicate any steps you need to take or do differently next year

- Good instructors always make reflection notes as they know how helpful they are to their growth in the class and with their students

H. Tips for Reducing Planning Time

1. **Plan ahead of time.** A good rule of thumb is at least a week before the class, but more lead time is always better.

2. **Plan a few classes at once**. This will give you a sense of direction for a few weeks and it will be much easier to just refine each week's class as it gets closer.

3. **Plan a skeleton outline of all of your classes at the beginning of the term**. Duplicate the template, date them all, insert the appropriate objectives for each class, and start fleshing out what will happen each week. Even if you jot down a few points for each class you will begin to feel less overwhelmed about planning and start seeing the whole semester taking shape.

4. **Do not write down everything you are going to say; you will just end up reading off of your notes and putting your class to sleep.** Good instructors plan big idea concepts and jot down a few key points they need to remember. How you deliver the content should be in a variety of forms from storytelling to asking questions to engaging students in activities to discover the content themselves. If you are nervous and require more detailed notes, try to highlight key topic titles and create notes that contain key details and concepts.

5. **Plan when you are awake and ready.** Planning when you are tired or after a full day of teaching will make any task take forever and seem unfeasible. Set aside a specific time each week to sit down, without interruptions, and think through your class.

6. **Share your plans and discuss with a colleague.** When you verbalize your thoughts and get feedback from others, you may find yourself putting the pieces together much quicker and in a more enjoyable manner. Seek out a colleague who would not mind taking approximately 30 minutes a week to chat about your class. It may also be inspiring to acquire new ideas.

Top Ten Takeaways

1. **Planning**: One of the secrets to having a successful class is having a well-planned class.

2. **Time**: Planning does take time but it benefits both you and the students. If you set aside time to effectively plan, you will see results in your teaching.

3. **Planning Template**: Planning using a template helps you organize your

ideas in a consistent fashion. However, the template is just a guide and should be modified if you feel it would work better another way.

4. **Order of Planning vs. Order of Instruction**: The order in which an instructor plans is not the order in which an instructor teaches. Many instructors make this mistake and plan in the same order as they deliver the content.

5. **Plan with the End in Mind**: Start planning by taking into consideration the objectives along with assessment and evaluation. This is called "planning with the end in mind" and produces a better class when you figure out where you want students to end up and then plan the steps to get there.

6. **Pre-assessment**: Pre-assessment is a planning step that involves thinking about your students' needs (those with learning disabilities, experience with taking notes, prior academic knowledge of content) and remembering this when planning the class.

7. **Chunking Content**: Chunking content into 10-15 minute segments allows students to grasp material easier and take better notes. The brain also is able to process content and will not be overwhelmed. Students will be more engaged and able to pay attention if a lesson is chunked.

8. **Application of Content**: Including application opportunities after content has been presented assists students in practicing and interacting with the content. Include examples, problems, discussions, review games, and videos to enhance the application of content.

9. **Consolidation of Content**: Good instructors always spend 5-10 minutes at the end of a class recapping the key points from the class, checking to make sure students have grasped concepts, and eliciting feedback from students about what they are learning.

10. **Assessment Methods**: Even if you are just observing students working in small groups or giving feedback to individuals, providing informal assessment is very important.

Next Steps

1. Copy the template and start filling in sections for your next class. See what parts work for you and how it might help in organizing your content.

2. Go over the sample class plan and consider how it would look with the specifics from your class.

3. Look at your content for your next class. Are you able to break it up into 10-15 minute chunks? Do you include application activities between content to allow your students to work with the new material and practice? Could you try chunking your content for your next class and see how it goes?

References and Resources

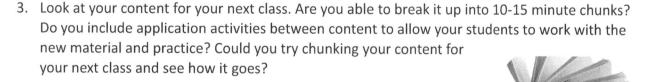

Wiggins, G. & McTighe, J. (2005). *Understanding by design*. Alexandria, VA: Association for Supervision and Curriculum Development.

Chapter 9: Starting with a Full First Day

Chapter Overview

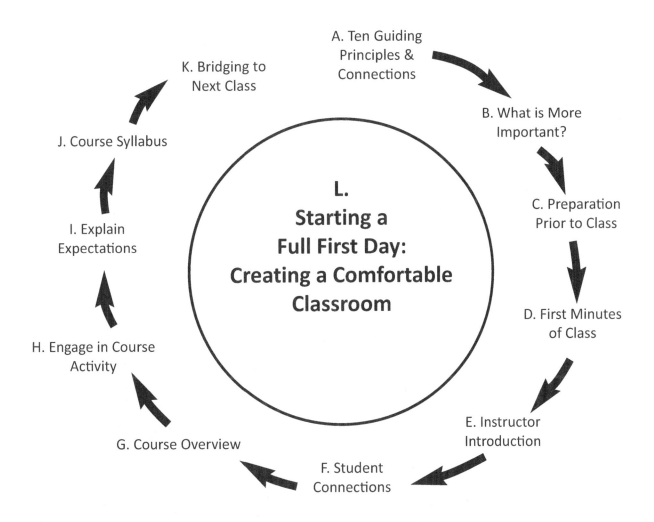

The first class, the first time you see the students, or the first day of a course is a very important day. On the first day you set the tone and atmosphere of how the course will be conducted. On the first day you let the students find out about you, the instructor, and their peers. On the first day you start establishing rapport with your class. On the first day you go over expectations and give students a solid start on course content. And, on the first day you set things in motion for a successful term. The first day is so important! The circle diagram above is just one possible way to look at conducting a first class, progressing from one item to another all the while considering the building of rapport, class atmosphere, and learning the students' names. This chapter will present ideas and suggestions for each item in the cycle to help you build a solid first class.

A. Ten Guiding Principles & Connections

The following ten principles are good to keep in mind as you plan your first full class for a course. Try not to squander the first class on just sharing the syllabus, going over assignments, and letting students out early. The first class is so much more!

1. Provide a **well thought-out** full first class

2. **Assist students** in making a smooth transition from previous schooling or holidays to an immersion into learning

3. Establish a **sense of community** and **communication** within the classroom

4. **Excite students** about course content

5. Aim for a **positive first impression**

6. **Encourage** students in an **active learning** environment

7. **Engage students** in immediate learning

8. **Introduce yourself and the course** effectively

9. Obtain **feedback** from students

10. Provide **support to students** to aid them in learning how to be successful

The first day of class is about the connections created between the students, the instructor, and the course.

The students must get to know the instructor, each other, and learn about the course. The instructor must get to know the students and engage them in course activities, while explaining course specifics and class expectations.

When you are planning your first day's activities, ensure you consider these three components and how they will connect with each other.

B. What is Important to Include on the First Day?

The following activity asks you to consider which activities are important to conduct on the first day of a course. Read both parts of each question. Circle which part is more important for you to consider on the first day of a course.

Which part of each question is MORE important to you?

- **Q1.** Covering the syllabus contents **OR** learning students' names?
- **Q2.** Ending class earlier than normal **OR** starting class on time?
- **Q3.** Engaging students in an course activity **OR** explaining course expectations?
- **Q4.** Presenting an overview of the course **OR** presenting an overview of the textbook?
- **Q5.** Covering assignment and test information **OR** showing the course website?
- **Q6.** Having students get to know each other **OR** explaining class rules and policies?
- **Q7.** Being organized and clear in your delivery **OR** showing your competence with the content?
- **Q8.** Empathizing with student situations **OR** being firm around class behaviour?
- **Q9.** Sharing your research and content experience **OR** sharing how you will teach the class?
- **Q10.** Assigning homework at the end of class **OR** asking students for any feedback on the first class?

The questions listed above may not have been easy to consider. Perhaps you were stumped on a few questions thinking both parts of the statement were equally important? You may have strong feelings about what is important on the first day developed from your teaching experience and what has worked for you.

You will find a variety of ideas and opinions about what constitutes a solid first class. However, many instructors and expert teaching facilitators tend to agree on similar components. Taking into consideration the characteristics of today's student, who craves a connected and communicative environment in which to learn, this chapter presents a set of ideas to get your term started!

C. Preparation Prior to First Class

1. Investigate your classroom (data projector/audio/visual materials to ensure they work; most effective arrangement of desks/chairs, consider entire layout of room, etc.)

2. Read through class names (going over them in your head will allow you to pre-think through class list and make connections when you meet students), if you get photos learn names/faces

3. Obtain a camera to take photos of students on the first day to learn names

4. Create an agenda of what your first class will look like; ensure it isn't just going over the syllabus and ending class early! Pack your agenda with a variety of activities that are similar to how you will be teaching the course (e.g., include discussions, an engaging activity, etc.)

5. Examine examples of active learning activities, talk to colleagues about ideas, etc.

6. Be prepared. Gather materials, arrive a bit earlier, and be ready for a great first class!

D. First Minutes of Class

1. Arrange tables, podium, chairs, or any other room items before your students enter the class.

2. Organize items to be picked up in a convenient location as students enter class (e.g., syllabus, handouts, attendance).

3. Play music while students enter room (adds to aura of the class, fills in dead air, and allows students to feel a bit more comfortable). Use current music or just choose a radio station and listen to it live through the computer.

4. Display the agenda or outline of the class so your students know what to expect.

5. Ensure title of course and your name are both clearly evident so students know if they are in the correct class.

6. Post instructions that tell students what to do immediately (e.g., pick up syllabus, a handout, and an index card on the table at the front of room – then read syllabus while you await the start of class).

7. Look happy and excited to see your students!

8. Greet students as they enter room (stand outside room and welcome them as they come in, or just when they get inside room) and ask them to pronounce their names too!

9. Circulate around room to chat with your students as the class is beginning.

10. Start class on time. This will set expectations for future classes.

E. Instructor Introduction

1. **Clarify any administrative details** about the course in case students are in the wrong class or thought they could attend class without being on the current class list, etc. Cover the following:

   • Prerequisites for your course

   • If and when you are signing in additional students

   • Directing students to agenda to let them know the syllabus and course expectations will be covered later in the class but that a course overview will happen earlier

   • Progress quickly through any other announcements

2. Share a bit about yourself

- Qualifications (so students have faith in your ability to teach content, your knowledge)

- Your beliefs and strategies about teaching/learning (so students know what to expect in terms of how you teach, how class will unfold, how you will evaluate them, etc.)

- Formal/informal nature (so students can gauge how approachable you are)

- Contact Info (so students know your email, office hours, how to make appointments, etc.)

3. Avoid

- Indicating you have never taught the course before

- Telling students this is your least favourite course to teach

- Being tired and upset about the class location or hour you are teaching

- Divulging any personal information that will not benefit you

4. Qualities to Demonstrate:

- Organization, Clarity, Enthusiasm, Fairness, and Empathy for Students

  ◦ These are key qualities students appreciate in a good instructor that should come through in your first class.

  ◦ Further down the list of qualities you will find comfort and competence with the subject matter. Show you are organized and are clear with your course.

F. Student Connections

Connecting Students: The more students feel connected to each other, the more likely they will come to class and have peers they can work with during class. The following ice-breaker activities will not only help students get to know each other, but also allow you to learn names.

These are low-risk activities that do not require much planning and will immediately engage your students. By focusing activities on fun facts and favorites, students will feel comfortable to participate. It may not be a good idea to ask students to stand up in class, introduce themselves and tell what program or year they are in, or what they hope to get out of the class. Putting students on the spot like this can make some students very vulnerable and embarrassed.

1. **Name Tag Symbols**: Have students write their name on both sides of a folded piece of paper (or stiffer cardstock paper). Then ask them to draw a representative symbol at the end of their name. Have students introduce themselves to the class in 30 seconds or less and explain the symbol. Try to have groups of 15-20 if you have larger classes. This activity will help with everyone learning names!

2. **Intro Tags**: Have students divide a sticker (or a piece of paper) in half. The top half is for the student's name. The bottom half needs to include 4 circles in a row. Give out a collection of 4 different coloured stickers (stars, happy faces). For each circle on the sticker, ask the stu-

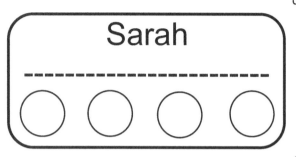

dents a multiple choice question with 4 possible answers proceeding from left to right. For each answer, there is a corresponding coloured sticker (e.g., A = orange happy face, B = purple happy face, C= green happy face and D= blue happy face). After all four circles are filled with a coloured sticker, have the students get up and mingle around the classroom to find students with similar patterns in coloured stickers/same answers to the questions. Multiple choice questions could include favourite genre of music, dream vacation spots, free meal opportunities, favourite cars, etc.

3. **Pop Culture Chat**: In small groups, students discuss their favourite movies and/or television shows for 5-10 minutes. Have a few groups share with the rest of class and ask for a show of hands if other students share the same favourites. You should share your favourites too. This shows students you are interested in their culture and that everything does not have to be serious and course-related all the time!

4. **Group Chat**: Post a question on the overhead/board and ask small groups of students to form and share their opinion on the answer. It could be an opinion-type of question based on course content or on something that happened in the news that is related to the course, or it could be a question with a correct answer. Allowing students to chat in small groups gives them a chance to share their thoughts in a low risk environment. You could wander around the room and listen to their conversations or stay at the front of the class and allow them the freedom to discuss.

G. Course Overview

Students come to class to learn something and the first class is an opportune time to get started. This is a great chance to model how you will excite them about learning! Here are some ideas:

1. **Slideshow of Images/Text/Audio:** Consider making a mini-movie showcasing your course. With some text, audio, and images, you can really provide a simple multimedia introduction to the course. Try to stay away from bulleted lists of information and lots of text. Instead, opt for slides/screens full of course images which will engage students more.

2. **Practical Examples/Relationship to Career/Courses:** Consider presenting a topic or two from the course and demonstrating how the topics relate to students and their lives. If students can connect with the content and see practical applications, they are more likely to stick with the course. Through demonstrations or stories, share how the course has practical applications and how it fits with other courses in the program.

3. **Tell a Personal Story:** When students hear you tell a story that relates to the course, they are engaged and attentive.

4. **Concept Map:** Create a concept/mind map of the course topics and present to students. Include connected links on the mind map that open up with an image or example of that topic. Students will appreciate seeing an overview of whole course.

H. Engage in Course Activity

As soon as you have presented an overview of the course, be sure to engage students immediately. This will serve as a model for students to know what to expect in your course and how you will run the class.

Here are some suggestions:

1. **Case Study**: Create a simple case study based on your course. Read the case study and ask students to discuss how they would solve the case based on what they already know. While students will not know much at this point, it will pique their interest and draw out what they already know. Ensure you take up the case by providing some quick answers to students before activity is done.

2. **Misconceptions Questions**: With clickers or a laptop, have students answer questions about their perceptions about aspects of the course content. If you do not have clickers, have students write their answers on a scrap piece of paper. Once the students have written down or keyed in their answer, have them discuss their answer with peers. This discussion time helps students clarify why they chose a certain answer and learn about other possible answers. After 3-4 minutes of discussion time, have students write their answer down (and hand in their answers without names) or key in again. Share correct answer with class. Make sure you collect responses to get a sense of how to plan for future classes. This also engages students in thinking critically about their misconceptions about the course content. It may also stimulate thinking outside of class.

3. **Question and Answer**: Pose a few well-structured questions about the course content and give students a few minutes to discuss in small groups. Then ask for students to participate by giving their input on the questions. Allowing students to discuss the answers first gives them a chance to think and participate more.

4. **Diagnostic Quiz**: Prepare a short diagnostic test about components that are covered in the class. Be sure to inform students that this is not a test and that marks will not be taken in. In fact, you might not require names just to assure students you are more interested in their answers and not who wrote them. This quiz will show students what the course is about and possibly interest them to find out more.

5. **Worksheet Activity**: Have a handout with questions about the course. Ask students to work in pairs or groups to see if they can answer any of the questions. These questions might review items from a previous course or from secondary school. The worksheet could be completed for homework and submitted the next class to see how much they already know. Students could also switch papers and mark it themselves to get an idea of how much they need to study this term.

I. Explain Expectations

Setting expectations with students is an appropriate thing to do during the first class. These expectations are more general and not often in the course syllabus. Try not to sound like the 'heavy enforcer' when you discuss expectations. Students want to know you have some guidelines, but you do not need to come down hard the first class. Consider sharing the following considerations:

1. What is an appropriate amount of study/homework time for your course?

2. Why it is important to hand in assignments on time? What can they expect in terms of return time for their assignments and tests?

3. How should students conduct themselves in your class (e.g., talking, cell phones, distracting activities, respecting peers, etc.)?

4. How will you deal with late and absent students? What department and/or class expectations will you set around this topic?

5. How will you encourage participation from students (e.g., randomly calling upon students, seeking hands, giving time to discuss/think first)?

6. How will you communicate with students (e.g., email, office hours, office location, what is your reasonable email reply time, etc.)?

7. How will classes be run in terms of teaching/learning strategies (e.g., how much instructor instruction vs. student interaction)?

8. How will you show you are a fair evaluator? (e.g., marking, assignments)

9. How have previous students felt about your class? (e.g., any tips or advice you feel previous students have mentioned)

10. What value do you place on frequent student feedback from students?

J. Course Syllabus/Course Outline

Ensure you cover the syllabus or course outline. A well-constructed syllabus should stand on its own. Ensure your syllabus has course expectations, contact details, assignment/test dates and percentages, along with details on textbook and academic policies. Bring a copy of the textbook to class to show students what it looks like. Students could be instructed to read over the whole syllabus prior to the second class and come prepared with any questions. For the first class, you should just highlight the key areas (evaluation, participation, etc.).

Here are some suggestions for covering the key components of the syllabus:

1. **Give students a mini scavenger hunt**. Write questions on the board and ask students to work in pairs or small groups to find the answers. The questions will focus on the most important points of the syllabus that they have to find and rephrase in their own words. Take up and elaborate upon any part to ensure all are clear.

2. **Test Questions**: Ask students to work in groups of three or four to create a few 'test' questions about the syllabus. Ask each group to write the questions (along with the answers) on a piece of paper. This makes students think critically and devise challenging questions, but also properly write out the answers. Choose a few good questions and post on the board/screen at beginning of the second class to act as a review of the first class.

K. Bridging to The Next Class

Ensure you have a proper ending to the class, rather than realizing you are out of time or telling students you have nothing else and letting them go early.

The ending of the class can be so important in establishing a positive feeling with students and reminding them of what the course will be about.

The final moments of the class should recap the big ideas. You want to excite students about coming back and you should share what will be covered in the next class.

Here are some ideas for the final moments of your first class:

- **Summary Slide**: Provide a slide on the screen that summarizes the key points of the class. This would consist of items you definitely want students to remember upon leaving your class.

- **Glimpse of Next Class**: Provide some 'teasers' about what the next class will entail. This will encourage students to see that attending is important.

- **Homework/Reading**: Provide students with a short homework activity to get them engaged in the course material and responsible for coming to next class to hand in the homework or report on it. Additionally, you could have a quiz the next class that is tied to a small percentage of their final mark. This will help with student participation and ensure there is accountability for doing their homework.

- **Ticket-Out-The-Door**: Ask students to find a piece of paper and write the answers to these 2 questions on it (with no name):

  - Question 1: What is one question you have about this course or course content?
  - Question 2: What is one thing you learned today that you feel will be helpful for your success in this course?

Collect the papers from your students on their way out the door (say thanks to them and call them by name if you can), analyze the responses, and provide a summary at the beginning of the next class. This demonstrates that you are willing to listen to your students and appreciate their thoughts and questions.

L. Creating a Comfortable Classroom

Building Rapport: This involves constantly letting students know you care, are willing to listen to their questions, and have an open line of communication with them. Here are some examples:

- **Invite students to a 5-10 minute mini-interview with you**. Post a sheet in class and have students sign up for a time that suits them. Tell your students you just want to meet them, find out what they are expecting from the class, and answer any questions they have. This will allow your students to find out where your office is, meet with you in a more comfortable setting, and start an open line of communication. Coming to meet you could be presented as the first 'homework' assignment!

- **Index Card Info**: On an index card, ask students to provide details about themselves such as email, phone number, pronunciation of name, challenges or questions they have about course, program/faculty, etc. Additionally, you can ask students to list ways they feel the course may benefit them. These cards will come in handy if you are able to attach a photo of the student for learning names.

- **Culture of Feedback**: Show students you value their feedback. Tell students that you will use a variety of anonymous methods to obtain input on how the class is going. Start this culture of feedback by ensuring you elicit some form of feedback the first day of class.

Setting a Comfortable Tone and an Engaging Atmosphere

- When you have a class atmosphere that allows students to feel comfortable to approach you at any time, you have magic happening. From the first class onwards, ensure you connect with students by playing some music, asking about their interests, showing a cartoon or short video, or finding ways to connect the content to the students' lives. Make efforts to create an inviting classroom where students feel comfortable to put up their hands or take risks. When you have an open and engaging classroom environment, you will find it easier to manage off-task behaviour and build respect.

Learning Names

- Take group photos of students during the first class. Ask each student to hold up a sheet of paper in front of them with their first and last name clearly written in large printing. If you explain to students that you are the only one using the photos and for the main purpose of learning names, few students will object. Line up 5-10 students holding their names, take a picture, and download photos/print them for learning names.

- Ask for student names before answering questions. This will help reinforce the names and faces. Ask students to be patient as it may take a few classes.

Top Ten Takeaways

1. **Attitude:** Am I excited and enthusiastic about teaching my first class?

2. **Preparation:** Have I arranged the classroom and put up the agenda before my students arrive?

3. **Get-to-know-you Activities:** Do I have at least one ice-breaker activity planned to connect students to each other?

4. **Learning Names:** Do I have a system for learning names?

5. **Course Overview:** Have I prepared an overview of the course to share with my students?

6. **Course Content Activity:** Do I have an engaging activity to allow students to interact with some of the course content?

7. **Course Expectations:** Am I clear on my own expectations of the course and of the students?

8. **Syllabus:** Have I created a well-detailed course syllabus that practically stands on its own?

9. **Bridging to Next Class:** Have I considered a solid ending to the first class which bridges nicely into the second class?

10. **Rapport:** Am I building rapport and setting the classroom atmosphere as a comfortable place to learn?

Next Steps

1. Plan at least one student ice breaker activity that will not take too long to create or implement.

2. Consider how you could provide a 5-10 minute overview of your course that will excite students and give them a glimpse of what they will learn.

3. Create an activity students could do that will immediately get them working with the course content and interacting with each other.

4. Look at your syllabus. Make sure it is able to stand on its own and includes all of the essentials for the students to understand what is expected of them in your course.

References and Resources

Honolulu Community College. (n.d.) *Faculty Development: Teaching Tips Index – The First Day*. Retrieved April 2, 2010 from http://honolulu.hawaii.edu/intranet/committees/ FacDevCom/guidebk/teachtip/teachtip.htm#firstday

Chapter 10: Building Rapport & Managing the Class

Chapter Overview

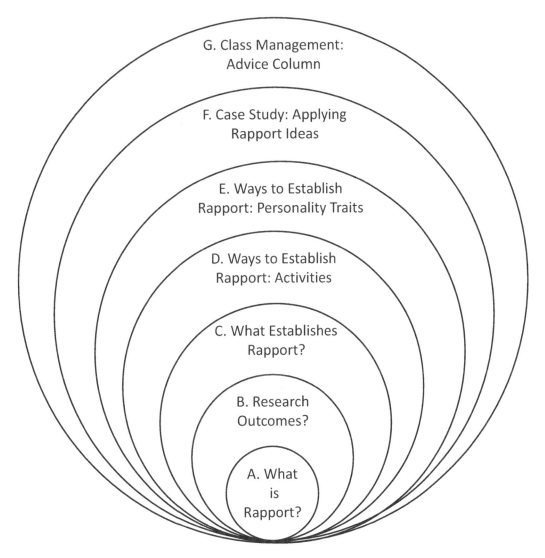

G. Class Management: Advice Column

F. Case Study: Applying Rapport Ideas

E. Ways to Establish Rapport: Personality Traits

D. Ways to Establish Rapport: Activities

C. What Establishes Rapport?

B. Research Outcomes?

A. What is Rapport?

Students appreciate instructors with whom they feel a connection.

In a 2004 research study of undergraduate students, rapport was the number one theme most expressed by students when asked what makes an outstanding professor (Faranda & Clarke). A stunning 36% of responses were related to rapport (e.g., approachability, accessibility, personality, and empathy), and a close relation to rapport—delivery (e.g., communication, personal style and pedagogy)—ranked second with 30% of all responses. Two-thirds of all comments made by students related to the relationships teachers need to build with their students. In a similar study, Buskist et al. (2002) revealed that 42% of students surveyed put rapport at the top of their top 10 qualities of an excellent instructor whereas only 7% of faculty put rapport in their list.

When instructors were asked what makes effective educators, they often report it is their knowledge of the subject matter, whereas students feel it is the ability of instructors to communicate (Grunenwald & Ackerman, 1986) and build relationships that are important considerations for learning.

Rapport is a connection that is built between student and teacher and has to be started from the first day of class. The topic of rapport and class delivery provokes a wide range of thoughts, yet rarely do we find chapters devoted to this topic in most teaching books and resources (Murphy and Valdez, 2005).

How Students Feel

Here are some fictitious, but based on real accounts of students talking about their instructors.

- *"I find when I have a prof I really like and can relate to, I enjoy the class so much more. I had this one prof who told us funny stories and had great examples to share. It just seemed as if he totally wanted us to like the course."*

- *"Instructors who are easy to talk to are my favorite ones. It really helps when I can ask a question or go to his office and not feel that I am bothering him."*

- *"The best instructors I have had are those who bring the class to life. They are totally passionate about their subject matter but also understand how to make it interesting for us to learn. For example, I love the instructors who have lots of activities and games to break up a class. I also love it when the profs join some of our small groups and share their thoughts. This means that the instructor isn't just standing at the front of the room talking – he likes to get involved in our activities too."*

- *"To me the best instructor I had was a very enthusiastic and dynamic lady. I just sat in awe most classes and wondered how she did it. It was a special thing she had where we all felt comfortable to ask any question, or make a mistake, or change the course of our class discussion. She was just real, yet also knew when to get more serious and make us work. It is hard to describe how she did it, but her ability to communicate and share her passion was incredible."*

- *"An instructor who takes the time to learn our names is one I will always remember. To me, learning our names means that they care about us."*

- *"I've had maybe a handful of fantastic instructors in all of my university years that had a strong rapport with the students. These instructors just had so many small things that they did to make the class a great spot to go each time and to feel comfortable to ask questions. I can't put my finger on exactly what they did, but it was more their personality and how open and caring they were."*

When rapport exists, managing class distractions and inappropriate behaviour becomes much easier. Rapport is the secret ingredient that helps you have a successful term. This chapter presents suggestions for establishing rapport and managing your class.

A. What is Rapport?

Activity: Think about this for a moment. What does rapport mean to you? How is it established in your classroom? What do you do to build rapport between you and your students? What is the connection with class management? What benefits do you gain with good rapport?

Jot down a few thoughts here:

Rapport has many definitions. The following quotes are from research studies on rapport and related literature describing the nature of rapport.

> "Warmth and liking between an instructor and students, a bond nurtured by a positive attitude toward students"
>
> *Wilson, J. H. & Hackney, 2006, p. 233*

> "The ability to maintain harmonious relations based on affinity for others"
>
> *Faranda & Clarke, 2004, p. 274*

> "Rapport appears to be linked closely to immediacy, the extent to which teachers establish a supportive and caring learning environment through their verbal and nonverbal behavior, which includes establishing eye contact, smiling and calling students by name"
>
> *Benson, Cohen and Buskist, 2005*

> "A three-component definition of rapport:...mutual attentiveness = mutual interest in what the other person is saying or doing....positivity = mutual friendliness and caring....and co-ordination = balance, harmony and synchronization in the actions of the participants."
>
> *Granitz et.al., 2008; Tickle-Degnan & Rosenthal, 1990*

Let's now look at some thoughts from instructors in the field.
What do they have to say about rapport?

> "Rapport is based on a number of characteristics – sense of humor, warmth, willingness to listen to the students, understanding, and approachability. Most of all, it is a reflection of how much an instructor cares about the students. To some instructors, building rapport comes naturally, however there are a number of steps that can be taken to build connections including greeting students warmly at the door, being readily available for questions through email and office hours, listening to students and being careful not to make quick judgments, gathering feedback from students 3-4 times during the term and addressing their needs and challenges, giving clear and ample feedback on assignments and tests, and showing your human side every now and then. In short, if you take time to regularly communicate to your students that you care about them and their progress in the course, a good rapport will be established. Finally, do not discount the little things you can do – they can make a huge difference. I recall one of my instructors personally handing out every final exam and wishing each student good luck as he did. I loved that and it was such a simple thing to do."
>
> *Dr. Robin Kay (personal communication, October 21, 2009)*

> "I believe rapport has a lot to do with having a sense of humor. It also involves getting to know students outside of class and offering assistance to them when needed. Rapport is developed when you are there for students: to assist with assignments, to listen to personal insights, to be flexible when situations arise, to write a reference letter etc."
>
> *Cliff Moon (personal communication, October 24, 2009)*

> "One conclusion I have is that it takes time to build rapport with students; it requires building connections and, often more than just 'what's the course material'. When I try to show how the content connects to their lives...I've established meaning for the content. I tend to be passionate about what and how I teach, so I hope they see what it means to be...in my life. It's also taking the time to listen; to be available at times outside office hours. It's about talking with them outside the class time; realizing that they have hectic lives and how can we work together."
>
> *Dr. Shirley Van Nuland (personal communication, October 19, 2009)*

"I believe that rapport between a professor and students helps establish a learning environment where students feel comfortable in asking questions, participating, and engaging in the online and face-to-face environments. If students are more engaged in their learning, I believe their potential to optimize learning is enhanced. I also believe that part of my own personal ease in developing rapport reflects my personality, and the manner in which I deal with others. Do I believe that people could learn how to develop rapport?

Absolutely. It just may require practice and a conscious effort to communicate and apply strategies that enhance rapport. Typically I try to establish rapport by:

In the beginning...

- Sharing a brief biography at the beginning of term, as well as providing them with contact information and my times of availability (i.e., office hours)

- Inviting students to drop by during office hours

- Acknowledging that students' schedules may not allow them to drop by during office hours, so I do encourage them to email me and we can make appointments outside of the established office hours if needed

Throughout the term...

- Greeting students at the beginning of class rather than launching into the lecture (i.e., good morning/afternoon, hope you had a nice weekend, how about that news story? How about that basketball game? etc.)

- Addressing students by name and using name tag tents they place on desks

- Being transparent by explaining or providing the rationale for course topics, decisions, assignments (i.e., providing context to make it more meaningful)

- Soliciting constructive feedback regarding various components of course

- Incorporating feedback into my planning/teaching if and where appropriate

- Sharing how I incorporated feedback (if and where appropriate) and providing rationale for not incorporating some of the feedback (if and where appropriate)

- Connecting stories or personal experiences to particular class topics

- Stepping away from the podium during the lecture and moving around the room into the student seating area (i.e., using a remote presentation device to advance through slides on computer, wireless microphone if necessary)

     Dr. Diana Petrarca, Assistant Professor (personal communication, October 29, 2009)

B. What are the Research Outcomes When Rapport Is Established?

Instructors know that establishing good rapport with students has a positive relationship to many classroom activities. Much research has been conducted on the topic of rapport. This is just a brief overview of the research that exists.

If rapport is established between students and instructor, the following research-based outcomes may occur:

- more **motivation by students** to **perform and learn**
  Buskist & Saville, 2004; Christensen & Menzel, 1998; Frymier, 1993, 1994;   Huff, Cooper & Jones, 2002; McCombs & Whistler, 1997; Wilson & Taylor, 2001

- students more likely **to attend class** and **pay attention**
  Benson, Cohen & Buskist, 2005

- students more inclined **to study for class**
  Benson, Cohen & Buskist, 2005

- students will **attend office hours/email professor**
  Benson, Cohen & Buskist, 2005

- students indicate they **enjoy** the **subject matter** more
  Benson, Cohen & Buskist, 2005; Christensen & Menzel, 1998; McCrosky et. al., 1996

- studies show that students **learn more**
  Benson, Cohen & Buskist, 2005; Wilson, 2006

- students experience **more comfort in** answering questions, requesting feedback, and seeking clarification
  Benson, Cohen & Buskist, 2005; Howard-Hamilton, 2000

- there is a high correlation of increased rapport with **higher teaching evaluations**
  Anderson et al., 1977; Perkins, Schenck, Stephan, Vrungos, & Whants, 1995; Thomas et al., 1982

C. What Establishes Good Rapport?

Activity: Look at the following squares. Put a "1" on those you think would be excellent activities to establish rapport. Put a "2" on those you feel would be satisfactory activities to establish rapport and put a "3" on those you do not feel would help in establishing rapport. Peruse the rest of this chapter to see how you did on this activity.

Learning **Student Names**	**Chatting** with Students Prior and Post Class	Sending Students a **Welcome Email** Prior to Class
Empathizing with Student Concerns/Issues	Showing **Humorous** video clips/cartoons	Inviting Students to **Email or Visit** You
Explaining **Course Expectations** in Detail	**Smiling** a Lot	Sharing **Personal Experiences** and **Stories**
Including **Class Discussions** in your Teaching	Sharing your Background **Expertise and Knowledge** for Content	Including **Active Learning Techniques** in your Teaching
Giving **Supportive** and **Encouraging Comments** to Students	**Moving** Around **Classroom**	Providing **Real Life** and **Meaningful Examples** of Content
Doing **Ice-Breaker** Type of Activities Beyond First Class	**Rewarding Student Comments** with Verbal **Praise**	Having Well-Written **Tests and Quizzes**
Having **Good Eye Contact** with Students	Learning about **Student Interests and Activities**	Being **Enthusiastic and Spontaneous** with Your Teaching

D. Ways to Establish Rapport: Activities

If you are seeking greater rapport between you and your students consider a combination of the following suggestions. Almost all of these ideas will work in larger classes where establishing rapport and classroom management is even more important.

1. **Use 'Ice-Breaker' Activities**

   Ice-breaker activities do not just have to happen during the first class. Play a short game or plan a quick activity where students get to share common interests, learn more about each other, or just engage in a few minutes of non-content related discussion. The more chances students and instructors have to interact with each other, the greater the chances rapport will be established.

2. **Learn Your Students' Names**

   Learning student names not only helps you relate to students, but allows students to learn each others' names too. Here are some ideas for learning names:

   - Videotape your students saying their names (and you repeating their names into microphone for clarity) so you can view the video and learn as many names as you can. For a large class, you can have groups of 10 come up at a time to be taped.

   - Ask for student names before answering questions. This will help reinforce the names and faces in your head. Ask students to be patient as it may take a few classes for you to know their names.

3. **Learn About your Students' Interests**

   Getting to know a bit about students beyond the classroom shows you care about them and are interested in who they are as human beings. For example:

   - On an index card, ask students to fill out details about themselves such as email, phone number, pronunciation of name, challenges or questions they have about course, program/faculty, special interests and hobbies etc. Additionally, pasting a student photo on the index card will assist in learning names.

   - Ask students to list ways they feel the course may benefit them or why they may have chosen to be in your class.

4. **Arrive to Class Early**

   Arriving to class early shows you are approachable and are there to answer any questions. If you are there early, play some music or put up a few slides with quotes or pictures. This allows students to sense they can approach you in a relaxed atmosphere.

5. **Be Available After Class**

   Hang around after class if students want to chat (even if you have to move the discussions to the hallway or the cafeteria). Invite students back to your office after class or tell them you are walking there so they can follow and join you. Try not to rush off after class. If you have to leave quickly, let students know and provide alternative times they can see you.

6. **Have Office Hours that Work for Students**

   Consult with students or your course director as to good times for holding office hours. Encourage students to email if they prefer another form of communication.

7. **Use Relevant and Meaningful Examples**

   Student learning will progress rapidly when course examples relate to the real world, their lives, and their future careers. Examples also bring the content to life and allow for connections to be made in the learning process. Try to include personal stories or examples from related careers. Students will appreciate you making learning more meaningful.

8. **Employ Active Learning Strategies in Your Teaching**

   Students appreciate instructors who use a variety of teaching and learning strategies. Not all students can sit and take effective notes for an hour or two. Using active learning strategies allows students to engage with the course content in a variety of formats. Try changing up your class every 15-20 minutes (e.g., lecture/cover content for 20 minutes, then have a discussion for 20 minutes, then put students in a small group activity for 20 minutes, etc.)

9. **Use Supportive Comments**

   When you are interacting with students, use phrases such as those listed below:

   - I like that idea. Can you tell me more about it?

   - Can you give me an example of what you mean?

   - Can anyone help us get back to what we were discussing?

   - I do not know the answer either. Let me get back to you on that.

   - I am not sure I understand you. Are you saying, X....

   - Super answer. I really like how you connected X with Y.

   - I appreciate all the hands up – feel free to contribute to the discussion.

10. **Praise Students**

    Give students positive comments when they participate or contribute to the class:

    - Thank you for your answer. That was well thought out.

    - Wonderful response. It shows you really understood the reading.

    - Super – that was what I was looking for in a response.

    - Wow – that is a great observation [insert name]!

11. **Be Creative and Spontaneous**

    While students appreciate a routine in how a class is conducted, they also love something out of the blue and different from the typical day-to-day activities. For example, have an activity where students are directing the learning or play a song or show a video which emphasizes the content. Come to class dressed in a costume related to your topic or have a spontaneous drama/acting activity with students you select on the spot!

12. Be Enthusiastic

If you come to class with energy and excitement, your students will feel that enthusiasm. Tell students you are excited about the class and the neat things you have planned for them to do. Students will appreciate hearing your interest and enthusiasm about the content.

13. Be Encouraging About Student Success

Focus on providing as much encouragement to assist students in being successful. Tell students how they are doing and what they can do to improve. Ensure the comments you write on papers and assignments have constructive feedback along with suggestions for how they can improve the next time. Students will feel you care about them and their academic successes.

14. Share Something About Yourself

When instructors share elements of their life beyond the content, students feel a greater sense of rapport. You could share information on your own schooling in the subject matter, your real life experience in the work world, challenges and triumphs you've had in life with the course topics, and even share what you did on the weekend. You don't need to become too personal with your information or share private details, but if students hear about your activities beyond the classroom they are more likely to feel comfortable approaching you.

15. Promote Class Discussions

Students like having discussions and hearing different points of view. An instructor who is in favor of having class discussions is more likely to have greater rapport opportunities with his/her students.

16. Make Eye Contact with Students

Walk around the classroom if you can and look at a variety of students. Look at the students when you are talking.

17. Have Positive Non-Verbal Behaviors

Always look at a student when he/she is answering a question. Always smile and possibly nod your head in encouragement. You may walk closer to the student or take a few steps in his/her direction. Look relaxed when you are listening to students (e.g., sit on a desk, lean against a wall, sit on a chair). This shows students you care and are attentive.

18. Smile

Smile, even if you are having a bad day. By smiling, you are showing students you are projecting a positive image and enjoying the class. Students also like to a see an instructor who emits happiness when they come to class.

19. Solicit Feedback from Students

When students see you are interested in their opinion about the course or interested in what they are learning, they see you as a caring individual. On a scrap piece of paper ask students to write a short answer to a couple of questions such as:

- "What was the most interesting point you learned today?"
- "What part of today's class is confusing and needs further explanation?"
- "What part of today's class did you enjoy?"

As students leave the classroom, have them hand in their anonymous responses. Browse through the responses and share a summary the next class, as well as address any common issues or areas that need more clarification. Students will appreciate an instructor who seeks feedback from students.

20. Never be Condescending toward Students

When instructors joke around or have a more sarcastic sense of humor, students can be offended. It often is not the intent of instructors, but it is the perception and reaction of students that may differ. With so many ways a joke can be interpreted by different genders, religions, or ethnicities, it is best to avoid being sarcastic or putting students down.

E. Ways to Establish Rapport: Personality Traits

21. Be Friendly and Approachable

Students like an instructor who is easy to talk to, personable and is calm and patient in his/her dealings with people. This creates a comfortable environment in which to approach an instructor.

22. Show a Sense of Humor

Use your voice, your face, and your laughter to evoke a sense of humor in the classroom. You could show a cartoon, tell a joke, or show a funny video every now and then to lighten the mood, but having a good sense of humor is also important.

23. Be Humble

Instructors who talk at length about their wonderful skills, experience, or awards tend to be viewed less positively by students. Try to be humble when talking about your experiences and accomplishments and focus on what is important for the students to know.

24. Be Empathetic

When students feel you are on 'their side' and respect who they are, they are more likely to have respect for the instructor. Students also appreciate instructors who can relate to what it was like being a student (e.g., having to study a lot, attend classes, do assignments) and are empathic to life situations (e.g., deaths, sickness, needing money).

25. Be a Caring Instructor

Show you care about students. Meet with students to assist them with content acquisition and application. Give an extension to a student you just found out has a family death. Students positively view instructors who have a caring, considerate, and generous personality.

26. Be Truthful and Fair

Students appreciate instructors who don't go back on their word and keep the class and their assessment systems fair and equitable for everyone. For example, keep your word on homework and assignment topics and always be fair with your due dates and extensions.

27. Be Open to Admitting Mistakes

Admit you don't know something or admit you made a mistake. If you are open to learning new things, changing your ways, and seeing where you may have been wrong, students will see a real person in front of them modeling that not everything is perfect.

28. Be Willing to Take Risks

Teaching is full of risks. Try being open-minded to experiment with new teaching strategies or engage in some of these ideas for building rapport. When students see you as an instructor who is willing to see things from another angle or to try something new, they have a greater appreciation for you.

29. Be Positive About Others

Even if you have negative thoughts or opinions about administration or your fellow instructors, it is important to be positive and professional at all times. Students are very quick to pick up on negative or inappropriate comments or facial expressions when you are talking about others. Ensure you have a positive personality in the class.

30. Enjoy Your Job

When you make an effort to just enjoy yourself and forget about racing through the content, you give students a much more inviting class atmosphere. If you tell students you woke up excited about the class or you share with them how much fun YOU had in class, students will pick up on this energy and be excited to come to class too!

F. Case Study: Applying Rapport Ideas

Activity: **The following story is based on real accounts from today's instructors. Read the story. Consider the case and questions either on your own or share with a colleague. See if you can identify the problems and some solutions based on the suggestions in this chapter.**

Diane Jenkins is serious about her teaching. She teaches introductory economics and marketing. She looks forward to her time in the classroom. She is in her fifth year of teaching.

Diane has a comprehensive syllabus that is very clear on all expectations and what the course is about. She spends a number of days organizing and planning each lecture. She arrives to class on time, lays out all of her notes at the podium, and often has very detailed PowerPoint slides to present her materials. Since students do not need her help after class, she often leaves immediately to head home to plan or mark assignments.

Diane does try out new active learning techniques and aims not to lecture all the time. She creates meaningful assignments for her students that allow for showcasing their knowledge and understanding. She thinks about her students and strives to find the best way for them to be successful in her course. Diane also reads a lot and stays on top of new innovations and information pertinent to her courses. She feels she is trying her best to be a good teacher.

However, Diane is not really comfortable in her classes. On her drive home, she has difficulty pin-pointing what is going wrong. She often feels that there is a lack of connection between herself and the students. She does not feel that they are with her when the material is presented and that they do not like how she is as a teacher. She feels very much alone at the podium, but figures that this is who students are today and that if they have a question they will ask. She always asks if there are questions, but gets little response. She feels confident she is giving students a good education and that she is teaching them all she can.

When questioned, her students say she is very knowledgeable and organized and presents applicable and current content. They generally like her assignments and tests, which shows she has put thought into their construction and marking. Yet, her students also say she is not approachable and they do not feel comfortable putting their hand up in class to ask or answer a question.

Her students often do not visit her during office hours and tend to not communicate much with her. Her students are sometimes late to her class and often she has more than half not in attendance. They say they respect her as their teacher, but they do not really know much about her to comment further. They feel like she is 'there' and the students are 'here' – sort of like "she's the teacher and talks and we are the students and listen". The students indicate that she is like most of their instructors and that this is likely the norm for post-secondary education.

But something is niggling away inside of Diane that tells her something isn't quite right.

Can you help Diane?

Consider the answers to these questions on your own, or share the case with a colleague and have a discussion over lunch one day about the problems and solutions.

> Q. What is the **main problem** in this case?
> Q. What are some of the **secondary problems** in this case?
> Q. What might be some **next steps** for Diane?

G. Class Management Advice Column

Once you have established rapport with your students, managing your class will be a lot easier. Rapport is the secret ingredient in allowing you to connect with your students. You will now be able to navigate with greater success through the ups and downs of a semester. If you have good rapport with your students, they will feel more comfortable coming to talk to you about problems and likely will have greater respect for you. With strong rapport, students will be more responsive when you ask them to quiet down or refrain from a disrupting activity. Class management is just a whole lot easier when you have a good connection with your students and show them that you care, want to listen to them, and are open to their suggestions.

Some Tips for Effective Class Management
1. **Stay calm** when a challenging situation arises. You can easily escalate a situation if you react inappropriately.

2. When in doubt about problems arising in class, realize that it **takes two people to arrive at an interpersonal conflict or problem**. Consider what you, the instructor, are doing that may have affected the students when you are deciphering any class management problems.

3. **Determine** if it is an **academic situation** (e.g., student does not understand material or is having problems learning), an **emotional situation** (e.g., student's reaction is more about a personal problem or crisis outside of the classroom), a **behavioral situation** (e.g., student is really just an attention seeker and is acting inappropriately to gain attention), or a **learning disability situation** (student is not able to hear, understand, take notes fast enough, is uncomfortable in seat, etc.). Most often, what we immediately think is the problem often turns out to not be the case. Have a chat with any student who is causing disruptions in the management of your class.

4. To get more information, have a **private conversation** with a student outside of class time in order to resolve a situation. Confronting a student in class just makes a bad situation much worse! Approach the meeting as an opportunity for you to work together.

5. **Laptops, PDAs, cell phones, portable music devices** are all common in our classrooms today. Banning them from your classroom may seem to solve a problem for the short term, but definitely not for the long term or even the next class! As instructors, we need to understand how such equipment might be used within our classes or find ways to work with students to prevent distractions to their peers.

If you require more advice on how to manage your class, try consulting with experienced colleagues. They often have discipline-specific tips or examples of how to handle common situations you will encounter.

The following section on class management is presented in the form of an advice column. Answers to common questions are presented with solutions and tips for managing a variety of situations.

Dear Class Manager,

How can I establish ground rules for my class? I want the students to all abide by the same rules and know the consequences should they break any of the rules. Shall I just post my rules the first day and tell them to follow them or else?

Sincerely, Rulelover

Dear Rulelover,

Coming off too strong or forceful is not going to be a good start to your class. It will also begin to erode any rapport you have developed. Having some common rules or guidelines is a good idea in any class environment. How about having the students discuss what rules they think would be appropriate for the class? By involving students in determining acceptable and unacceptable behavior, you are giving them an opportunity to have a voice in the class, be part of designing and developing their classroom environment, and be more committed to the rules once they are established.

Sincerely, Class Manager

Dear Class Manager,

I have a number of students who bring a laptop to class and watch videos, instant message or 'chat' with their friends, and do an assortment of other activities. They are disrupting their classmates who sit behind them and can see what is on the laptop. I have heard that this is a common occurrence in most classrooms with students who bring laptops. I would like to ban laptops altogether in my class, along with cell phones and other digital devices that are complete annoyances to me and other students. What do you think?

Sincerely, Laptop Banner

Dear Laptop Banner,

The use of laptops in the classroom and the disruptions they can provide is a topic high on the list of complaints from many instructors. While banning all digital devices sounds like a simple task to do, you would be alienating most of your students and ruining the chances for a great class. While I realize there are students using digital devices in non-academic ways, and certainly in very disruptive ways, do not forget that there are just as many (if not more) students who use a laptop to benefit their learning (e.g., students with learning, physical, auditory, and visual disabilities). Laptops are also used by many non-disabled students because of the ease in taking notes, accessing online materials, and engaging in class activities. Banning laptops could be preventing a larger number of students from learning! Take a look at what you are doing in the classroom to cause students to become distracted, bored, and needing to engage in off-task activities. If you have students constantly involved in active learning activities, doing research, answering questions, and participating in discussions, there might be little time for them to be off-task. Additionally, they might be able to use their laptop for academic uses if you structure activities to use online resources. If you move around the room a bit more, you might be able to pinpoint the specific students and speak to them individually about refraining from disrupting their peers. These are just some tips. I hope they help in understanding the situation from a different angle.

Sincerely, Class Manager

Dear Class Manager,

I have a handful of students in my class of 75 who consistently dominate class discussions by putting their hands up first, always giving answers, and contributing way more than other students. What do I do? I try to call on other students, but they do not always have an answer. I also try to give the class more time to think, but it seems as if the same hands are always up. Sometimes when these students speak, other students roll their eyes or appear disinterested in their response. I don't know what to do! Help me.

Sincerely, **Dislike Discussion Dominators (aka Triple D)**

Dear Triple D,

I see two problems with your situation. The first problem deals with the need to get more students to participate, thereby outnumbering the frequent hand raisers. Consider the types of questions you are asking. Are they simple "yes-no" answers, or are you asking more deep questions that might take a bit longer to formulate an answer. If you are asking questions that require some thought, how about having students think about the answer for a few minutes on their own first. Then ask them to partner up with one or two other students and discuss their answers. When students are given more time to think on their own, as well as discuss with their peers, they often have an answer to share because they have had it reaffirmed through peer discussion and also through time to consult materials or their notes. When you have a class of 75, it is going to be more challenging for students to feel comfortable to respond. However, when you have smaller groups, students are more likely to participate. If you want a large class discussion, how about

having smaller groups of students responding as a team rather than having everyone respond as individuals? These are just some ideas to try. As for the students who seem to dominate class discussions, why not chat with them briefly after or before class. The conversation need not be one of punishment or negativity. Rather, why not say to them, "You have lots of great answers and contribute so well in class. However, the other students are depending on you to do all the work here and that is not fair to you. Let's work together to make them participate more. When I ask questions in class, why don't we see if the first 5 questions can be answered by your peers and on the 6th question I'd love to hear your response? How does that sound?" In this way, you are working cooperatively with the students in an effort to get them to refrain from participating for a portion of the class. Good Luck.

Sincerely,

Class Manager

Dear Class Manager,

I have a student in my class who likes to challenge me on many points or issues I am teaching. I don't believe she is being deliberately hostile, but it is quite unnerving to me as I am teaching. I am not sure how I should respond, or if I should respond at all!

Sincerely,

Choking on the Challenges

Dear Choking on the Challenges,

There are two important points that come up when you have such a student in your class. First, this is an opportune time to get into the topic in more depth. For every one student who verbally expresses their disagreement with what you are teaching, there are sure to be others who are wondering the same thing. This is what learning is all about! You need to take a few minutes and respond with more information to clarify your topic or subject, ask a few good questions about the students' underlying beliefs and knowledge, and you could also involve the class to see what they think about this topic. It is a moment to rel-

ish, not fear! Students need the chance to see both sides of a topic or issue and when they challenge you they are really asking for more learning. Secondly, it is important for students to see how you handle this situation. In other words, you are modeling for them how to handle challenging situations in the real world and how to professionally respond and carry the dialogue in the classroom. Ensure you carefully listen and ask good questions of the student. This is a moment for you to have a scholarly debate and educate the rest of the class while you are at it! I realize not every instructor has the confidence or courage to delve deeper into a topic in front of hundreds of students or immediately realize they are a role model for how to handle confrontation, but the more you practice the easier it will become!

Sincerely,

Class Manager

Dear Class Manager,

I consistently have 5-10 students who come late to class every day. I have tried talking to them, but they don't seem to care that they miss the first few minutes of class or disrupt their peers. They often say they have slept in or missed the bus and it will never happen again. I am not sure what to do.

Sincerely,

Instructor Latehater

Dear Latehater,

While it is important to be sensitive to the variety of students we have in our classes, the distances they travel, the jobs they hold outside of class, and the expectations they have, it seems as if you have talked to these students and are getting nowhere. How about having a short quiz within the first few minutes of some classes? Tell the students the quiz will be handed out as they walk in the door and that they will only have 5-10 minutes to do it. The quiz could include questions from the final exam or mid-term. You are therefore making the first few minutes of class very valuable to attend. Ensure you tell the class the period prior of this new procedure and what they will need to review for the quiz. If they miss the quiz, or come in late, indicate the consequences in terms of time lost to do the quiz or the inability to get a few more marks.

Sincerely,

Class Manager

Dear Class Manager,

I have a lot of students who whisper and talk during my lectures. It is very disrupting to the students in the class and it always gets me off my game. I don't understand why students can't sit and be quiet for an hour and take some notes. I sometimes see them showing each other cell phone pictures too! What should I do?

Sincerely,

Professor Talkintext

Dear Professor Talkintext,

The students of this generation are very social beings. Some students love to chat on their phones, text message their friends, and conduct full length discussions during presentations and lectures at school. However, they are being very disruptive of their own and others' learning. I would hopefully have set some class guidelines around talking during class or other disruptive behaviors and would take this time to reference those guidelines. If you have not set any guidelines, why not pose the problem to your class and ask them how they would solve it? You could do this as a small group activity asking each group to come up with a few solutions they could live with. This would take the heat off your shoulders and put the students and their peers on the spot for offering up solutions.

But the crux of this problem is that students, adults, or anybody for that matter, have a

(cont'd)

hard time sitting still and paying attention for 60 straight minutes. Try breaking up your lecture into 15-20 minute chunks and stopping for a few minutes in between each chunk. Also consider using other teaching and learning strategies to have students more engaged in their learning such as an activity, a case study, or a group activity. Give a short survey asking if students understand the material or are having problems during class. Getting student feedback will be valuable in determining if they are academically struggling and really are asking their neighbor to clarify points you are raising in your lecture or whether they are really off-task talking about non-class topics. Moving around the class also lets students know you are not glued to the front of the room and that you will be walking near them at some point. Additionally, you might want to try having students sit in different locations for some classes through a seating chart or just randomly moving some students around for activities. Give those suggestions a try!

Sincerely,

Class Manager

Dear Class Manager,

I have some angry students in my class. Well, I think it is anger. They look really mad at me when I glance their way in class and they seem to spout off in an angry way when they answer questions or talk to me. I am not sure what I am doing to make them so angry.

Sincerely, I.M. Confused

Dear I.M. Confused,

Having students look and act angry in class is not fun at all. It throws you off your lesson. The easiest way to solve this problem is ask the student(s) to drop by for a short chat. Indicate to them that you want to get to know them a bit better and find out if you can be of more help with their learning. Having a short chat in your office may allow them to open up as to why they are angry and then you can deal with the situation. It may not be you; they may have come to this class or program begrudgingly or they may have misunderstood something on day one. Get to the bottom of it!

Sincerely, Class Manager

Top Ten Takeaways

1. **Definitions:** Rapport has a variety of definitions.

2. **Results of Good Rapport:** Positive teaching and learning outcomes may arise if you establish good rapport between you and your students.

3. **Activities & Personality:** Rapport consists of conducting class activities along with exhibiting personality traits.

4. **Names:** Learning student names is a good start to establishing rapport. Take an interest in student hobbies, music, favorite movies and activities too.

5. **Time to Chat:** Making time for students (before class, after class, or holding office hours) is another way to show you care about your students. It is also a good time to deal with any class management issues.

6. **Revealing Reasons Why**: Teaching strategies such as providing meaningful examples, sharing the reasoning behind activities, and connecting content to the real world all help in establishing rapport. It also helps prevent a lot of class management issues. When students know why an instructor is doing something, or they see the relevance to another course or a career, they are more likely to be engaged.

7. **Active Learning:** Using active learning activities within your classroom will allow students to learn in different ways and interact with each other. When you include more engaging activities, you may prevent students from becoming bored, taking part in off-task activities, and possibly being disruptive to their peers.

8. **Obtaining Feedback:** Soliciting ongoing formative feedback from students is a way of showing you are listening to them and appreciate their thoughts and comments on their learning and the course. You can also be proactive about class management by getting regular and informal updates from your students about what is going well and not so well in the class.

9. **Positivity:** Smiling, being positive, and having a good sense of humor are good traits to have. Students will feel more comfortable approaching you to talk about any problems or concerns.

10. **Class Management is Not the Same for All:** There are some common situations most every instructor experiences. A few examples were presented through the 'advice column' questions. Ensure you do not jump to conclusions. Talk to the students, get their story, and discuss in the privacy of your office to work out solutions. Remember, each instructor handles class management situations his/her own way depending on personality and experience.

Next Steps

1. Reflect on things you are already doing to establish rapport in your classroom.

2. Consider trying a few new ideas from this chapter.

3. Ask a colleague how they would define rapport. In other words, ask them what they do to establish rapport in the classroom.

4. Think about a situation that arose in one of your classes that was challenging to handle. Would you do the same thing next time? What would you do differently?

5. Try to be proactive about classroom management issues. Consider what possible reactions students might have to a test, a topic, or an activity and ensure you are clear and honest with them. Fewer problems might arise if you have good rapport with the students.

References and Resources

Anderson, T. W., Alpert, M. I., & Golden, L. L. (1977). A comparative analysis of student-teacher interpersonal similarity/dissimilarity and teaching effectiveness. *Journal of Educational Research, 71*(1), 36-44.

Benson, T. A, Cohen, A. L. & Buskist, W. (2005). Rapport: Its relation to student attitudes and behaviors to teachers and classes. *Teaching of Psychology, 32*(4), 237-239.

Buskist, W., Sikorski, J., Buckley, T., & Saville, B. K. (2002). *Elements of master teaching.* In S. F. Davis & W. Buskist (Eds.), The teaching of psychology: Essays in honor of Wilbert J. McKeachie and Charles L. Brewer (pp 27-39). Mahwah, NJ: Lawrence Erlbaum Associates Inc.

Buskist, W., & Saville, B. K. (2004). *Rapport-building: Creating positive emotional contexts for enhancing teaching and learning.* In B. Pearlman, L.I. McCann, & S. H. McFadden (Eds.), Lessons learned: Practical Advice for the teaching of psychology (Vol. 2, pp. 149-155). Washington, DC: American Psychological Society.

Christensen, L. J. & Menzel, K. E. (1998). The linear relationship between student reports of teacher immediacy behaviors and perceptions of state motivation and cognitive, affective and behavioral learning. *Communication Education, 47,* 82-90.

Faranda, W. T. & Clarke III, I. (2004). Student observations of outstanding teaching: Implications for marketing educators. Journal of *Marketing Education, 26*(3), 217-281.

Frymier, A. B. (1993). The relationships among communication apprehension, immediacy and motivation to study. *Communication Reports, 6,* 8-17.

Frymier, A. B. (1994). A model of immediacy in the classroom. *Communication Quarterly, 42,* 133-144.

Granitz, N. A., Koernig, S. K. & Harich, K. R. (2008). Now it's personal: Antecedents and outcomes of rapport between business faculty and their students. *Journal of Marketing Education, 31* (52).

Grunewald, J. P. & Ackerman, J. (1986). A modified Delphi approach for the development of student evaluations of faculty teaching. *Journal of Marketing Education, 8,* 32-38.

Howard-Hamilton, M. F. (2000). Creating a culturally responsive learning environment for African-American students. *New Directions for Teaching and Learning, 82,* 45-54.

Huff, L.C., Cooper, J. & Jones, W. (2002). The development and consequences of trust in student project groups. *Journal of Marketing Education, 24,* 24-34.

McCombs, B. L. & Whistler, J. S. (1997). *The learner-centered classroom and school: Strategies for increasing student motivation and achievement.* San Francisco, CA: Jossey-Bass.

McCrosky, J.C., Frayer, J. M., Richmond, V.P., Sallinen, A., & Barraclough, R.A., (1996). A multicultural examination of the relationship between nonverbal immediacy and affective learning. *Communication Quarterly, 44,* 297-307.

Murphy M. & Valdez, C. (2005). Ravaging resistence: A model for building rapport in a collaborative learning classroom. *Radical Pedagogy, 7*(1). Retrieved March 22, 2011, from http://radicalpedagogy.icaap.org/content/issue7_1/murphy-valdez.html

Perkins, D., Schenk, T. A., Stephan, L., Vrungos, S., & Wynants, S. (1995). Effects of rapport, intellectual excitement, and learning on students' perceived ratings of college instructors. *Psychological Reports, 76*(2), 627-635.

Thomas, D., Ribitch, F., & Freie, J. (1982). The relationship between psychological identification with instructors and student ratings of college courses. *Instructional Science, 11*(2), 139-154.

Tickle-Degnen, L. & Rosenthal, R. (1990). The nature of rapport and its nonverbal correlates. *Psychological Inquiry, 1,* 285-293.

Wilson, J.H. (2006). Predicting student attitudes and grades from perceptions of instructors' attitudes. *Teaching of Psychology, 33,* 91-94.

Wilson, J. H. & Hackney, A. A. (2004). In W. Buskist & S.F. Davis (Eds.), *Handbook of the Teaching of Psychology.* Maiden, MA: Blackwell Publishing.

Wilson, J. H., & Taylor, K. W. (2001). Professor immediacy as behaviors associated with liking students. *Teaching of Psychology, 28,* 136-138.

Section III: Refining and Improving Strategies and Resources

Chapter 11: Supporting Student Success

Chapter Overview

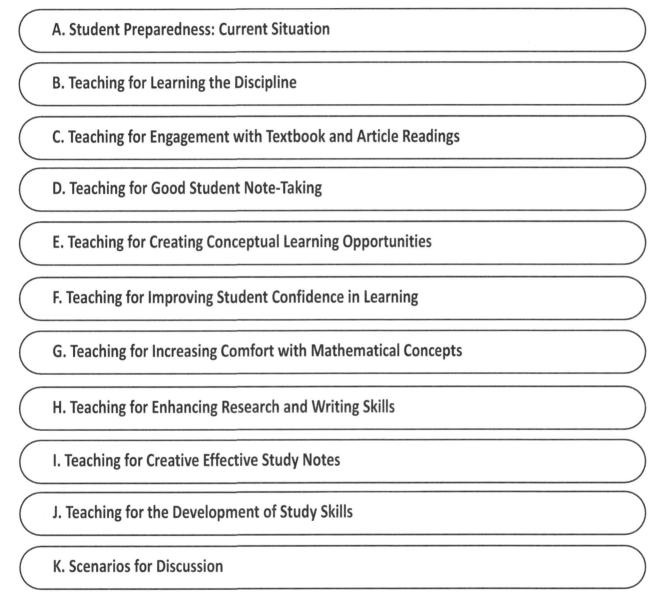

A. Student Preparedness: Current Situation

B. Teaching for Learning the Discipline

C. Teaching for Engagement with Textbook and Article Readings

D. Teaching for Good Student Note-Taking

E. Teaching for Creating Conceptual Learning Opportunities

F. Teaching for Improving Student Confidence in Learning

G. Teaching for Increasing Comfort with Mathematical Concepts

H. Teaching for Enhancing Research and Writing Skills

I. Teaching for Creative Effective Study Notes

J. Teaching for the Development of Study Skills

K. Scenarios for Discussion

This chapter covers simple techniques instructors can use to assist unprepared and "at-risk" students in being more successful in learning activities such as actively reading textbooks and articles, taking proper notes during lectures, understanding discipline-specific concepts, producing well-researched and well-written assignments, as well as creating useful study notes and employing effective study skills. These techniques provide instructors with practical ways to structure the class to provide helpful hints so that all students will be successful.

A. Student Preparedness: Current Situation

While record numbers of students are attending post-secondary education institutions, studies about student preparedness (National Survey of Student Engagement (NSSE), 2008; Faculty Survey of Student Engagement (FSSE), 2008) are consistently showing that many students are not ready to take on the challenges and expectations of a university or college education. Students are not sufficiently prepared for learning beyond high school. First year students are reported as having poor note-taking skills, weak study habits and writing skills, and low math readiness abilities (Liu, Sharkness & Pryor, 2008; Sanoff, 2006).

Some blame the lack of student preparedness on grade inflation from high school and lack of proper instruction from teachers. Registrar's offices are seeing a greater number of higher grades of incoming students. Some educators feel this is significantly impacting the first years of post-secondary education whereby students are shocked at their academic struggles and lack of A's and B's to which they were accustomed. Others contend that students are not spending enough time preparing themselves for classes. Students are continuing to follow the same pattern of work and play they used in high school.

Studies of student satisfaction (NSSE, 2008; FSSE, 2008) indicate that, on average, many students are spending about 2-3 hours per course a week on readings, note review, assignments, and studying. Instructors expect students to be doing twice as much per course per week (approximately 6-7 hours). *The American Freshman*, a yearly national survey of first year college students, reports an increase in learning disabilities among students (Pryor, Hurtado, DeAngelo, Sharkness, Romero, Korn, and Tran, 2009). Clearly, the need for student support is increasing.

Students are working more part-time jobs than ever before while attending school, and are increasingly having to support and care for family members (NSSE, 2009). With the increase in students attending post-secondary education and the associated desire to become educated to obtain a fulfilling career, there are more students who are requiring support with the challenges of fully understanding concepts and taking on the rigors of academia in obtaining a degree, diploma, or certificate in higher education.

The essence of this chapter is to provide some easy strategies you can use to help students. This shouldn't be perceived as 'handholding'. The goal is to make learning less like a 'scavenger hunt' for students; as instructors we should seek to provide a clear outline for learning and achievement. This chapter contains strategies for promoting student success.

Activity: *Looking at the 9 bubble quotes, how many resonate with you?*

A. **All**   *(and maybe write a few more while you are at it!)*

B. **Most** *(and you are sure you might relate to a few more in due time)*

C. **Some** *(but those that do resonate are still troubling)*

D. **A couple** *(maybe you have great classes)*

E. **None**

What are they taught in high school? Most are not prepared for post-secondary learning at all!

Many students have weak writing skills from poor sentence structure to atrocious spelling!

Some think Wikipedia is a mostly truthful research site!

Some spend class time chatting online, texting their friends and not taking proper notes!!

Many students have weak study skills. They don't use their time well to really study.

Most of my students do not know how to take good notes in class.

Among some, there is this sense of entitlement for getting good marks based on their effort.

They came from high school with supposedly As or Bs, but are struggling now. What's going on?

Many students don't take enough time to prepare for their classes, read the text or do homework.

Even if you can relate to a couple of these statements, you are experiencing the lack of student preparedness that many instructors are talking about these days. Students are struggling and we need to help them.

The following sections provide you with simple tips and strategies for slightly modifying your teaching to enhance student learning.

B. Teaching for Learning the Discipline

Oftentimes, student support centers engage students in analyses of learning styles. This learning style inventory activity (e.g., Kolb, Myers-Briggs, Dunn and Dunn, or any of the 70 different models available to instructors) expose students to an array of questions designed to categorize each student into a particular learning format or methodology—often with informative labels and descriptions. Some researchers (Pashler et al., 2008) caution using learning styles inventories at all, as there is little empirical evidence to support their use.

Not without the inherent merits of self-awareness of how one learns, the inventories are often one-time events that are rarely followed through later on in the term or later in the student's post-secondary education. Students often do not understand the real reason such inventories are conducted in the first place: to focus on how one learns and to become more aware of the learning process.

Researchers (Coffield et al., 2004) feel that the use of learning style inventories should focus on the discipline itself. Instructors should be customizing student assistance as it will be more likely to have a significant effect on learning than the one-size-fits-all learning style versions used in most courses.

Instructors should seek to help students learn a discipline by focusing on discipline-specific ways to acquire knowledge and apply it for optimal learning. While there are many generic suggestions for improving learning (shared throughout this book), consider the following questions to ascertain if there are discipline specific guidelines you could share with students for being more successful learning your discipline.

- What are the **essential concepts** to be learned in your course? Do you share those concepts with students?

- Is there are **progression of learning** that students need to acquire early on before grasping concepts and content later on in the course? If so, ensure you structure the course and scaffold learning so that students can be successful.

- Is **memorization** required (e.g., of formulas, definitions, dates, procedures) and if so, do you share **memorization aids** to help students?

- Are there **key chapters or readings** that provide **an understanding** of the main components of the course that you could direct students to read?

- Are there problems that require students to **apply learning**, and if so, **where** are **more problems** to practice?

- Is there a **framework** that will help students understand how all the pieces of the course fit together? If so, share the framework and **reference it each class**.

- Do **former students** of this course have **suggestions** on how to take notes, study, and grasp concepts? **Poll students** and **share responses** with next years' students.

- Are there **discipline-specific tips** for learning course concepts? If there is anything you know that will help students acquire a deep understanding of the course and its related concepts, share it students either verbally or in writing. Students will appreciate it!

C. Teaching for Engagement with Textbook and Readings

Instructors use textbooks, articles, and reading assignments in various ways:

- **before lecture/class.** The lecture often refers to the textbook content, yet is presented with instructor emphasis.

- **before lecture/class.** The lecture doesn't specifically refer to the textbook content, but it may be related or is an application of it.

- **around the time the lecture topic is happening.** The lecture makes no reference to the textbook, but may include additional material to know for an exam.

- **after lecture/class.** The lecture may be the introduction to the material and the reading is meant to reinforce the content learned.

Whatever the purpose of the reading/textbook chapter, many students often engage in 'passive reading'. This means they sit and read portions of the textbook, but they are not entirely grasping the content. They may be reading in front of a television or while talking to friends. Or they may be in a library study carrel trying to focus on all the work they have to do and trying to read too. Often, they do not understand what 'active reading' is or how to do it. Instructors can help them become active readers by trying these simple steps in the classroom.

1. Share Purpose of Reading

- Tell students **why** they are reading, **what** they are reading, **when** they should read it (before/after class), and **how** it will **relate** to the class

- Let students know if the class is an **application** of textbook reading or if the class covers **additional** material outside of the textbook

- Indicate to students if they should **skim** the textbook reading or **thoroughly read** it. Sometimes skimming is more purposeful

  - Students may be more likely to read/skim if they know the purpose of the material and how it relates to class work

2. Provide Active Reading Tips

- Pose a few **questions** for students to answer while they are reading

- Share a situation, context, or problem revolving around the reading; maybe students have to read to find solutions to a problem

- This will force them to conduct **'active reading'** whereby they will be interacting with the content

- Introduce the reading in class by **directing** their **attention** to key areas

- Inform students if they should **make notes** on readings prior to class

  - If they are to take notes, suggest to students that they should make notes with gaps for adding more content from the lecture

  - Suggest **key headings** for their **notes** so they can focus on key portions of the reading and structure content accordingly

D. Teaching for Good Note-Taking

Taking notes during a lecture or class will likely rank as one of the most common activities students do. Taking good notes helps students learn and do well on tests and exams. Most students' notes are word-for-word accounts of the class and often miss sub-sections, titles, big ideas, and often lack coherence. Students end up focusing on capturing everything and not necessarily processing it as they are copying. Here are suggestions to assist students in taking better notes.

1. Supply an Agenda or Class Outline

- Agendas or class outlines (written on the board or via a presentation slide) **provide** students with **details** about **what to expect** during the class, when there will be a break to catch up on note-taking, when they need to refer to the textbook, etc.

- Agendas serve as a **guide for both instructor** and **students** to know where the class is heading and provide direction for taking good notes

- If you can, provide **digital agendas** with links/readings/tips prior to class. Some students will be able to **prepare better** and know what to expect/be prepared/have downloaded, etc.

- Share agendas through a **learning management system** (e.g., Moodle, Blackboard, Desire2Learn) or a course web site

- Students will be **more likely to attend class** if they see an **organized plan** with specific sections and activities. Like a 'movie trailer' of your class, an agenda gives students a **preview** of what is to come

- If **posted at least a day in advance**, students can **copy** the **agenda** into their own digital notes or make handwritten sub-titles in their notebooks

- Some **students may read** the digital agendas a **day before class** and sometimes even skim through the material in order to be thoroughly prepared for learning

- Not every instructor is able to plan with a great deal of detail, but if **some detail** was provided students would be appreciative

2. Provide Gapped Handouts or Partial PowerPoint Slides

- When you provide gapped handouts or partial slides with key headings of the class content, students have a **head start** in **organizing their notes** and knowing the key themes of the class

- Consider giving students the **main headings** and **sub-headings** of the class and include **enough space** for students to fill in information

- Students will see the need to attend the class to get the full note and also will recognize the big ideas and supporting ideas within the class

- **Provide instructor notes** (partial or full handouts) only when the topic is **too complex** to copy (those with learning disabilities/language challenges will benefit more from complete notes)

- Students with laptops can **download digital versions** of gapped handouts/partial slides into **OneNote** (PC) or **Notebook Layout of Word** (Mac) so that they can start to format notes for ease in reading/studying

  - OneNote is a **digital version of a notebook** that is part of the Microsoft Suite of software. If students have access to a laptop they can structure and format their notes with greater ease than using a word-processing program. It allows students to effectively take digital notes.

  - OneNote is a **digital canvas** where a student can type, write, or draw notes in the form of text, graphics, and images—all common formats for taking notes in the classroom.

  - Using a system of **tabbed menu headings** and **sub-tabs**, a student can add new content, divide it up, and rearrange additional content.

  - It is even more powerful than a paper notebook in that you can **easily move pages** around and **add** online attachments, website links, and other digital references

3. Share Objectives of The Class

- Students need to know **what is important** in class. We want them all to know the target.

- As part of the **first few minutes of class**, either verbally or in written format share the main objectives/outcomes of the class

- Be up front about **key themes/big ideas** and concepts that are central to the class. Don't make your class a guessing game

- Possibly suggest to students **when to take notes** and when you want them to listen or participate; many students just copy word-for-word as they are unsure what is important for learning

4. Slow Down: Pacing and Pausing

- **Speak** at a **speed** that your students find acceptable for taking notes

- Speaking too fast, particularly on new and detailed information, will not give students enough time to think, process, and write down all the key components. Student notes will lack a lot of detail

- If you are unsure if you speak too fast or not, **ask your students**. Give them an anonymous survey question and determine if you are meeting their needs. Ask a colleague to sit in on your class and give you feedback

- While speaking, you should **pause** and **give students time** to properly write notes and **ask questions** for clarification

  - Tell students you are not going to talk for a minute or two so that they can get their notes caught up and/or copy down more info

5. Share Note-Taking Tip Sheets and Exemplary Sample Notes

- There are many books and websites written for students about how to take class notes and manage with their classes, but students rarely read them

- Provide a **note-taking tip sheet** emphasizing some of the key points for success in taking notes, especially in first and second year courses

- Partway through a class ask students to get into **small groups** and **share their notes**. Discuss what **observations** students are making. Possibly share what 'good notes' should look like. This will help students to see what is reasonable and what they are missing

- Ask permission from a student who takes very good notes if you can share his/her notes with the class (remove student's name)

  - It is extremely helpful for students to **see what exemplary notes** should look like in terms of content, layout, design, etc.

Sample Tip Sheet for Students:

Make a digital copy and share with students

Study Skill Tips for Students

Preparing For Class

- ▶ Download materials/do activities given by instructor so you are adequately prepared for class

- ▶ Do your readings in a spot with few distractions and at a time you are alert

- ▶ Reference your course syllabus for topics and upcoming assignments

- ▶ Gather all materials required for note-taking (notebook or laptop). A laptop is a valuable tool for taking notes. Try using OneNote (MS Office) or Notebook layout (Mac Word) to easily take notes in a digital notebook format with multiple formats and uses

- ▶ Arrive to class on time and get a seat where you can hear and see instructor – avoid any distractions and sit away from classmates who like to talk or engage in other activities during class

Make the Most of In Class Experience

- ▶ Look for structure/outline of the lecture either from a written agenda or the instructor's overview of the class as this will help you format your notes

- ▶ Be an active listener during class: ask questions in your head, watch for verbal cues referencing important content, listen for key phrases, take note of what the instructor emphasizes/ writes on board or suggests you read/do for homework

- ▶ Actively format your notes (e.g., skip lines, indent words, draw arrows, create concept maps, sketch diagrams, and leave lots of space between topics for future notes and readability)

- ▶ Copy down all examples the instructor provides. Leave space after each example so you can redo the examples as part of your studying

- ▶ Try the 'Question-Evidence-Conclusion' format for your notes by a) labeling in the margin the question the instructor is addressing b) labeling in your notes the evidence that answers or supports that question and c) labeling the conclusion/answer to the question

To Do After Class

- ▶ Read over your notes for gaps or misunderstandings; consult with peers or text for more info

- ▶ Reorganize/format your notes so they are visually accessible for easy studying later on

- ▶ Actively study your notes for mid-terms and exams (e.g., explain concepts out loud, teach the material to a classmate, do a practice quiz, rewrite notes to a more condensed study guide)

- ▶ Try to study in 30-60 minute chunks and take 10 minute breaks

6. Organize Your Class into Chunks

- Try not to give the **non-stop, hour-long lecture**. Your students' brains cannot handle all the information. Retention and understanding of content often declines after the first 20-30 minutes. Note-taking quality will decline too with often the best notes taken in that first half hour.

- **Organize** your class into unique **10-15 minute chunks**. Ensure each chunk is easily defined and evident

- For each chunk, try to **vary the format** (e.g., lecture, pose a few questions for content discussions, show a video clip related to content, etc.) This will **help students pay attention** and **take better notes** because they will be more engaged and awake

- **Write headings** and 'chunk' titles on the board (or show on each slide) so students can focus on making notes on each chunk

- **Summarize/reinforce** each **chunk** before you move onto the next one

---

Sample Chunked Class Outline:

▶ Review Key Points of Previous Class – Board Note *(10 mins)*

▶ Introduction/Hook for New Content – Video or Class Survey *(10 mins)*

▶ New Content – Direct Instruction Lecture *(15 mins)*

▶ Problem to Solve – Students Work in Pairs *(10 mins)*

▶ New Content – Direct Instruction Lecture *(15 mins)*

▶ Break (10 mins)

▶ Application of Content – Group Discussion *(15 mins)*

▶ New Content – Direct Instruction Lecture *(10 mins)*

▶ Consolidation of Content – Game *(10 mins)*

---

7. Provide Application of Content through Examples

- Examples should **clearly demonstrate characteristics** of the concept

- Students need **more than 1 or 2 examples** to help achieve deeper understanding; aim for a handful of the best examples you can find

- **Application activities**, which include practicing with examples, help students **feel confident** with new content

- **Provide 'worked examples'** (sample questions worked through by students and instructor together)

- Ask students to **paraphrase concepts** as this will allow them to better understand material and make appropriate notes, which they can use later (paraphrasing increases higher order thinking)

8. 'Bulletproof' Your Slides

- PowerPoint (or Keynote for Mac) is **declining in its novelty** for **students,** yet instructors are still excited about its abilities or use it as a form of "integrating technology"

- Slides with lots of text are often more for the instructor than students – the detailed text acts as a 'teleprompter' rather than effectively presenting concepts and content

- **Avoid** creating **heavily-bulleted**, content-dense, or text-dependent slides
    - The brain is unable to make the connection from bulleted information to concepts at a later date
    - Students get caught up in copying every point and don't pay attention to the instructor and what they are saying

- Avoid the use of templates that often have dull, boring or commonly-seen backgrounds. Students will be bored quickly as they are less 'wowed' by slideshows today

- **Increase the number of visuals** (graphics, pictures, diagrams, charts, graphs, videos, cartoons). Visuals help students to remember content and help focus their attention on you and what you have to say!

- Place a **few words/phrase** along with a **graphic** on a slide and talk about the rest of the content in your discussion with the students. Students will listen and take better notes rather than trying to copy down bullets that do not make a lot of sense on their own

E. Teaching for Creating Conceptual Learning Opportunities

Educational experiences must focus on conceptual learning. There is an increased call by many educators to focus on conceptual learning happening in classrooms. Conceptual learning is tied to deeper and more persistent learning. Here are some sugestions for instructors:

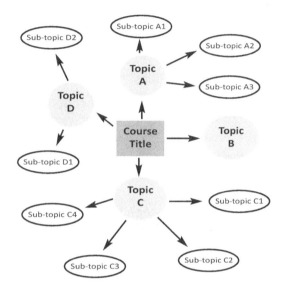

1. Create Concept Maps

- Whether done digitally in concept mapping software (e.g., Smart Ideas, Inspiration), in a word processing programs with textboxes and arrows, or on a piece of chart paper, sharing a course concept map assists students in their learning

- Early on in the course, a concept map is like a big map of all that is to be covered in the course and helps clarify the objectives

- Later on in the course, the concept map helps with reviewing

2. Consider a Course Framework/Diagram

- Students will appreciate having an overview of the course

- Is there a diagram, image, or format you know will suit your course material and present it in a visual manner so that students can see where they are headed? (e.g., flowchart, timeline, Venn diagram)

- Would this framework/diagram also be helpful to include in syllabus or on your course web site?

3. Provide Many Applied Learning Opportunities

- Students **learn concepts by applying them** in many situations, problems, case studies, role plays, or examples

- Create many **applied learning opportunities** for your students to practice to learn

4. Move Beyond Textbook – Create Your Own Questions/Problems

When instructors **move beyond the textbook questions** (or bank of questions that come with the text), there are greater chances for addressing more specific concepts and allowing students to really delve **into understanding** the course material

5. Give Pre-Test on Course Concepts

- Create a **short pre-test** on the **concepts** inherent in your course (possibly framed in case studies or mini-scenarios). This could be an online or paper test, but it must address the conceptual learning you wish students to have. Make sure you take up the no-mark test

- Indicate to students that these are the **concepts to be explored** and learned throughout term. Refer back to pre-test as the course evolves

- Students will appreciate seeing the **reason for attending class.** The pre-test acts as an overview of what to expect in the course. Emphasize how the in-class activities will enhance their understanding of the concepts

F. Teaching for Improving Student Confidence in Learning

Sometimes the simplest things an instructor does (smile, welcome a student by name, give some feedback) helps at-risk or unprepared students. It is all about increasing student confidence in learning and the discipline. Here are some tips for supporting students.

1. Setting the Tone the First Day

- The first day of a course is so important. If the instructor sets a welcoming tone with intent to support all students, then the term is off to a great start

- Be forthcoming with **live** and **virtual office hours** so students know how to contact you

2. Build a Strong Rapport With Students

- Throughout the term it is important to constantly work on **building rapport** with all students

- **Learn names**, get to know students, be **approachable, arrive early** to class, and stay for any questions. Ask students questions and take interest in them

- **Share a bit about yourself** so students see you as a human being who is there to laugh, share stories, and teach the course

3. Give Lots of Informal Feedback to Students – All Term

- **Talk** to students, **write comments** on their papers, ask them questions, **wander** around while they are working in groups, **watch** and listen, and **give informal** feedback when appropriate

- Provide **no-mark quizzes** or **questions** students can do in class (or for homework). This gives students an idea about how they are doing

- Always **take up problems** and questions to provide **immediate** feedback on learning

- Use **clickers** or **online surveys** to gauge student understanding of concepts and content. Allow students to know correct responses

- Give lots of **positive encouragement**

4. Provide Opportunities for Self and Peer Assessment

- Create **checklists**, use **rubrics,** and provide **samples** of excellent assignments so students can conduct a **self-assessment**

- When students are presenting or working in a group, create **peer assessment** opportunities for students to give feedback to each other

- **Teach students** how to properly conduct self and peer assessment

G. Teaching for Increasing Comfort with Mathematical Concepts

Some students have weak mathematical and problem solving skills. Educational institutions are responding with summer 'math boot camps' or transition courses to brush up on basic math skills. Regardless of whether your students took these 'courses' or have signed up for more help at the learner support centre, here are a few ideas for supporting weak math students at the classroom level.

1. Create Math Mini Clips

- For common math questions as they pertain to the content of the course, **create** a short **screen capture video** explaining the steps and key points

- Mini clips can be **uploaded** to your course web site (or free online storage web sites) for frequent access

- Encourage students to **replay** the clips to help learn the math concepts

2. Provide Web Links to a Few 'Math-Help' Sites

- If there is an existing web site that has mini-clips, web learning tools, or videos of how to do math related to your course **provide a link**

- Spend a few minutes **in class showing** students the web sites

$$sin(\alpha - \beta) = \sin \alpha \cos \beta - \cos \alpha \sin \beta$$

$$ctg^2 \alpha + 1 = \frac{1}{\sin^2 \alpha} = \csc^2 \alpha$$

$$f'(x) = \lim_{x \to 0} \frac{f(x + \Delta x) - f(x)}{\Delta x}$$

$$\cos 2\alpha = \cos^2 \alpha - \sin^2 \alpha$$

$$\sin^2 \alpha + \cos^2 \alpha = 1$$

$$\sin x = a; \quad x = (-1)^n \arcsin a + \pi n,$$

$$\log_a b = \frac{1}{\log_a}$$

3. Supplement Class with Quick Review of Key Math Concepts

- Most students will appreciate a **short review** of some **key math** concepts at a time that is appropriate and related to an assignment or test, as long as it is short and is presented with a focus

- Provide a one-page digital **handout** for students to review the key concepts, if you don't have time in class

- Every now and then **write a math question** on the board/slide for students to **solve** in the first few minutes of class. Be sure to provide the answers

- This provides **constant practice** for all students, but will be a clear indication for others that they need more help

4. Encourage Students to Attend Math Help

- Share **workshop** times and locations for **remedial math** help

- If you share with the whole class, those who need it are not singled out and can choose to attend

- For those students who are really struggling with course work, send **private emails** or ask to see the students out of class

- Bring in a math **workshop instructor** to **speak** to your class to share workshop times

H. Teaching for Enhancing Research and Writing Skills

Instructors often complain that students lack good research and writing skills. Writing, for post-secondary education assignments, is often quite different than writing for secondary school work. If instructors assume that all students can write and research effectively they will likely see poor quality work and will have to deal with frustrated students. Here are some tips:

1. Have Library Conduct a Research Workshop in Your Class

- Plan to have a **class** (or part of a class early on in the term) **devoted** to explaining how to do a **research paper** (for an assignment which requires brainstorming, finding and retrieving articles, citing resources, etc.)

- **Contact** the **library** to set up a day/time

- Have an **in class-library session** for your students

- Take the **time to teach students** where and how to gather data (specific to your class and assignment). This will give students a leg up in starting your assignment and they often produce better work!

2. Demonstrate Research Skills as Part of Class

- If you do not have time to schedule a library session, at least show the **library web site** and location of tips for searching databases

- Provide **journal** and **book** suggestions that might be good **starting points**

- **Download** a research **article** and **demonstrate** how to **summarize** the information for a paper

- Share **library workshop information**, encourage attendance

3. Share and Show Student Samples

- Show an **exemplary piece** of work from a previous student(s). This will indicate how paper/essay should look (e.g., layout, paragraph structure)

- Sample work should be **linked** with **rubrics/marking schemes**

  - You aren't giving away answers, you are providing support!

  - Removes guesswork for students and often provides better quality work; you benefit by having an easier time marking their papers!

4. Promote Learner Support Center Services

- Most institutions have **"learner support"** centers where student workshops are offered on study skills, writing skills, referencing, time management, note-taking, English language support, etc.

- Arrange to have **someone** from your **support centre come in to your class** to share information on the workshops offered

- Better yet, **ask the staff to present** a **short set** of **tips** on writing a good paper or take **part of a class to deliver workshop components**!

I. Teaching for Creating Effective Study Notes

Students often are challenged to make good study notes because they are unsure what to study and unable to focus on the big ideas . The following strategies take very little of your class time, but help students to construct effective study notes and know what to study for mid-terms and exams.

1. Consistently Consolidate Class Content

- Take 5-7 minutes at the end of each class to **summarize the main points**

  - Put students in **small groups** and ask them to name the top 3 items they learned. One person per group shares the answers with the class; record student responses

  - Give class a **sample test question** or **problem** and ask them to solve on their own before they leave and provide answer either before end of class or beginning of next class

  - **Turn to another peer** and share the key points of class

  - Explain a short situation or **scenario and** ask students to think on their own about the solution. After a minute, ask them to share solution with a small group of students. Explain answer focusing on key points they just learned

  - Instructor provides a **slide** or **overhead outlining the key points** of the class and gives students time to record in notes

- Students will be able to **make effective study notes** as they will have content consolidated and reinforced

2. Provide Opportunities for Ascertaining Student Learning

- Are students leaving your class with confidence to do their homework and readings? Are they grasping the key concepts essential to learning and building upon for your next lesson? How can you find this out?

    - Ask them to complete a "**Ticket out the Door**" with 1-2 questions to be answered such as

        ◦ What were the main points of the class today?

        ◦ What points did you not fully understand?

        ◦ Solve this problem/question as best as you can.

    - In the last 5 minutes, ask them to get out a piece of paper and answer the **questions you have posted**

    - Tell students this is **not for marks**, it is just to see how well they understand the class

    - **Collect 'tickets'** as they exit and share summary of the answers at the beginning of next class (or post online)

- Ascertaining whether students have "caught what you have taught" helps you know how to **plan next class** and what to questions/emails to expect

3. Summarize Key Points from Previous Class

- At the **beginning of each class**, conduct a **5-10 minute summary** of the **key points** from the previous class re-emphasizing main learning components

- Produce a **board note** that students can copy to add to their study notes

- Alternative: Provide a **short podcast** or video capture of yourself talking about the key points of the class so students can use another medium to learn

- **Reviewing** and **repeating** aid in long term memory acquisition of material and lead to deeper understanding of the content

4. Conduct Review Session for Mid-Terms and Exams

- Conduct a **review session in class**

- Review **key concepts**, answer questions, provide additional examples, have classmates quiz each other on questions, etc.

- Create and share a '**study guide**' outlining key components of test

- **Interact with students** and find out how deep their learning is on the topic

- "**Millionaire**" and "**Jeopardy**" templates (found on Internet) can be fun activities for in-class review sessions where questions you insert into the template focus on key concepts and possible mid-term/exam questions

5. Have Students Create Concept Map of Course

- Have students **work together to create a concept map** of the entire course. This activity brings out key points and content for studying

- In **small groups**, give students a large sheet of **chart paper** and markers. Ask them to make a concept map of the course drawing the relationships between items

- Give each group some **tape to affix to a wall or front boards.** Have students **wander around for 10 minutes** and look at each group's chart paper

- **Discuss** as a large group or a combination of small groups

- Take a **picture** with a **digital camera** of a few **concept maps** and **post** on **class web site** for students to access and review for making study notes

J. Teaching for the Development of Study Skills

Even if your students have good lecture and study notes, they still might not know how to properly study. Students tend to engage in 'passive' studying techniques, whereby they think that looking at their notes or skimming content will somehow make content sink into their brains. Students need to have a plan for studying and do a little bit each day. Here are suggestions to assist your students in developing good study skills.

1. Share Information About What to Study

- Give students **tips** on **what to study**, **types** of **exam questions**, **how long** they should spend on certain content, what questions will be from the text vs. notes, some sample questions. They will appreciate this information; it will assist them in making a plan for studying

- Indicate how much the test or exam requires **memorization vs. understanding content/applying knowledge**. This informs students that they need to employ different study techniques for different types of questions

- Can they bring in **formula sheets** to a test/exam so they don't have to memorize them? If students know that basic facts, formulas, and procedures are either made available on the test or they can bring in a 'cheat sheet', they will focus on other areas to study

2. Share a Personal Story or Tips on How To Study

- Sometimes **personalizing the experience** and sharing what you did will help students focus on how to study. Story telling is an effective way to engage students

- Suggest a **timeline for studying**. Spend a few minutes suggesting a timeframe and set of tasks that should be done to prepare for the exam or test. For example, indicate how far in advance students should review notes and start organizing into categories

- Sharing some **study tips** could benefit some students who don't read self-help books or attend workshops or have any study skills for this subject matter, especially first year students!

3. Have Students Create Sample Test Questions

- In class, or for homework, have **students create some sample test** questions. In small groups have students share the questions and discuss how best to study for them

- **Share sample test questions** from **previous years**. Give students **time in class** to work through one or two questions. In a **class discussion**, have students share what they think will be the challenging content, what they believe they need to spend their time practicing, and what questions will be easier to grasp.

K. Scenarios for Discussion

Activity: Read the following scenarios structured around commonly heard student quotes. From your own experience and/or the ideas presented in this chapter, determine the answers to the questions. Discuss with a colleague.

Scenario 1: Organic Chemistry 252 (Instructor Schmidt)

Students were overhead saying...

"Second years always fear Schmidt's Organic Chem because it is a tough class."

"The material is difficult to get and you have to learn it over and over yourself before it makes any sense."

"While the content isn't the easiest, it is more how the instructor presents it to us that gets us confused."

"Prof Schmidt is really passionate about organic chem; apparently he's been teaching this course for 20 years. You can tell – he has a lot of overheads with formulas, definitions, and structural diagrams we copy down at lightning speed. Class is basically copying notes and listening to him."

"I really need this course for my degree; however, I struggled in high school with chemistry. Now I am really not doing well. I have a difficult time concentrating – my mom thinks I might have ADD."

"The prof is a really kind guy. He answers questions and gives more detail and content is asked."

"We take tons of notes in this class. I know a number of students are struggling and appear frustrated. I don't know what to do when I get home. I just look at my notes and freak out."

"Organic chem is really a tough subject and you basically have to teach yourself the content after you sift through your notes or make the TAs go over all the content in labs."

"I wish we had more problems to practice in class so I felt confident when I went home. He's a great prof so maybe if we asked him he might give us more problems."

Question: What **3 strategies (from this chapter or your own ideas)** might Instructor Schmidt use to support the unprepared and at-risk students in his class?

Scenario 2: History of the World 110 (Instructor Detaile)

Students were overhead saying...

"History of the World 110 is a class with a lot of stuff to remember! But the instructor seems really passionate about the content and teaching the course. That is good."

"I hate the hugely expensive textbook. It is a requirement of the course but the instructor often just goes over the same stuff in the textbook. I am not a good textbook learner – I need examples and activities to make sense of what is going on."

"I wish the prof would explain what parts of the chapters we need to focus on. We are told each class covers 3-4 chapters of our textbook, but it would take days to read and understand those chapters. We are told to read the chapters before class but the prof just covers them anyway. I am confused."

"Don't get me wrong. I don't mind PowerPoint – at least the prof is trying to do something with technology or make it less boring than just talking – but his slides are so jammed full of text and it is really hard to copy everything down and make sense of it. I sit close to the front and try to pay attention but it is hard."

"Yeah, the slides are full of bullets flying in all over the place. It is just like most of my profs so I am used to it, but there are a lot of dates and names and places in history to get down. We get the slides after class (he says this so we'll come to class to listen) but many people skip class as they know they'll just get them later. I have skipped some classes as it just makes me frustrated trying to keep up."

"The mid-term and final are a lot of memorization for me. I find this course stressful because of that. I can't memorize because it all just flows out of my head."

"I am a slower learner than others and really need to take my time to understand what is being said and make some sense of it. I have asked him to slow down but he says I should just read the textbook to get a better sense before class starts."

Question: What **3 strategies (from this chapter or your own ideas)** could Instructor Detaile use to support the unprepared and at-risk students in his class?

Scenario 3: Business Basics 202 (Instructor Gates)

Students were overhead saying...

"Instructor Gates is a fun instructor – but she talks really fast!"

"We have this big business project that takes the whole term. A number of my class-mates are not sure how to get the data we need –maybe half of our class of 50. We are in second year but no one has taught us how to find business information for projects or do proper research on the Internet."

"I like the prof, but she doesn't give us many examples of what she means. She talks fast and jams a lot of information into a lesson and I don't get it some days. I have auditory processing problems and while I do tape record her lecturing, I still find it frustrating when I get home to make sense of it."

"When I go to study for one of her business tests, I just have all this information from class and am not sure what she thinks we should study. She tells us that to be good business people we have to figure it out for ourselves. I am really frustrated by this and try to think it through but it is not easy."

"I find the math parts of this course hard. I am not strong in math and didn't know that so much math would be part of a business course."

"I want to be in business but this is a basics course and it seems pretty hard to me. I mean there are so many 'basics' that I am having a hard time understanding what they all are. They are just sort of clumped together into big lessons that are full of things to know."

"I am an adult learner returning to school after being out for 20 years. My processing isn't as fast as these 'whipper snipper' students. I am caring for two children at home and holding down a part time job so I have a hard time meeting in our groups and managing the flurry of information coming my way."

"I wish things were clearer. This project we have to work on must use all that we learned in class. But when working with my group we find it hard to know what we need to focus on. We spend half our time some days just sorting out what we need to do."

Question: What **3 strategies (from this chapter or your own ideas)** could Instructor Gates implement to support the unprepared and at-risk students in her class?

Scenario 4: Psychology 101 (Instructor Freud)

Students were overhead saying:

"Psych 101 is a required course for me but I don't see the point in it."

"Instructor Freud covers a lot in a class. Most of us, I think, are unsure where one topic ends and the next one starts. He just keeps going and going."

"We all know Instructor Freud is just a part-time instructor and is getting a lot of content and material from other profs. I think all the PowerPoints are made by the other profs and he just uses them – it doesn't seem like he makes it his own."

"Prof Freud isn't easy to approach. He is usually arriving just as class starts and you can hardly find him in his office between classes. He doesn't always seem keen on teaching this large class."

"Our class is huge – 500 students. Prof Freud tries his best to present all the material but it is hard to concentrate when we have to listen so carefully. Some of my friends text message or play on laptops during class as it is hard to stay focused. You can get away without him seeing you."

"I have no one at home who can help me with my studies. I am in this big class and office hours and finding the prof or TAs is hard sometimes. No one in my family has ever gone to university so they don't understand what I am going through."

"I have a learning disability. I am identified and have brought in my paperwork to the instructor but not much is really any different. I have slow cognitive processing with language. I basically need a longer time to process stuff and think it through and then write it – I have a tutor who helps me out but this class is killing me!"

"There are many sample Pysch 101 exams and tests in the library. However, I have no idea how to take all of my notes and make studying worthwhile. In high school we never had to study this much content. I can practice answering the sample test questions, but after that I am lost."

Question: What **3 strategies (from this chapter or your own ideas)** might Instructor Freud use to support the unprepared and at-risk students in his class?

Top Ten Takeaways

1. **Textbook Reading and Notes:** To ensure students are 'actively' reading, share details about how the textbook fits into the class notes/lecture, as well as how to make good notes.

2. **Agenda:** Supply an agenda or class outline for your students clearly detailing the parts of the class, indicating when there is a break, and when they will be doing activities.

3. **Partial Handouts and Slides:** Provide gapped handouts or partial slides so students have all the major headings and sub-sections and can focus on taking notes using their own words.

4. **Class Objectives:** Inform your students about the objectives of the class. This will help them know what to expect and what major points you will be covering.

5. **Speak Well:** Speak at a speed that allows your students to take proper notes. Pause when students need time to copy detailed information.

6. **Chunk Content:** Organize your class into 10-15 minute chunks. This method of teaching greatly increases student attention and interest in the class.

7. **Examples:** Provide many examples and opportunities for students to practice in class.

8. **More Visuals on Slides:** Bulletproof your slides by trying to ease away from multi-bulleted slides and focusing more on using key phrases and visual images.

9. **Consolidate:** Summarize and review content at the end of each class and review it again in the first few minutes of the next class.

10. **Mid-Term and Exam Clarity:** Clearly explain to students what they need to study for a mid-term or exam. Try to be clear about the number and types of questions.

Next Steps

1. Consider where your students need the most help: Reading the text book? Taking good class notes? Writing and researching papers? Making study notes or studying for tests and exams? Determine which area needs the most help and focus on those strategies.

2. Start small. Try one of the strategies.

3. When planning a new class, build in a few minutes to either summarize or review content.

4. Put an agenda on the whiteboard or post online. Try it for one class.

5. Make a gapped handout for one class and tweak the process after getting feedback from students.

References and Resources

Coffield F., Moseley D.V., Hall E. & Ecclestone K. (2004). *Learning styles and pedagogy in post-16 learning: A systematic and critical review.* Learning and Skills Development Agency, London. Retrieved May 10, 2009, from https://crm.lsnlearning.org.uk/user/order.aspx?code=041543

Coffield F., Moseley D.V., Hall E. & Ecclestone K. (2004). *Should we be using learning styles? What research has to say to practice.* Learning and Skills Development Agency, London. Retrieved May 10, 2009, from https://crm.lsnlearning.org.uk/user/order.aspx?code=041540

DeZure, D., Kaplan, M. &Deerman, M. A. (n.d.). *Research on Student Note taking: Implications for Faculty and Graduate Student Instructors.* Retrieved May 7, 2009, from http://www.math.lsa.umich.edu/~krasny/math156_crlt.pdf

Erikson, B. L., Peters, C.B. & Strommer, D. W. (2006). *Teaching First-Year College Students.* San Francisco, CA: Jossey-Bass. (see Chapter 6)

Faculty Survey of Student Engagement (FSSE). (2008). *Comparing NSSE and FSSE Results: Student and Faculty Expectations.* Indiana University Centre for Post-Secondary Research. Retrieved May 1, 2009, from http://fsse.iub.edu/index.cfm

Gabriel, K. F. (2008). *Teaching Unprepared Students: Strategies for Promoting Success and Retention in Higher Education.* Sterling, VA: Stylus.

Liu, A., Sharkness, J., & Pryor, J.H. (2008). *Findings from the 2007 Administration of Your First College Year (YFCY): National Aggregates.* Los Angeles: Higher Education Research Institute, UCLA. Retrieved May 22, 2009, from http://www.gseis.ucla.edu/heri/PDFS/YFCY_2007_Report05-07-08.pdf

National Survey of Student Engagement (NSSE). (2008). Promoting Engagement for All Students: The Imperative Look Within – 2008 Results. Indiana University Centre for Post-Secondary Research. Retrieved May 1, 2009, from http://nsse.iub.edu/NSSE_2008_Results/

Pashler, H., McDaniel, M., Rohrer, D., & Bjork, R. (2008). Learning styles: Concepts and evidence. *Psychological Science in the Public Interest*, *9*(3), 105–119.

Pryor, J. H., Hurtado, S., DeAngelo, L., Sharkness, J., Romero, L.C., Korn, W. S., & Tran, S. (2009). *The American Freshman: National Norms for Fall 2008.* Los Angeles, CA: Higher Education Research Institute, UCLA.

Sanoff, A. P. (2006). What Professors and Teachers Think: A Perception Gap Over Students' Preparation. *The Chronicle of Higher Education*, *52*(27). Retrieved May 16, 2009, from http://chronicle.com/free/v52/i27/27b00901.htm

Chapter 12: Honing Skills for Effective Questioning

Chapter Overview

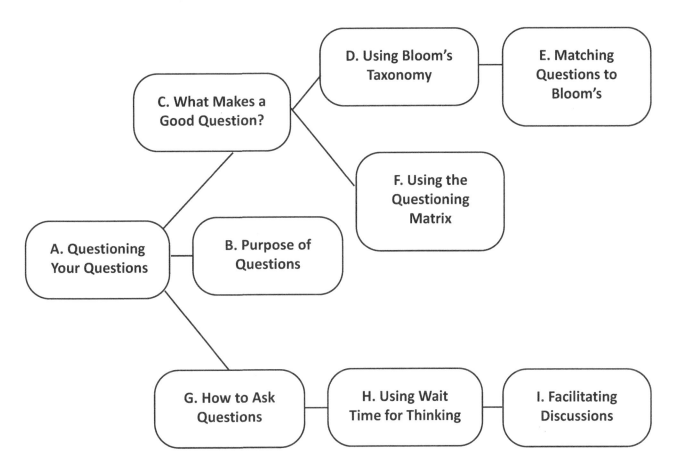

Asking good questions may seem like a simple task when teaching. You just ask a question, right? You wait for a hand or two to go up and you get an answer. What can be so hard about that? You may not have spent much time thinking about what questions you ask.

This chapter will shed light on tips and tricks for asking questions that stimulate all levels of thinking. The chapter will also give you insights on how to properly ask a question, how long you should wait before choosing a student to answer, and how to probe and prompt students for more detail.

The art and skill of questioning are important components to being an effective educator.

A. Questioning your Questions

Here is a short activity to get you thinking about your experience with questions. Check off those questions to which you can answer "yes". If you feel your answer would be better categorized as 'only once or twice' and not all the time, still check it off.

- ☐ Do you create questions prior to class?

- ☐ Do you consider anticipated responses to your questions so you can provide direction should something not go as planned?

- ☐ Do you ask a variety of questions (e.g., lower order and higher order?)

- ☐ Do you display your questions prior to asking them? (e.g., with readings for homework, on board/slide, or on handouts?)

- ☐ Do you employ good 'wait time/think time' after you have given a question? (e.g., 3-5 seconds?)

- ☐ Do you allow pairs/groups of students to discuss a question prior to asking for a response?

- ☐ Are you able to get most students involved in class discussions?

- ☐ How often do you challenge your students with higher order questions? (e.g., asking them to analyze, judge, see things from new angles, evaluate a response)

- ☐ Are your questions able to elicit feedback on student comprehension levels?

- ☐ Do your questions encourage students to listen to each other and contribute to the answers?

- ☐ Are you able to build rapport and class cohesion through your questioning?

- ☐ Do you encourage your students to ask questions either in small or large groups?

- ☐ Do you use various response methods (other than verbal response) to your questions? (e.g., written post/email, written paper handed in, group response on whiteboard?)

Count how many checkmarks you have from this list. If you have approximately half to almost all, you are on your way to being a good questioner! Learn more in this chapter.

If you have less than half checked off, hopefully you are open to learning a bit more about questioning and expanding your questioning strategies. Changing the quantity and quality of your questions can have a significant improvement upon student learning.

This chapter will provide more detail and strategies on questioning for your class teaching.

B. Purpose of Questions

What purposes do questions serve? Why take the time to embed them in your class? Why consider questions for student learning and achievement?

Here are some reasons why instructors use questions. What might be your reasons for using questioning in your class? Count how many relate to your use of questions.

- ✓ Introduce a Topic
- ✓ Engage Students in Class
- ✓ Facilitate a Discussion
- ✓ Focus Attention on a Topic or Problem
- ✓ Review Important Information
- ✓ Stimulate Thinking and Learning
- ✓ Assist in Organization and Sequence for Class Content
- ✓ Develop Concepts / New Learning
- ✓ Promote Reflective and Critical Thinking
- ✓ Clarify Feelings, Values, Goals, Beliefs
- ✓ Assist in Managing and Keeping Class Moving Along
- ✓ Personalize Learning for Students
- ✓ Clarify Ideas
- ✓ Establish and Test Facts
- ✓ Assess a Topic's Progress
- ✓ Assess Students' Knowledge of Content / Gaps for More Learning

C. What Makes a Good Question?

The characteristics of a good question:

- should be related to the class' focus and the students' experiences.
- ensures the words are ordered in such a way that the thinking is clarified, both for the students and the instructor. The question is stated clearly and is easily understood with little need for rephrasing/rewording.
- has appropriate intonation and non-verbal signals to enhance the meaning and intent which helps in being clear with your students.
- strives to challenge the current knowledge base of students.

- encourages reflective thought, even after the question is asked.

- is seen as part of an on-going dialogue between the instructor and students.

- can surprise students, but it should not be seen as a weapon to embarrass or call-out students.

- maintains student engagement, stimulates thoughts, and evokes feelings.

D. Composing Thought-Provoking Questions: Using Bloom's Revised Taxonomy

Benjamin Bloom was a university professor and in 1956 he and his colleagues devised three domains of learning: cognitive, affective, and psychomotor (Bloom, 1984). Bloom's cognitive domain has become highly referenced in terms of teaching and learning as it relates in this chapter to the art and skill of designing and asking good questions. These domains were briefly explained in Chapter 2: Determining Goals and Objectives as they pertained to designing learning objectives and aligning with assessment and evaluation methods.

The cognitive domain outlines six levels of thinking skills. The lower end of the spectrum is often referred to as "lower order thinking skills". The higher end is called "higher order thinking skills". When asking questions either in oral or written form, try to vary your questions across all six levels. Instructors tend to ask more questions that involve remembering, understanding, and applying. It is important to include higher order thinking questions in courses. Students need opportunities to analyze, evaluate, and create in order to stimulate good problem solving and critical thinking skills.

Higher Order Thinking Skills		
Evaluation		Creating
Synthesis		Evaluating
Analysis	↑	Analyzing
Application		Applying
Comprehension		Understanding
Knowledge		Remembering
1956 Version	**Lower Order Thinking Skills**	*Revised Version*

Bloom's Taxonomy has undergone a few revisions since its creation in 1956. In 2001 Lorin Anderson, Bloom's former student, revised the taxonomies along with a colleague of Bloom's, David Krathwohl. The nouns (e.g., Knowledge, Comprehension, Application, Analysis, Synthesis, and Evaluation) were replaced with verbs (Remembering, Applying, Evaluating, etc.) and the last two categories were switched around (from Evaluation to Creating in the highest category).

However, a more significant change involved the addition of four knowledge dimensions that Bloom had originally included but which had not been used or understood by educators throughout the years (Anderson & Krathwohl, 2001). Designed as a two dimension format, the inclusion of the knowledge dimension allows instructors to see that learning is not just limited to one level of thinking.

Cognitive Process Domain							
		Remember	Understand	Apply	Analyze	Evaluate	Create
	Factual						
	Conceptual						
	Procedural						
	Meta-cognitive						

(Left vertical label: Knowledge Dimension)

It is not the aim of this handbook to delve into a deep explanation and analysis of the knowledge dimension (please consult Anderson Krathwahls' 2001 book called *A Taxonomy for Learning, Teaching and Assessing: A Revision of Bloom's Taxonomy of Bloom's Educational Objectives*—a very helpful book), but the following examples will highlight how good questions can be created across the knowledge dimensions.

Factual Knowledge: *The facts, definitions, key terms, specific details, and information that students must know to understand the discipline or solve a problem.*
For example, asking a question about

- Remembering + factual knowledge = the list of the materials required for an experiment

- Evaluating + factual knowledge = ranking performance of each material from experiment

Conceptual Knowledge: *The relationships amongst the basic knowledge of the discipline including classifications, principles, generalizations, theories, models, or structures*
For example, asking a question about

- Understanding + conceptual knowledge = the interpretation about the symbolism in the story

- Creating + conceptual knowledge = designing a new character to fit into the structure of novel

Procedural Knowledge: *The knowledge about how to do something, the process of inquiry, the use of algorithms and techniques, and the processes around using them.*
For example, asking a question about

- Applying + procedural knowledge = calculating an answer based on using proper formula

- Analyzing + procedural knowledge = show differences in results when you use formula X vs. Y

The following pages outline the six cognitive process dimensions of Revised Bloom's Taxonomy. While some subject-specific examples are included, a series of "cooking" related sample questions are also given to present a non-educational example for ease in understanding.

Remembering   Basic Recall of Facts/Knowledge – Often a short answer

 At this level, you ask basic questions about identification and recall of information such as knowledge of events, places, dates, and major ideas. The questions are very simple in that they merely ask for the students to remember a fact or piece of data. Instructors may use this type of question to ensure students know the underlying key points.

Questions may include the words "list, define, tell, identify, label, examine, tabulate, quote, name, who, when, where," and so on.

Sample Questions:

Cooking Example:
- What is the name of this recipe?
- How many ingredients are there in this recipe?
- Name all the ingredients.

Other Examples:
- What year did _____ happen?
- How many people were affected by _____?
- Name the person who_____.
- What is the definition of _____?
- List all the authors who wrote about _____.

Understanding   Understanding facts – Short sentence answer

 At this level, you ask questions about how well students understand information. It is a step above just recalling simple facts. This level asks students to demonstrate comprehension of a concept, show understanding of the order, organization, or process of information, etc. Instructors use this type of question to ensure students have grasped a procedure or a concept. Having students rephrase concepts in their own words leads to greater understanding.

Questions may include the words "summarize, describe, interpret, contrast, predict, associate, distinguish, estimate, differentiate, discuss, extend," and so on.

Sample Questions:

Cooking Example:
- What do you need to do first to make this recipe?
- Summarize in your own words what this recipe is about?
- Predict how long this recipe will take to make?
- Describe the texture of the batter.

Other Examples:
- Retell _____ in your own words.
- What is the main idea of _____?
- Predict what will happen after_____.

Applying

> Applying knowledge of facts, principles to an example – showing you understand by doing.

At this level, you ask questions which involve applying new information /data /details to already given formulas, concepts, or situations. Students are being asked to solve problems using required skills and knowledge to determine if they can apply their learning. This level also has questions that ask students to show reasoning and demonstration of basic concepts.

Questions may include the words "apply, demonstrate, calculate, complete, illustrate, show, solve, examine, modify, relate, change, experiment, discover," and so on.

Sample Questions:

Cooking Example:
- Why is baking powder an important ingredient?
- Why do we preheat the oven?
- How do we measure liquids?
- If we doubled the recipe, how many cookies would we have?

Other Examples:
- How is _____ an example of _____?
- Using the new information and the formulas given, determine the amounts now required for this experiment.
- If you had a situation with half the costs, what would the formula look like?

Analyzing

> Breaking down whole into parts, analyzing parts, comparing one to another (charts, tables, graphs)

At this level, you ask questions about the subdivision of a whole into component parts. You want to know if students see patterns, can identify components, are able to categorize information into separate areas, can compare and contrast data, etc.

Questions may include the words "analyze, separate, order, explain, connect, classify, arrange, divide, compare, select, explain, infer," and so on.

Sample Questions:
Cooking Example:
- Classify all the dry ingredients in one column and all the wet ingredients in another column.
- How does this recipe compare to this one?

Other Examples:
- What are the parts or features of _____?
- Classify _____ according to _____?
- How does _____ compare/contrast with _____?

Evaluating (Making decisions, judgments and evaluations – usually longer answers)

 At this level, you ask questions about students' opinions judgments, or decisions. You want students to compare and discriminate between ideas, assess value of theories, make choices based on evidence, and be able to recognize subjectivity.

Questions may include the words "assess, decide, rank, grade, test, measure, recommend, convince, select, judge, explain, discriminate, support, conclude, compare, summarize," and so on.

Sample Questions:

Cooking Example:

- Rate these three recipes in terms of taste?
- Which recipe would you select to make from this list of winning recipes? Why?
- What criteria are important to you in rating the chefs' meals?
- Convince the panel that your recipe is the best.

Other Examples:

- Do you agree _____?
- What do you think about _____?
- What is the most important _____?
- Prioritize _____ according to _____.
- How would you decide about _____?
- What criteria would you use to assess _____?

Creating (Adding new ideas and information and considering the outcome – usually longer answers)

 At this level you ask questions about using old ideas to create new ideas. You want to know if students can design, postulate, hypothesize, or generalize about something based on a new situation, new materials, new plans, etc.

Questions may include the words "combine, integrate, modify, rearrange, substitute, plan, create, design, invent, what if, compose, formulate, prepare," and so on.

Sample Questions:

Cooking Example:

- If you didn't have any eggs in the house, what might you substitute?
- What solutions might you suggest for a cake that doesn't rise?
- Instead of using bananas, could you use another fruit?
- Is it possible to design a new recipe that produces a similar product

Other Examples:

- What would you infer from _____?
- What ideas can you add to _____?
- How would you create/design a new ____?
- What might happen if you combined ____ with ___?
- What solutions would you suggest for _____?

E. Matching Questions to Bloom Level

Activity: Read each sample question and decide which of the following 6 cognitive domains of Bloom's Revised Taxonomy you would appoint to that question? See bottom of page for answers.

Remembering   Understanding   Applying   Analyzing   Evaluating   Creating

Lower Order Thinking Skills   **Higher Order Thinking Skills**

#	Question	Bloom Level
1	How would you rank, in terms of accuracy, the three responses just given by your classmates?	
2	Describe, in your own words, how you focus a microscope.	
3	By comparing heterogeneous and homogenous mixtures, what are the similarities and differences?	
4	What kinds of graphs can a spreadsheet produce?	
5	How would you redesign the pasta bridge so that there isn't as much sagging in the middle and there is a stronger truss system on the top?	
6	Why do you feel that answer B is correct? Explain your thinking.	
7	Who was the inventor of insulin?	
8	Categorize all the characters in the story into two columns A. Characters who have a direct impact on story outcome OR B. Characters who have an indirect impact on story outcome	
9	What new thoughts can you add to the answers already given about why we need to study this topic?	
10	How do you solve this formula using the new data given?	

Answers: 1) Evaluating; 2) Understanding; 3) Analyzing; 4) Remembering; 5) Creating; 6) Evaluating; 7) Remembering; 8) Analyzing 9) Creating; 10) Applying

F. Varying Your Questions Using the Questioning Matrix

Another format for considering the creation of questions is the use of the 'Questioning Matrix' or 'Q-Matrix' as seen on the following page. It is a grid with two-word-question-starters that encompasses lower order to higher order thinking categories.

Steps to Using the Q-Matrix:

1. **Identify** the level of thinking (as related to Bloom's Revised Taxonomy) you want your question to elicit. For example:

   - "remembering and understanding" word pairs – upper left portion of matrix

   - "evaluating and creating" word pairs – lower right portion of matrix

   - As you move from the "What is?" (upper left portion of matrix) to "How Might?" (lower right portion) ….you are moving toward questions which require **more in-depth** thinking

2. **Consider** the "**subject**" of the question versus the "**process**" of the question.

   - The **horizontal items** represent the **subject** of the question *(event, situation, choice, person, reason, means)*

   - The **vertical items** represent the **process** *(present, past, possibility, probability, prediction, imagination)*

3. **Choose the word pair and use them** in your question followed by the appropriate content.

   - Example—Begin question with the pair of words "What might"
     - **What might** be the best way to solve this problem?

   - Example—Embed pair of words within question "What might"
     - Of all the solutions we've discussed, **what might** provide the best solution for being environmentally conscious?

Quadrant Version of Matrix:

The matrix could be also viewed as broken into 4 distinct quadrants (top left 9 squares, top right 9 squares, bottom left 9 squares, bottom right 9 squares). It might be easier to visualize the levels of thinking better by seeing the distinct quadrants as they relate to Bloom's Revised Taxonomy. See shaded quadrants.

- Top Left 9 squares would be Remembering and Understanding (e.g., What Is? Where/When Is? Which Did? Which Can?)

- Bottom Right 9 squares would be Creating and Evaluating (e.g., Who Would? Why Would? Why Will? Why Might? How Might?)

- Those quadrants in between are a combination of the lower and higher order categories.

Questioning/Q-Matrix

Subject → Event ↓	Event	Situation	Choice	Person	Reason	Means
Present	What Is?	Where/ When Is?	Which Is?	Who Is?	Why Is?	How Is?
Past	What Did?	Where/ When Did?	Which Did?	Who Did?	Why Did?	How Did?
Possibility	What Can?	Where/ When Can?	Which Can?	Who Can?	Why Can?	How Can?
Probability	What Would?	Where/ When Would?	Which Would?	Who Would?	Why Would?	How Would?
Prediction	What Will?	Where/ When Will?	Which Will?	Who Will?	Why Will?	How Will?
Imagination	What Might?	Where/ When Might?	Which Might?	Who Might?	Why Might?	How Might?

G. How to Ask Questions

1. Prepare Questions and Anticipated Responses Prior to Class

Preparing Questions: Take time to create well-constructed questions; you will be better prepared to conduct effective questioning. Consider composing a variety of questions. Types of questions can be labeled as follows:

- **Convergent** (narrow correct answer, answer is short, requires little thought and may be just recalled from memory) **vs. Divergent** (open-ended, requires a lot of thought to explain, analyze or further develop a situation, may have more than one answer)

- **Bloom's Revised Taxonomy** (from Low Order Thinking Skills: Remembering and Understanding to High Order Thinking Skills: Evaluating and Creating)

- **Questioning (Q) Matrix** (4 quadrants elicit various types of thinking) Use the question starters asking what, where, when, which, who, why, and how. As you work through the matrix, the questions become more complex and open-ended

- **Preparing Anticipated Responses:** If you take a few minutes to write down what responses you may expect from students, it will help you anticipate and respond to any answers. Anticipating student responses will allow you to prepare better prompts/probes to more fully engage students.

2. Ask the Question

Let students know when you are going to ask a question

- If you are lecturing/directing the learning, are you interjecting questions within your class? Or are you stopping and having a question period or a discussion?

- Students appreciate knowing when they can ask questions and when you are going to ask questions. Do you have an agenda for when questions are going to be posed or do they just appear as the class progresses?

- Will you write the question on the board or have it on a slide to be visible while the question is being asked? Sometimes having the question visible helps students concentrate and realize that their attention should be not on note-taking, but on thinking about the question.

Inform students of the expectations during questioning

- Should students have their books/laptops open or closed?

- Will they be able to think about it first, consult notes, or chat with a peer?

- Should they put up hand, write something down, or shout out the answer?

- Who are you going to choose? The first hand up, or will you wait for a few hands? If the class is in a large classroom, how loud do they need to speak?

- Is this part of participation mark? Are you grading them? Are you making notes on who responds and who doesn't?

3. Sequence Questions

- Start with easier/lower order questions so as not to intimidate students

- Sequence questions to allow each one to build on the previous one

- Give feedback as you go along with your questioning to indicate that they have achieved the correct response and that you are moving onto another question

- Avoid starting a class with a higher order question; you will likely get many students confused and afraid to try and answer later on

4. Employ Wait Time/Thinking Time

- Count 3-5 seconds after you ask the question. Dead air is tough to handle, but insist on giving students time to think

- Do not talk while you are waiting, ensure there is no noise. This will allow students to focus and to think about the question

5. After Asking A Question, Use Probes and Prompts

- If you are not getting any participation by the class or you feel your question may have been unclear, you may need to use a **prompt**

  - A prompt is a little 'hint' to get the students thinking about the answer

  - It could be a reference to something that you talked about in class, a reading they were to do, or something that is similar to the answer you are seeking

  - Prompts are good to use, as long as you use them sparingly and do not give away the answer. You are using a prompt to encourage more participation

- **Probes** are what you use to get a more detailed answer out of a student

  - A student may have just given a partial answer or a fairly close answer and you want to probe a bit further to see if they know more or if another student can build upon their answer

  - Probes are little questions that take what was given and request the students to think a bit deeper, a bit broader, or just expand on the answer that was given

6. Fairly Choose Students to Answer

Ensure you choose a **variety of students (gender, race, age, seating location, etc)** to be fair in your questioning. Often, without thinking, we choose the same students each class to answer questions because they are the ones with their hands up. We need to find ways to indicate that others will be called upon or that you'd like to see more engagement in the class. Using some of the wait time/think time techniques might help with more students responding, but ensure you choose a variety of students to answer each class.

7. Respond without Repeating

It sometimes is so natural to repeat a student's answer because you want to ensure everyone in the class heard it. Often this is just wasting time because everyone likely did hear the answer. It sometimes infers that the student did not articulate it well enough and you, the instructor, have to repeat it. Try to **refrain from repeating a student's answer and instead give positive feedback** on the answer, ask a probing second question, or build upon the answer with some additional information.

8. Have Students Create and Ask Questions

- Not all question-asking has to come from the instructor. You could ask different students each week to prepare a question for the next class.

- Having students feel comfortable enough to ask question in class is a sign of rapport between the instructor and the class

H. Using Wait Time for Thinking

The Facts

When you give students 3 or more seconds of quiet wait time/think time after a question has been posed (and after an answer has been given) these things might happen:

- The length of their responses increases

- The correctness of their responses may increase

- The number of "I don't know" or "no hands" responses decrease

- The number of students who choose to reply increases

- The scores on tests tend to increase

- Instructors tend to have more variety to their questioning

- Instructors decrease how many questions they ask and increase the quality (i.e., more higher order) questions

- Instructors tend to ask more follow up questions of students to engage learners in a dialogue about the question's concept (Cotton, 1988)

What does Wait-Time/Think-Time Look Like?

Tip: If the question is particularly challenging or has many words in it, post it on the board or on a slide. This will allow visual learners to read the question again and process it another way. Here are 3 ways to allow time for your students to think:

1. **Wait 3-5 seconds** (or more) **after you pose a question**.

    - Let your students know you are giving them time to think

    - Do not talk, do not repeat the question, do not make any noise to disturb thinking

- Try counting in your head or on your hands for assistance with waiting the full 3-5 seconds

- Keep eye contact with the students as this will let them know you are still there and are just waiting/giving them time to think

- Look at the class as if you are looking for responses and that you are not giving up on the question and moving on. Hands should begin to surface

2. Plan a "**think-pair-share**".

- Indicate to your students that you are going to give them 30 -60 seconds to think alone about the question first

- They can jot something down or consult their notes, but they must be silent

- After the minute is up, pair them up with a nearby classmate and ask them to share their thoughts on the question

- After a few minutes of sharing, ask for individual hands for a response to the question

3. Allow students to **discuss the question in a small group** (that you arrange or they arrange) for 2-3 minutes.

- Ask for individual hands or indicate that you are going to choose various people from within the groups

- Given that they have had time to discuss, they will be able to share the group's response and make a contribution to the discussion

I. Facilitating Discussions Through Questions

Many instructors have anxiety about facilitating discussions in their courses:

- What if no one replies?

- How will I keep the discussion going if there isn't interest?

- What if a student says an inappropriate comment? How will I get the class back on track?

- What if the discussion doesn't go the way I intend it to go? How do I keep the discussion focused?

- How do I handle a discussion with so many in a class? Everyone won't be able to speak.

- What if students speak so softly that I have to repeat answers?

- Maybe my students will be too shy to put up their hands and speak.

Facilitating a discussion isn't an easy task, but it does get better with experience. In the first place, you have to be sure having a discussion will benefit student learning. Sometimes instructors do not properly prepare their class for a discussion and things then tend to fall apart. Here are a few tips for facilitating a discussion in any class and with any number of students.

1. **Plan for Enough Time to Have a Discussion.** This means setting aside adequate time within the class to get enough responses to warrant a good discussion.

2. **Prepare Students.** Ensure you give material for students to read, reflect, and consider prior to the discussion. You will have a much richer discussion if students are prepared to participate. Give them some sample questions you will be asking and suggest they formulate some possible answers prior to class. If students have time to think about the content, they are more likely to participate with worthy answers than if a discussion arises unexpectedly.

3. **Warm Up**. Often starting a discussion in class, even if students have been prepared, is akin to inertia. You have to get the ball rolling somehow. Try posting the first question on the board/slide and asking students to talk about the answer in small groups (4-5 students) first. This will get them thinking about various answers. Many students are not comfortable putting their hands up in large groups. Allowing them to share within a small group first might give them more confidence to share.

4. **Set Guidelines.** Indicate how you are going to facilitate the discussion. Consider the following: How long will the discussion go? What sorts of questions will you pose? How will you choose people to participate? Can students just shout out the answers? Will you be providing feedback? If you don't know all their names, how will you be choosing students (e.g., will you ask them to state their name first?) Let the students know the answers to these questions so they know the parameters of the discussion.

5. **Assessment or Evaluation?** Consider the following: Will you be marking student participation for grades? How will you be able to give participation marks with large classes if you don't know all their names? Will this be part of your assessment of students? Will the discussion shed light on answers for a mid-term or an exam? Is there impetus for the students to attend? You need to consider these answers to ensure students know what/how their participation affects their grades and/or their understanding of content. Be honest and up front with them.

6. **Problems? How do you deal with inappropriate comments?** Certainly this is bound to happen and your expression/reaction dictates the outcome and class reaction. The simplest answer is to just indicate that the comment was inappropriate and not give it any more 'airtime'. Students who make inappropriate comments are often looking for attention. The more attention you give them or the topic/situation the more you are playing their game.

7. **How do you end the discussion?** Sometimes good discussions can go on beyond your allotted time. This may be a good thing if the discussion helped clarify content and students were engaged. The loss of the rest of the class can be compensated by the fact that you were engaging your students and they were enjoying the discussion. Maybe this might lead to having more discussions to build on their enthusiasm. However, you need to end a discussion at some point. If there is an online component to your course, allow students to continue the discussion online. You could also indicate that you'll continue the discussion the next class or you may just say that the discussion is done and move on.

Top Ten Takeaways

1. **Purposes:** Questions serve many purposes from introducing a topic to assessing students' understanding of material. Consider how you use questions in your class.

2. **Compose Questions Beforehand:** Take time to compose thought-provoking questions before class. Often, good questions are not easy to think of on the spur of the moment. Anticipate student's answers so you can probe better.

3. **Ask a Variety of Questions:** Vary your questions from lower order to higher order thinking (or convergent to divergent) questions by using Bloom's Taxonomy or the Q-Matrix chart.

4. **Lower Order Questions:** They ask students to remember, understand, and apply their knowledge to learned content. They are good to use when trying to get student feedback on the understanding of basic concepts.

5. **Higher Order Questions:** They ask students to analyze, evaluate, and create new answers based on content. They are good to use when you trying to get deeper student answers that contain rationalizing, synthesizing of new material, and making informed judgments.

6. **Questioning (Q) Matrix:** Use this chart with its easy-to-use 'question starters'. Put the chart beside you while you are teaching to easily access for composing a variety of questions.

7. **Use More Higher Order Questions:** Instructors need to ask a lot of higher order questions as this is the only way students can get practice with critical thinking skills. Ask at least one higher order thinking question a class.

8. **Employ Wait Time!** Count 3-5 seconds after you ask a question to allow students time to think and compose an answer. Do not talk or rephrase the question during this time. Increasing 'wait time/think time' allows students to process questions and think of better responses. Aim to add more wait time into your teaching.

9. **Small Group Discussion First:** Consider giving students time, in small groups, to think and discuss a question before you ask for answers. Allow students time to chat amongst themselves as this gives them time to process the question.

10. **Plan Discussions:** Set the parameters of how a discussion is going to happen, how you will ask for responses, and how you will manage the time.

Next Steps

1. Consider a class topic. Compose a couple of lower order and a couple of higher order questions on the topic, along with anticipated responses.

2. Next class, tell your students you are going to give them a longer time to think after you ask a question. Count for 3-5 seconds (or more) and see what kind of response you get.

3. Look at some of the questions you normally ask. Categorize a few of them according to Bloom's Revised Taxonomy. Do you vary your questions or ask thought-provoking questions already?

4. Give students a couple of the questions you will be asking them the next class. Give it to them in digital form or have them copy the questions off the board.

5. Ask colleagues how they handle questioning in their class. You might get a few ideas about how to better ask questions related to your discipline.

References and Resources

Anderson, L.W. & Krathwohl, D. R. (Eds.) (2001). *A taxonomy for learning, teaching and assessing: A revision of Bloom's taxonomy of educational objectives.* New York, NY: Longman.

Bloom, B.S. (1984). T*axonomy of educational objectives. Book I: Cognitive domain* (revised edition). New York, NY: Longman.

Cotton, K. (1988). *Classroom Questioning.* Northwest Regional Educational Laboratory (NWREL). Retrieved November 12, 2008, from http://www.learner.org/workshops/socialstudies/pdf/session6/6.ClassroomQuestioning.pdf

McComas, W. F, & Abraham, L. (2004). *Asking More Effective Questions.* Retrieved May 22, 2009, from http://cet.usc.edu/resources/teaching_learning/docs/Asking_Better_Questions.pdf

Stahl, R. J. (1994). Using "Think-Time" and "Wait-Time" Skillfully in the Classroom. *Eric Digest.* Retrieved May 12, 2009, from http://www.ericdigests.org/1995-1/think.htm

Chapter 13: Writing Well-Constructed Test Questions

Chapter Overview

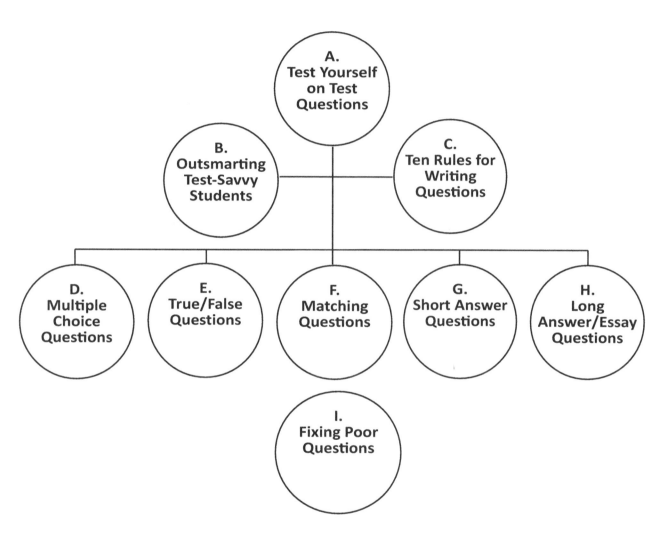

Mid-terms, tests, and final exams have a huge role in education. They provide instructors with a means to formally evaluate knowledge and application of content. Most instructors tend to rely on textbook question-banks or use questions from web sites. Instructors also create their own questions gathered from years of teaching experience. Many instructors are unaware of guiding principles in constructing proper questions. When workshops are offered on 'test construction' specifics, instructors are often amazed at how many errors exist in their questions. One research study found a statistical significant drop of up to 25 percentage points in the marks of students who answered flawed multiple choice questions (Downing et al., 1995). When we so drastically affect the validity and reliability of student assessment, it is imperative that test questions are well-written. This chapter addresses the principles and guidelines that many agree form the basis of writing good test questions.

A. Test Yourself on Test Questions

Activity: This is a fun self-assessment to answer before you progress further in the chapter. Answers are at the bottom of the page.

1. Objective questions encourage guessing more than essay questions.   T   F

2. Circling answers in true-false questions is better than writing the words.   T   F

3. It is best to use lower case letters a. b. c and d. (vs. CAPITALS – A. B. C. D.) for multiple choice questions.   T   F

4. The following are examples of words that should be avoided in true-false and multiple choice questions: "all", "none", "never", "sometimes", "generally", and "often".   T   F

5. It is nice to include a 'fun' or 'out there' answer for a multiple choice question.   T   F

6. According to students, which answer best summarizes their thoughts on length of multiple choice answers as a way to take tests.
   A. The longer and more descriptive answers are often the most correct.
   B. The shortest answers are often the most correct.
   C. Students don't have any thoughts on the length of answers in multiple choice.
   D. The medium length answers are often the most correct.

7. Put blanks at the _____ of the statement rather than the _____.

8. Below are four test item categories labeled A, B, C, or D. Following these test item categories are sample learning objectives. On the line to the left of each learning objective, place the letter of the most appropriate test item.
   A. = Objective Test Item (multiple choice, true-false, matching questions)
   B. = Performance Test Item (something a student has to do in person)
   C. = Long Essay Test Item (e.g., extended response)
   D. = Short Essay/Short Answer Test Item (e.g., short reply)

_____1. Name the parts of the human skeleton   _____2. Demonstrate safe laboratory skills   _____3. Cite four examples of satire that Twain uses in Huckleberry Finn

_____4. Describe the impact of a bull market   _____5. Diagnose a physical ailment   _____6. List important mental attributes necessary for an athlete

_____7. Categorize noteworthy Canadian authors   _____8. Analyze the major causes of learning disabilities   _____9. Match business definitions to correct terms.

Answers: 1. T; 2. T; 3. F; 4. T; 5. F; 6. A; 7 end, beginning; 8-1 A; 8-2 B; 8-3 D; 8-4 D; 8-5 B, C; 8-6 D; 8-7 A; 8-8 C; 8-9 A

B. Outsmarting Test-Savvy Students

When students do not properly study for tests, they often resort to test-taking rules and strategies for multiple choice questions. They may score accurately, but it does not mean they know the material. Outsmart your test-savvy students and respond with your well-constructed questions.

Student Test-Taking Secrets	How to Outsmart Students
If in doubt, pick "C"	Ensure you vary the correct response equally throughout all multiple choice questions
Choose "All of the Above"	Ensure you only use 'all of the above' only when it is absolutely necessary and vary it being the correct response
Choose "None of the Above"	Ensure you only use 'none of the above' only when it is absolutely necessary and vary it being the correct response
Pick the longest answer	Ensure you make all of your choices relatively equal in length
Never pick A – the professor will never put the correct answer as the first choice	Ensure you vary the correct response equally throughout all multiple choice questions
Do not pick a choice that has the words "always" or "never" in them	Since "always" and "never" indicate that the answer is likely incorrect, avoid using these words
Look for a choice that has vague words in it like "maybe", "usually", "typically" or "sometimes"	Since these words indicate that the answer is likely correct, avoid using these words or use similar words in all the choices
If you see words that you learned in class that are more technical in nature, choose that answer.	Use a variety of words in all choices
Never pick an answer that is too easy or simple – a professor will never give an answer away.	Sometimes make the simplest answers the correct ones
If in doubt, conduct a process of elimination. Remove any answers that are just too far-fetched to be true. You should have two choices to guess.	Never include far-fetched answers as choices and ensure all choices are equally plausible. If the student has studied they will see the correct answer immediately

C. Ten Basic Rules for Writing Effective Test Questions

Rule 1: Avoid confusing questions that create uncertainty about what is being asked.

All but one of the following is not a perennial plant. Which one is not?

A. Hosta
B. Coneflower   (Poor Question)
C. Day Lilly
D. Petunia

Which of the following is <u>not</u> a perennial plant?

A. Hosta
B. Coneflower
C. Day Lilly   (Better Question)
D. Petunia

Rule 2: Consider question type and level of thinking for students. Vary your questions to allow students a variety of ways to express answers.

Thinking Skills	Best Question Type
Remembering/Understanding (Facts, Events, Places, Dates, Terms, Definitions, Timelines etc.) – fairly low levels of thinking which involve short answers that may heavily rely on memorization	Multiple-Choice, True-False, Matching
Applying/Analyzing (Solving problems using rules and principles, Applying new information, Comparing, Contrasting, Connecting and Classifying) – some good levels of thinking which involve taking knowledge and applying it to new situations	Multiple-Choice, Matching, Short Answer, Long Answer
Evaluating/Creating (Developing new ideas, Ranking and Verifying choices, Making decisions, Designing new information) – high levels of thinking which involve going beyond what was taught	Long Answer

Rule 3: Ensure your questions have one definitive answer.

In what movie did Brad Pitt star?_____   (Poor Question)

What is the name of the lead male star from the movie
Mr. and Mrs. Smith?_____   (Better Question)

Rule 4: Keep questions short and to the point. Avoid extraneous details; focus on the intent of the question and the required information.

Megan and Eric were in the market for a condo rental down by the waterfront. The rental came in at $2075 per month plus utilities. It was a beautiful 9th floor unit in a two-year-old building with hardwood floors and floor-to-ceiling glass windows. Utilities would be equal to 15 percent of the rent cost and would include electricity, water/sewage, and natural gas. The air conditioner works off electricity but the nice new stove is gas. If Megan brings home $2000 net a month and Eric brings home $1600 net, what would each be contributing to the rent cost and utilities if they were splitting the costs.

   A. $1193.13
   B. $1203.55   (Poor Question)
   C. $1312.13
   D. $1332.15

Megan and Eric found a condo to rent for $2075 per month plus utilities. Utilities would be equal to 15 percent of the rent cost. What would each be contributing to the rent cost and utilities if they were splitting the costs?

   A. $1193.13
   B. $1203.55   (Better Question)
   C. $1312.13
   D. $1332.15

Rule 5: For long answer/essay questions, give information about the nature of the desired answer and related marks so students are clear and know what to provide in terms of an answer.

(Poor Question)

Why should students study science?

Describe three reasons students should study science. Provide one   (Better Question)
example to support each reason. 8 marks (1 mark per reason; 1 mark
per example; 2 marks for overall quality of written explanation)

Rule 6: Avoid grammatical clues that give away answers.

1. The sea creature which has eight legs is called an_____

   A. Sea Anemone
   B. Mussel   (Poor Question)
   C. Lobster
   D. Octopus

2. Compared to cars of the 1970s, cars in the 2000s _____.

   A. silver is the most popular color.
   B. smaller in size.   (Poor Question)
   C. to use more fuel.
   D. are more likely to be fuel efficient.

1. What do we call the sea creature that has eight legs?

    A. Sea Anemone

    B. Mussel   (Better Question)

    C. Lobster

    D. Octopus

2. When you compare cars of the 1970s to cars of today, what statement would be true?

    A. Cars built in the 2000s are likely to olive green or baby blue in color.

    B. Cars built in the 1970s are likely to be more fuel efficient.   (Better Question)

    C. Cars built in the 2000s are likely to be smaller and more fuel efficient.

    D. Cars built in the 1970s are likely to be silver in color.

Rule 7: Create questions that test for content and do not confuse.

According the food guide for proper eating, which of the following answers is what the food guide would say?

    A. Eat lots of fruits and vegetables every day.   (Poor Question)

    B. Eat meat (or substitutes) in moderate proportion.

    C. Avoid eating a lot of meat; but ensure you get your protein.

    D. A and B

    E. A, B or C

    F. A and C but not B

According to the food guide, which is the best answer about how to eat properly?

    A. Eat lots of fruits and vegetables every day.

    B. Eat lots of red meat.   (Better Question)

    C. Eat lots of breads, buns and desserts.

    D. Eat lots of cheese, eggs and frozen food.

Rule 8: Leave enough space for students to write answer.

Always give students enough room to write short and long answer responses. While trying to save trees by cramming questions on as few pages as possible, sometimes we do a huge disservice to students by not providing them with enough room to write the answer. Especially if students have larger printing/handwriting we are not being fair if we don't give them enough room to properly answer the question.

Rule 9: Put page numbers (page x of y) on all pages and label sub-sections.

By including page numbers at the bottom of your tests and exams you are allowing students to see if the photocopying process worked accurately. Many times a page or two gets missed in the collating process and this would be a bad situation to find out once the test is over. Additionally, label all sub-sections so students can see the breakdown of the test or exam and are able to gauge their time and attention to certain sections based on the total marks for that section, the type of questions in that section, or the topic of the questions.

Rule 10: Layout your test with adequate white space and proper font size.

When you are done putting all the questions together in a document, consider the font size and amount of white space used. Using too small a font size (10 point or lower) may hinder some students who have vision difficulties. Shrinking margins and trying to cram too many questions on a page—without enough white space—will actually decrease the readability of your tests and exams and cause problems for all students in being able to read and process each question. Adding just an extra line of space between questions, or increasing to 11 or 12-point font size or increasing margins (1 -1.5 inches) will greatly increase readability for all.

Poor Test Layout   Name:____
This is a small example of how a test can be too jammed.
Question 1: XXXXXXXXXXXXXXXXXX
XXXXXXXXXXXX
Answer:
Question 2:YYYYYYYYYYYYYYYYYYYYY
YYYYYYYYYYYYYYY
Answer:
Question 2:ZZZZZZZZZZZZZZZZZZZZZ
ZZZZZZZZZZZZZZZZZZZZZZZZZZZZZZ
Answer:

Better Test Layout   Name:____

This is a small example of how a test can be designed better.

**Question 1: XXXXXXXXXXXXXXXXX
XXXXXXXXX**

Answer:

**Question 2: YYYYYYYYYYYYYYYYYYY
YYYYYYYYYYYYYYYYYYYYYYYYYYY**

Answer:

D. Multiple Choice Questions

Advances in medicine; A. have happened because of improved knowledge,   b. are costly, c. increasing rates of diagnoses of cancer,   d. third world countries are benefiting, e. both a and c,   f. none of the above.

(Poor Question)

Which of the following is the best answer about the advances currently being made in medicine?

    A. More people are getting sicker.
    B. More people are getting proper treatment for diseases.
    C. Fewer people are living.
    D. More people in third world countries are isolated from health care.

(Better Question)

Multiple choice questions are very good for short item recall or factual questions. However, with some thought, instructors can write well-constructed multiple choice questions that can involve applying knowledge of formulas, principles, and laws to problems and mathematical questions. Additionally, short scenarios can be written where students have to rationalize, evaluate, and think on a higher level to make a choice among a variety of solutions, next steps, or diagnoses. While easy to mark, creating well-constructed multiple choice questions takes a long time.

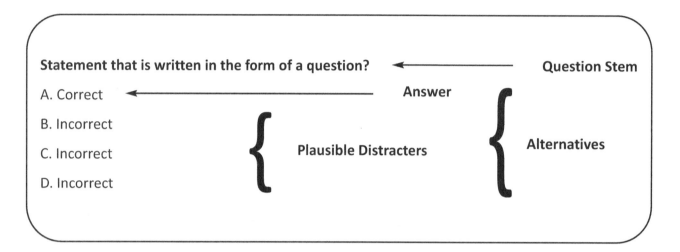

Fifteen Tips for Writing Proper Multiple Choice Items

1. The stem of the question should clearly indicate what the student is to do (e.g., identify the best answer, find the most recent accomplishment, identify the answer with the best order of events, etc.). Often, poorly worded questions do not clearly state what the student is to do.

2. Use the words 'best answer' rather than 'most correct answer' as there may be exceptions and this phrasing will avoid any arguments.

3. The stem should be in the form of a question and be worded positively if possible. Irrelevant material should be avoided.

4. Use capital letters (A. B. C. D.) rather than lower case letters (e.g., "a" gets confused with "d" and "c" with "a" for those with vision problems, poor photocopying, dyslexia, etc.)

5. Construct four suggested choices (alternatives). Research indicates 4-5 are a good number.

6. One alternative is the correct answer. This answer has to be clearly the best or only answer.

7. Three alternatives are incorrect or inferior alternatives (distracters). The purpose of the distracters is to appear as plausible solutions for those students who did not study. Do not use absurd or fun distracters as they would just give away the answer or make is far easier to guess from fewer plausible choices. Try to make all the distracters as closely related as possible. This is the most challenging part of creating multiple choice questions.

8. Make all responses fairly equal in length. Avoid making the correct response either the longest or the shortest in length.

9. Put options in a logical order, if possible. (e.g., alphabetical, chronological).

10. Make sure all the grammar, punctuation, and spelling are correct.

11. Avoid grammatical clues to the answer (e.g. an, a – which indicate a vowel/non-vowel word)

12. If "no" or "not" is used, underline it. Try to avoid using negative constructions in the stem.

13. Try to avoid using "all of the above" and use "none of the above" sparingly.

14. Avoid using the words "never, all, none, always" (they often indicate an incorrect response) and words such as "often, seldom, sometimes" (they often indicate a correct response).

15. Place the correct answer in each possible position equally often.

E. True-False Test Questions

Traffic congestion can be a result of drivers taking their eyes off the road for a short period of time and having to hit the brakes. Write the word true or false for this statement. _____

(Poor Question)

Instructions: Circle either T (True) or F (False) for the statement.

(Better Question)

Traffic congestion can be a result of drivers taking their eyes off the road for a short period of time and having to hit the brakes.   T   F

True or false questions are useful when the objective is to test whether students are able to evaluate the correctness/truthfulness of an assumption. True or false questions are also good for evaluating student understanding of popular misconceptions and misunderstandings.

Seven Tips for Writing Proper True-False Items

1. Make items absolutely true or absolutely false. There should be no possible challenge to the statements being true or false.

2. Avoid the words "all, always, never" as they can be dead giveaways for false items.

3. Avoid using the words "sometimes, maybe, fairly", etc. as these words often are giveaways for true items.

4. Make each statement roughly about the same length as much as you can.

5. Restrict each statement to a single idea. If there is more than one item in a statement, the student does not know what to indicate as 'true or false'.

6. Avoid long and complex statements. Keep sentences short and to the point.

7. Make more false than true (60/40) as students are more likely to answer true.

F. Matching Test Items

Directions: On each numbered line in Column A, print the letter (A, B, C, etc.) matching to the correct capital city from Column B. Each choice in Column B can only be used once. There are more choices in Column B than are required.

Column A	Column B
_____1. Czech Republic	A. Berlin
_____2. Denmark	B. Brussels
_____3. Finland	C. Budapest
_____4. Germany	D. Copenhagen
_____5. Hungary	E. Helsinki
_____6. Sweden	F. Prague
	G. Stockholm
	H. Vienna

Matching items are used to measure a student's understanding of the relationship between two sets of items. There should only be one answer for each in column A. Matching questions are great for testing students' abilities to analyze, categorize, compare, find similarities and differences, etc.

Ten Tips for Writing Proper Matching Items

1. Compare things that are similar. Do not include items from another topic/strand/concept as this decreases the effectiveness of the question.

2. All answers in Column B should be plausible or possible answers for the choices in Column A. In this way, someone who has studied is being tested for their knowledge and not for guessing.

3. Keep items in both columns short (a word, few words, or a short phrase).

4. Provide a few extra answers in Column B to avoid the final option being the correct answer by default. This will prevent students from guessing through elimination of remaining responses.

5. Make sure the directions are clear and state the relationship of both columns. Also remind students that there are extra answers and only each answer is used once (if that is the case).

Indicate where the students should place their answers (e.g., on lines, in another area of the test, etc.) to make marking easier.

6.   Arrange the lists in alphabetical or chronological order so that students do not think you have some secret reason why they are arranged.

7.   Ensure that all matching items appear on the same page to help with reading and comprehension of the question.

8.   Number one set of items (e.g., 1, 2, 3) and mark the other set with letters (e.g., A, B, C).

9.   Use 6-10 items in column A. After 10 items, the matching exercise just gets out of hand.

10. You can use graphical images in either column or have one large diagram students need to label given a set of choices.

G. Short Answer/Fill in the Blank Test Items

List all the reasons why leaves turn color.   (Poor Question)

Indicate two (2) main factors that are at work in changing
the color of deciduous tree leaves in autumn.   (Better Question)

Four Tips for Writing Proper Short Answer/Fill-in-the-Blank Items

1.   Questions must be clearly worded so that students understand what is being asked of them.

2.   Ensure the question can be answered in a few sentences or short phrases.

3.   When asking math questions, ensure you give details as to how specific the answer should be. For example, are units of measurement expected, how many decimal points should be shown?

4.   If using a 'fill-in-the-blanks' question, always put the blanks toward the end of the sentence. No more than 1-2 blanks per sentence. Ensure each blank (the line that signifies the blank) is equal in length so as to not give away clues to answer.

H. Long Answer/Essay Questions

Discuss global warming. (12 marks)   (Poor Question)

Discuss the current situation of global warming with respect to **three areas**
(**economical impacts, political involvements, and scientific advances**).   (Better Question)
Each area should include at least **3 examples**. Ensure you conclude with **2
personal thoughts** about your own efforts for global warming. (Total Marks = 12;
1 mark per each example, 1 mark per each personal thought + 1 mark for spelling/grammar).

Essays or longer answers are useful for addressing higher levels of thinking from students. They can also provide insights into writing ability and the ability to process information.

Eight Tips for Writing Proper Essay Items

1. Use several short essay questions rather than one long one.

2. Provide a clear focus of the desired outcome of the essay. Make questions specific with a clear marking scheme for students to see where their efforts should be focused.

3. Do not create essay questions that require a great deal of memory, as you likely want students thinking at a higher level in terms of concepts and content.

4. Aid students by focusing them with terms such as "state and defend the topic", "compare", "contrast", "explain why", "apply the principle to", "develop a valid conclusion", and so on. These kinds of instructions focus students and also help to focus the grading. Avoid starting questions with "what", "who", "when", and "list". These types of things are better measured with multiple choice questions.

5. If answers will be graded in other areas (e.g., grammar, punctuation, organization, etc.) as well as content, be sure to be clear about this in the instructions or marking scheme.

6. Include a few sentences to set the stage and introduce the question.

7. Require students to demonstrate complete understanding by specifying that answers include supporting evidence for any assertions they make.

8. Develop a scoring rubric for essay questions such as a checklist point system.

I. Fixing Poor Test Items

Activity: **Can you find the mistakes in the following questions?** Browse through the chapter for the answers to these questions.

1. Rhode Island the only state that does not have a border with Canada. T   F

2. Switzerland_____
   A. is located in northern Europe.
   B. produces large quantities of snow.
   C. has no direct access to the ocean.
   D. is a flat, arid plain.

3. The _____ produced by the _____ is used by the _____ to make maple syrup.

4. Who is Angelina Jolie? _____

5. Match the correct phrase in Column A with the term in Column B. Write the number of the term in Column B on the line at the end of the correct phrase in Column A.

Column A
A. Type of flower _____
B. Poisonous snake _____
C. Capital city of Finland _____
D. Color of chlorophyll _____
E. Cooking spice _____

Column B
1. Cobra
2. Helsinki
3. Nutmeg
4. Green
5. Rose

6. Questions should not avoid using negatives none of the time. True or False

7. The correct question type for assessing remembering/recall of information is called a_____
   a. multiple choice question
   b. true-false question
   c. short answer question
   d. matching question

8. Washington, D.C. is the most important city in the United States.   T   F

9. The environment is very important to us. Discuss. (15 marks)

10. Which choice best describes the browsers available for searching the Internet?
    A. Internet Explorer, Firefox, and Google Chrome
    B. Internet Explorer, Firewood, Google Chrome, and Opera
    C. Internet Explorer, Firefox, Google Chrome, and Ballet
    D. Internet Experience, Google Chrome, and Opera

Top Ten Takeaways

1. **Writing Good Questions Takes Time:** The time you spend on writing good test questions will benefit you and your students!

2. **Question Banks:** Many questions from test banks, textbook test collections, and online test questions contain errors. It isn't always safe to rely on these types of questions for use with your students.

3. **Vary Questions Across Thinking Levels:** Consider the level of thinking and what you are expecting your students to demonstrate when you are choosing the type of question.

4. **Outsmart Test-Savvy Students:** Students have many test tips they will use when they are short on study time, and these tricks often work because test questions are poorly constructed. Try to outsmart these types of students by always writing questions that are well-constructed.

5. **Multiple Choice Questions:** They take the longest to write, but they are the fastest to score.

6. **Multiple Choice Question Format:** When writing multiple choice questions, it is best to provide three plausible distracters (possible answers) and one true answer. The distracters need to all look and seem correct. If a student has studied, the correct answer will jump out. If the student hasn't studied they will have a harder time of just guessing.

7. **True/False Questions:** When writing true/false questions, ensure the statement is clearly true or clearly false or you could open yourself to arguments and disagreements from students.

8. **Matching Questions:** When composing matching questions ensure that you have a few extra choices in one column to avoid students using process of elimination to match up all choices.

9. **Short Answer Questions:** When creating short answer questions, ensure that the question truly has a short answer (e.g., a few sentences or a phrases, mathematical calculation, etc.) and is not better in a longer answer format.

10. **Long Answer/Essay Questions:** When creating long answer/essay questions ensure you are clear with your expectations and provide a brief mark breakdown so students know what to write.

Next Steps

1. Locate a test or exam you frequently use.

2. Look at your multiple choice questions. Considering the suggested rules for properly constructing such questions, determine if any of your test questions could use a revision.

3. Look at any essay or long answer questions. Again, considering the suggested guidelines for long answer/essay questions, determine if your questions need a bit of work.

4. Practice writing a multiple choice question following most, if not all, of the guidelines.

5. If you can remember the questions that students tend to get wrong, determine if there is an error in the way the question was written. This may be the problem and not students' knowledge.

References and Resources

Airasian, P. W. (2005). *Classroom Assessment: Concepts and Applications*, 5th Edition. Boston College: New York.

Burton, S.J., Sudweeks, R. R., Merrill, P. F., and Wood, B. (1991). *How to Prepare Better Multiple-Choice Test Items: Guidelines for University Faculty*. Brigham Young University Teaching Services and The Department of Instructional Science. Retrieved October 1, 2008, from http://testing.byu.edu/info/handbooks/betteritems.pdf

Center for Teaching Excellence, University of Illinois at Urbana-Champaign. (no date). *Improving Your Test Questions*. Retrieved October 11, 2008, from http://cte.illinois.edu/testing/exam/test_ques.html

Clay, B. (2001). *Is This a Trick Question? A Short Guide to Writing Effective Test Questions*. Kansas Curriculum Centre. Retrieved, September 20, 2008, from http://www.ksde.org/LinkClick.aspx?fileticket=6PmcGOcdLB8%3D&tabid=1660&mid=8825

Devine, M. and Yaghlian, N. (2010). *Construction of objective tests*. Office of Instructional Support Retrieved December 11, 2010, from http://www.cte.cornell.edu/faculty/materials/TestConstructionManual.pdf

Downing, S. M., Baranowski, R. A., Grosso, L. J., & Norcinni, J. J. (1995). Item type and cognitive ability measured: the validity evidence for multiple true-false items in medical specialty certification. *Applied Measurement in Education, 8*, 189-199.

Frey, B. B., Peterson, S. Edwards, L.M., Teramoto Pedrotti, J and Peyton, V. (2005). Item-writing rules: Collective wisdom. *Teaching and Teacher Education, 21*, 357-364.

Haladyna, Thomas M., Downing, Steven M. and Rodriguez, Michael C. (2002). *A Review of Multiple-Choice Item-Writing Guidelines for Classroom Assessment. Applied Measurement in Education, 15*: 3, 309-333. Retrieved April 27, 2011, from http://dx.doi.org/10.1207/S15324818AME1503_5

Mandernach, B. J. (2003). *Developing Essay Items*. Retrieved October 12, 2008, from http://www.park.edu/cetl/quicktips/essay. html from Park University Faculty Development Quick Tips.

Mandernach, B. J. (2003). *Developing Short Answer Items*. Retrieved October 12, 2008, from http://www.park.edu/cetl/quicktips/shortanswer. html from Park University Faculty Development Quick Tips.

Mandernach, B. J. (2003). *Effective Multiple-Choice Items*. Retrieved October 12, 2008, from http://www.park.edu/cetl/quicktips/multiple. html from Park University Faculty Development Quick Tips.

Mandernach, B. J. (2003). *Writing Matching Items*. Retrieved October 12, 2008, from http://www.park.edu/cetl/quicktips/matching. html from Park University Faculty Development Quick Tips.

Murdock, J. (2006). *Basic tips for writing effective multiple choice questions (MCQ's): A compilation of most useful advice*. Retrieved September 12, 2008, from http://homes.chass.utoronto.ca/~murdockj/teaching/MCQ_basic_tips.pdf

Schuwirth, L.W.T. and van der Vleuten, C. P. M. (2003). ABC of learning and teaching in medicine. *British Medical Journal.* Retrieved October 11, 2008, from http://www.bmj.com/cgi/content/full/326/7390/643

The University of Tennessee at Chattanooga, (2003). *Designing Test Questions*. Retrieved November 3, 2008, from http://www.utc.edu/Administration/WalkerTeachingResourceCenter/FacultyDevelopment/Assessment/test-questions.html

Chapter 14: Designing Digital & Print Material

Chapter Overview

A. Digital and Print Material Examples

B. How We Access and Use Information

C. Basic Design Principles

D. Alternative Formats for Slide Presentations

E. Slide Design Tips

F. Handout Design Tips

G. Test Your Design Knowledge

At some point in a course, an instructor may create a slideshow presentation (with PowerPoint, Keynote or a similar product) or may create a handout. This chapter presents some basic tips for improving presentations or handouts by focusing on design principles that will aid students in learning.

Slideshow presentations are likely more common than handouts, but the design principles are the same and apply to both. Taking an extra 15 – 20 minutes to properly design your learning materials can greatly aid students in accessing information, reading with greater ease, and having a higher chance of using them again.

Most of this chapter is based on providing you with examples of how to progress from a poorly constructed slide or handout to a much improved one. Simple tips and tricks are included along the way.

A. Digital and Print Material Examples

Instructors use digital and print materials in many ways throughout a course. With the move to digitize more materials, almost any resource can be put online for students to download. Here is a concept map of five main uses of digital or print course materials. Examples are in the circles. This chapter will deal with basic design principles that will improve your materials so that students can learn with greater ease while accessing, reading, and processing information.

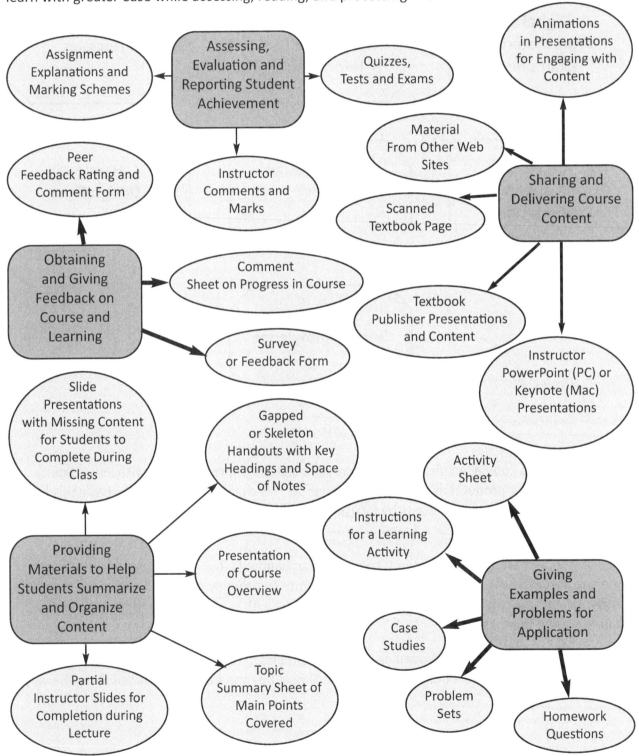

B. How We Access and Use Information

In our ever expanding world of information, we are getting very good at skimming and scanning digital and print materials to quickly access key details. No longer do we read every word or sentence or spend copious amounts of time on any one source. We consume information quickly. There is so much to consume that our heads often spin when trying to figure out where to start. Here is a chart of how society has adapted to the increase of digital information and how we process it today versus a decade or more ago.

Then	Now
Print dominated	Digital dominates
Good quantity of information available	Massive amounts of information available
Printed magazines, newspapers, and journals	Online databases accessing digital versions of newspapers, magazines, and journals
Physical exertion required – driving to libraries, bookstores, etc.	Little physical exertion required – click of a mouse to digital collections
Local – National access	International access
Sometimes a cost to access and use information	Often little or no cost to access and use information
Needed skills in locating information	Need skills in refining searches, using advanced search tools, finding specific information
More in depth coverage of content	Skimming and scanning of most content
Presentation and publishing of information done by graphical designers and publishers	Presentation and publishing of information done by anyone who can create a web page
Key skills: researching, writing, creating text	Key skills: synthesizing, distilling, filtering
Deep and concentrated reading	Surface and simultaneous reading
People had some spare time	People have little or no spare time
People had patience: willingness to wait for something	People have less patience: want things more immediately

C. Basic Design Principles

Below are six basic design principles that could apply to digital and print materials (e.g., handouts, tests, slideshow presentations, web pages, learning management system pages etc.).

1. **Preserve White Space**
   - Create as much white space as you can on a page
     - White space allows a spot for the 'eye to rest'
   - Create spacing between chunked content for ease in locating sections of content

2. **De-Clutter, Distill and Reduce Content**
   - Review your content and distill it down to the essence of what is needed for learning
   - Remove any content that really isn't needed and may contribute to clutter
   - Be concise. Better learning results when materials are concise and free of extra elements (Mayer, Bove, Bryman, Mars, and Tapangco, 1995).
     - Remove extraneous or repetitive words
     - Use as little text as you can on slides

3. **Signal and Draw Attention**
   - Create items that stand out through the use of bolding, increasing font size, shapes and lines and also through the creation of appropriate paragraph headings
     - Research studies indicate that this use of 'signalling' important points helps students learn better (Mautone & Mayer, 2001)
   - Avoid use of transitions to bring in bulleted information in slideshows
     - The brain is unable to handle the animated movements of bullets and students learn better when the information is presented at once without animation (Mahar, et al., 2009)

4. **Group Similar Items**
   - Using proper spacing and group content together so it looks like it belongs
   - Add extra spacing above and below paragraphs or blocks of text
   - Create sections of information rather than long lists of items

5. **Use Visuals to Represent Information**
   - Add appropriate visuals to text to improve learning
     - When visuals are aligned with the purpose of the instruction, improved learning happens and this is called "dual encoding" (Paivio, 1990). The brain is better able to process and store information (Vekiri, 2002)
     - Use graphs, charts, Venn diagrams, tables, arrows, circles, rectangles, and triangles to organize information differently

- Don't use visuals for 'decorating' your slides or handouts – choose appropriate visuals that directly relate to the concepts and assist in comprehension
  - When visuals are misaligned with the purpose of learning they can actually hinder the students' ability to learn (Harp & Mayer, 1997; Bartsche & Cobern, 2003)

6. **Be Consistent**
   - Whatever you do on one slide or page, be consistent and do elsewhere
   - Be consistent with fonts, colors, lines, spacing, layout, etc.
     - In slideshows, sans serif fonts tend to be more associated with being professional in appearance, comfortable to read and interesting, but serif fonts are okay to use as long as any font style is 24 points or larger (Mackiewicz, 2007)
   - Do not to center titles and then left align all the content – the eye likes to consistently see all the text with one alignment for ease in reading

D. Alternative Formats and Uses of Slide Presentations

In this section are six examples of slides which may provide suggestions for moving from the   traditional format to something more interactive and visual.

Traditional

- Bullets (many per slide)
- Long phrases of information or full sentences
- Many slides – presentation is more than 15 minutes
- Slides full to the edges with content
- Minimal use of graphics and visuals
- Dark backgrounds with white text
- Light backgrounds with multi-colored text

Title of Slide

- Bullet with content in long phrases or sentences
- Bullet with content in long phrases or sentences
- Bullet with content in long phrases or sentences
  - Sub bullet with more content
  - Sub bullet with more content
- Bullet with content in long phrases or sentences
- Bullet with content in long phrases or sentences
  - Sub bullet with more content

- Transitions used when bullet/content enters slide and also between slides
- Students copy text or are given the slides after class
- Instructor talks while slide is shown adding more info
- Used to help instructor organize class
- Primary used in lecture-based classes

Scaled-Back Traditional

- Bullets (1-5 per slide)

- Shorter phrases of information per bullet

- Fewer slides than traditional format

- Slide contains text and relevant image

- Some use of graphics and visuals

- Background and text color combinations are okay

- Transitions used when bullet/content enters slide and also between slides

- Students copy text or are given the slides after class

- Instructor talks while slide is shown adding more info

- Used to help instructor organize class

Title of Slide
- Bullet with content in long phrases or sentences
- Bullet with content in long phrases or sentences
- Bullet with content in long phrases or sentences
  - Sub bullet with more content
  - Sub bullet with more content

Missing Information Format

- Phrases or bullets (only some information included as the rest is filled in by the students during class time)

- Fewer slides than traditional format

- Slide contains some text or just an image

- Some use of graphics and visuals

- Background and text color combinations are readable

Missing Content Slide

Term and Application
  Term: Definition that students do not have to copy
  Application Example: *(missing info)*

Two Issues
  Issue 1: *(missing info)*
  Issue 2: Information included so students do not have to copy

- Minimal or no transitions of slides or content

- Students get a digital copy of the slide presentation or a 'handout' version to print/bring to class to fill in while the instructor covers missing info

- Helps focus students on elements they need to understand without students spending time copying everything

- Time given for students to comprehend content

- Discussion may happen to allow for application of new material

Activity Slides

- Slides contain activities for students to engage with content:
    - Terms in one column, definitions in another (students have to discuss in small groups how they would correctly match items)
    - Photograph or clip art image with missing labels (students have to think as to how the image would be labeled properly)

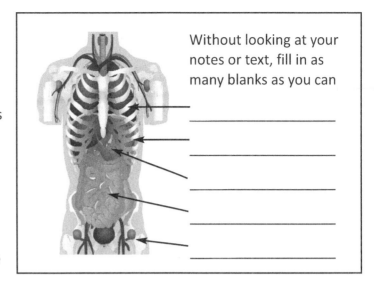

- Fill-in-the-blanks (students go through notes or previous slides to find answers)
    - True/False Statements on content just covered (students discuss in small groups)
    - Multiple-choice questions (students discuss or vote by raising hands)
    - Timeline, chart or graph that has missing labels

- High use of graphics and visuals on most slides

- Instructor may intersperse 'activity slides' between content slides

- Time given for students to discuss, ask questions, and work with peers

Animated Slides

- Slides contain simple animations for explaining content

- Steps in a process: Have an image or phrase for each step appear on screen with a description (students add in their own notes)

- Timeline: Have date and a key phrase appear showing students progress through time

- Conceptual diagram of connected parts: Have whole diagram appear at once but upon mouse click each part increases in size and emphasis is added with additional info

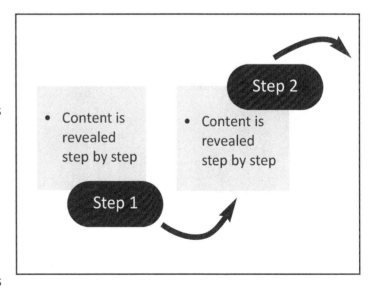

- Animation is used to emphasize the content, not as a fun element on page

- Instructor provides full slideshow to students so they can replay animations for studying

Creatively Visual

- No bullets

- One phrase or word per slide

- Most of the slide is filled with an image that is related to content

- No transitions

- Students listen to the instructor and create own notes

- Students may be given a notes version of talk so they focus on listening rather than copying information

- Instructor engages in discussion, possible activities, and group work focused on slide image

- Students likely to remember image and content associated with it long after the class is done

- Students are likely to have better class attendance and test scores when these types of slides are used as opposed to traditional bulleted slides (Alley et al., 2007)

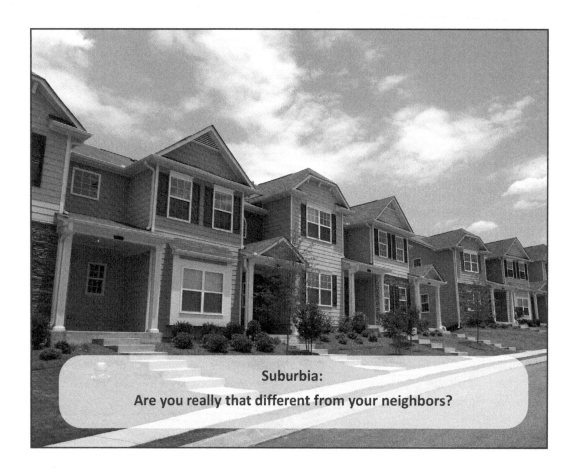

E. Slide Design Tips

Version 1 – This is an example of a typical presentation slide. At first glance, you probably don't see anything wrong with it. Or do you? Using a design template is not a bad idea, as long as you choose one that is cleanly presented and is easy to read. The main problem with this slide is the amount of text. It is very common for instructors to include a lot of text on slides as they act as "organizers" or "guides" for a lecture. They also give students the content for studying. However, a slide like this is just too much: too much text, too many bullets, too much going on, etc. The trend in slide presentations is to reserve most of the text for the speaking portion and put only the key headings or topics on the slide. You could provide a handout with content after the class, but the focus should be on engaging the students in discussions or activities about the content and not racing through too many slides of text.

The font size is fairly small, especially the second-level bullets

Tips for Slide Design

- Keep bullet content short as it just makes for a long and wordy slide
- Refine and distill the message you want to have on each slide
  - Break up content onto different slides if one slide gets too busy
  - You do not need to include everything you are going to say
  - The 'notes' for each slide can be shared with students after class
- Don't make the font size too small and the font type too difficult to read
  - A slide is not a handout to be jammed with a ton of content
- Use an appropriate and relevant image on some slides to convey meaning such as a graph or a table or a photograph
- Align your title with the rest of your content – in other words make it all left aligned
- Use sub-headings in a different font and style to separate content
- Chunk content into sections so the user knows what belongs together
- Avoid the use of transitions to bring in each bullet – it is just distracting and not really helping students learn

There is too much content on this slide. It just isn't needed.

Version 2 – This is a significant improvement over Version 1. A good deal of content was removed. A different slide design was chosen that is cleaner and presents the content in a straightforward way. A white background (or an off-white background color) makes for good contrast when used with a darker font.

The title is now aligned to the left to match up with the text and bullets

Tips for Slide Design

- **Make Bullet Content Short**
  - A slide is not a handout to be jammed with a ton of content
  - Avoid the use of animations to bring in each bullet

- **Refine and Distill Content**
  - Break up content on different slides
  - Do not include everything you say
  - The 'notes' for each slide can be shared with students after class

- **Consider Layout and Design of Slide**
  - Use images on some slides if they convey a better message
  - Align your content all left or all centered – not both
  - Chunk content into sections for learning
  - Use sub-headings to organize content

Content is grouped into sections to make it easier to read. Sections are then spaced apart from each other to make them more evident.

Sub-headings are bolded to grab the reader's attention.

Version 3 – The biggest change in Version 3 is the two column format and the inclusion of a graphic. For this content (but not for all content) the use of shorter bullets to present the content gives the reader the impression there is less to read. More content was weeded out as is often necessary to ensure clear and understandable text. The instructor should speak about each point and give more detail verbally. The color of the separating lines was changed in the color palette choices.

The words in the title were rearranged to be more succinct.

Slide Design Tips

■ Make Bullet Content Short

　▨　A slide is not a handout

　▨　Avoid the use of animations

■ Refine and Distill Content

　▨　Break up content into slides

　▨　Do not include everything you say

　▨　Cover content in spoken words

■ Consider Layout and Design

　▨　Use images on some slides

　▨　Align your content

　▨　Chunk content into sections

　▨　Use sub-headings to organize content

A graphic was added to bring more meaning to the content and break up all the text.

Version 4 – The trend in slide presentations is less text and more visuals. It is not a 'golden rule', but it is a way to present material without all the clutter of bullets and text. In this way, the instructor has the attention of the students and can talk about the content. Students either make their own notes on what is said or the instructor can provide them with his 'talk' as organized through the 'notes' portion of the software program. However the slides are used, students need to come to class to hear what the instructor has to say and not be frantically copying slide content.

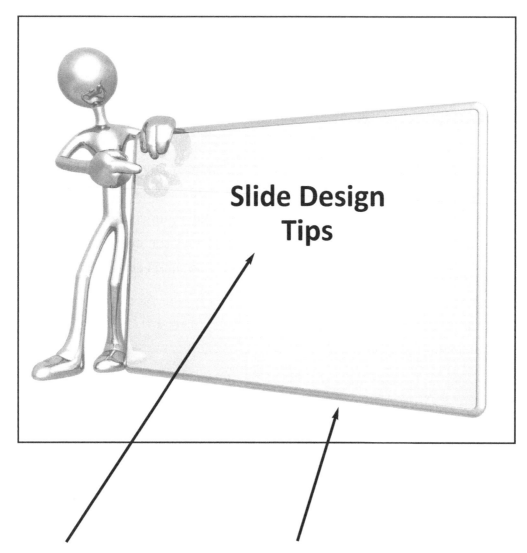

Keep the text—a heading, a phrase or a quote—clean and with a strong font. Whatever the background color of the image, make the text a strong contrast against it.

One single image or a few images make for a visually stunning slide. Other slides could contain some text, a comparison chart, a bar graph, or some numbers. Learning is further supported by discussions or interactive activities based on the slide content. Students are more engaged in the class rather than listening to an instructor read content from the slides.

F. Handout Design Tips: Four Steps To a Better Looking Handout

Version 1: This version looks like a typical handout. The margins are narrow so that all the content fits on the page. The text is standard Times New Roman, but quite small for readability. The use of some bolding and italics is an attempt at making headings stand out. There is still a lot more that could be done to improve the usefulness of this handout and make it more readable. **Note:** The content of the handout is actually based on good design tips for handouts! Check out versions 2, 3 and 4 for more!

Handouts: Design Tips

Title is bolded and centered.

Handouts are helpful teaching and learning tools in both the digital and face to face classroom. Handouts are useful for summarizing content from a complex topic, for presenting a specific set of steps or procedures or for giving to students in a 'gapped or skeleton' fashion to assist them in taking proper notes. With course web sites, instructors can easily share handouts with students in digital format. Today people tend to skim or scan written material and it is essential to present handout content in a fashion that makes it easy to read and doesn't cause the learner to hunt for valuable information. Handout design it isn't about 'decorating or prettying-up' material, it is about 'designing' materials that allow the student to learn the best. This page has some simple tips, which do not take much time, you can apply to making your handouts.

Purpose: Focus on the purpose of your handout as that will lead the way as to how to design it. For example, if your handout is for students to take some notes of their own, then ensure you leave enough space for them to write. If the handout is to capture some key content information that isn't found in the textbook, ensure you present the material for students to easily read and grasp the key points.

Spacing: All handouts should have plenty of space for students to jot their own notes, for the eye to 'rest' amongst data/information etc. Use wide margins (2.5 cm at most, 1 cm at least), space out your topics (leave space between sections) etc. "White space is your friend!" - it improves readability in a big way.

Headings: Use headings and sub-headings to show importance of points. This aids the learner in following the lecture. Change the size of headings (to 2 pts larger than the text under the heading) to emphasize items.

Graphics: Using graphics are very useful as they augment the verbal explanation much better than a ton of words. This is not to make the handout look pretty but rather to emphasize the message and increase comprehension.

Charts and Tables: We often forget that presenting material in a chart, table or in a graph might more easily convey the message than a lot of text and paragraphs.

Contrast: When there is contrast on the page, the eye can pick out key items much easier. You can create contrast by changing the size of font (larger for headings, smaller for content), varying the fonts used (chunky font for main title, cleaner font for content), and by using boxes and charts in some areas versus short text segments in other areas.

Refine and Chunk Content: Look at the content that is necessary for your students. Establish what content is not needed and get rid of it, then chunk (or group) the content into sections to help with skimming.

Title: Ensure there is a strong and relevant title and that students know what class/course it belongs to

Footer: Ensure that your name, course and Page X of Y is in the footer so students know how many pages are part of the handout and that you give yourself credit for the handout and material included. Also include the date of the handout – it will help students organize their papers and tie it to their class notes.

Short Phrases/Bullets: If you can reduce the number of sentences within your handout, this will make reading and learning much easier. Consider what you can write in short phrases, what could be a bullet or what could go in a chart.

Logo: a small graphic image you use on all of your handouts, allows students to more easily sort through any printed material and immediately identify it as belonging to your class. For example, a symbol or graphic item that you paste in the footer of all your materials is an appropriate way to use a logo.

Bolding/Italicizing/Font Size: Rather than underlining to bring attention to certain parts, titles, key words

Alignment: Try to focus on just one alignment on your page. Alignment refers to left justifying, centering or fully justifying your text. Best alignment is left justification with a ragged edge on the right. Do not use full justification (like a newspaper) as it is very difficult to read.

Proofread: Ensure you proofread your work, not just for spelling/grammar, but also for the layout and formatting.

v.1

Each sub-heading is in italics and each section has some space to set it apart.

Margins are a bit narrow and the footer could be improved with more detail.

Version 2: It took approximately 10 minutes to make the changes to this version of the same hand-out as shown in Version 1 (previous page). The title was made more evident, a graphic was added, the font was changed, and the sub-headings were bolded. The margins were increased, along with spacing between sections so the handout now flows to two pages. While it may be seen as a bad thing to have more pages, the benefits of increased readability and use of the handout will outweigh the disadvantages of an additional page. Since most people are posting handouts online, this isn't a waste of paper, but rather an effort to provide students with a document that presents material more clearly.

Font and size of title was changed to make it stand out more.

An image of papers was added as it relates to the topic. Adding a relevant graphic helps break up text and provide a visual element to distinguish amongst other handouts.

Sub-titles are bolded and put on a separate line. They stand out more than the use of italics.

Handouts: Design Tips

Handouts are helpful teaching and learning tools in both the digital and face to face classroom. They are useful for summarizing content from a complex topic, for presenting a specific set of steps or for giving to students in a 'gapped or skeleton' fashion to assist them in taking proper notes. On course web sites, instructors can easily share handouts with students in digital format. Today people tend to skim or scan written material and it is essential to present handout content in a fashion that makes it easy to read and doesn't cause the learner to hunt for valuable information. Handout design it isn't about 'decorating or prettying-up' material, it is about 'designing' materials that allow the student to learn the best. This page has some simple tips, which do not take much time, you can apply to making your handouts.

Purpose:

Focus on the purpose of your handout as that will lead the way as to how to design it. For example, if your handout is for students to take some notes of their own, then ensure you leave enough space for them to write. If the handout is to capture some key content information that isn't found in the textbook, ensure you present the material for students to easily read and grasp the key points.

Refine and Chunk Content:

Look at the content that is necessary for your students. Establish what content is not needed and get rid of it, then chunk (or group) the content into sections to help with skimming.

Title:

Ensure you have a strong and relevant title so students know what class/course it belongs to.

Short Phrases/Bullets:

If you can reduce the number of sentences within your handout, this will make reading and learning much easier. Consider what you can write in short phrases, what could be a bullet or what could go in a visual chart.

Spacing:

All handouts should have plenty of space for students to jot their own notes, for the eye to 'rest' amongst data/information etc. Use wide margins (2.5 cm at most, 1 cm at least), space out your topics (leave space between sections) etc. "White space is your friend!" - it improves readability in a big way.

Headings:

Use headings and sub-headings to show relative importance of points. This really aids the learner in following the lecture and knowing what the structure is of the lesson. Change the size of headings (to 1-2 pts larger than the text under the heading) to emphasize items.

Bolding/Italicizing/Font Size:

Rather than underlining to bring attention to certain parts, titles, key words, changing the font size

Graphics:

Using graphics are very useful as they augment the verbal explanation much better than a ton of words. This is not to make the handout look pretty but rather to emphasize the message and increase comprehension of concepts.

Charts and Tables:

We often forget that presenting material in a chart, table or in a graph might more easily convey the message than a lot of text and paragraphs.

Alignment:

Try to focus on just one alignment on your page. Alignment refers to left justifying, centering or fully justifying your text. Best alignment is left justification with a ragged edge on the right. Do not use full justification (like a newspaper) as it is very difficult to read.

Contrast:

When there is contrast on the page, the eye can pick out key items much easier. You can create contrast by changing the size of font (larger for headings, smaller for content), varying the fonts used (chunky font for main title, cleaner font for content), and by using boxes and charts in some areas versus short text segments in other areas.

Footer:

Ensure that your name, course and Page X of Y is in the footer so students know how many pages are part of the handout and that you give yourself credit for the handout and material included. Also include the date of the handout – it will help students organize their papers and tie it to their class notes.

Logo:

a small graphic image you use on all of your handouts, allows students to more easily sort through any printed material and immediately identify it as belonging to your class. For example, a symbol or graphic item that you paste in the footer of all your materials is an appropriate way to use a logo.

Proofread:

Ensure you proofread your work, not just for spelling/grammar, but also for the layout and formatting.

The spacing is still an issue in this version. Each sub-section needs to have the content and title closer together. This is called 'proximity' in design language. We tend to think that the title above relates to the content below, but check out the next version for a better way to use proximity.

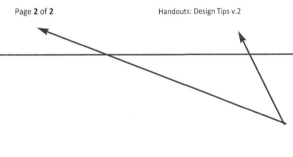

Page numbers and more detail are improved in the footer.

Version 3: This is a much improved version with a complete restructuring. The information is now grouped under three "steps" to help the reader see distinct chunks for learning rather than two pages of ideas. The use of shorter phrases and bullets means some content was removed to make it more readable. More white space and slightly larger margins help with the overall look. The new title is more meaningful to the purpose of the handout and a better graphic relates to the handout topic.

Photographs help make it look more professional.

Font for main title and sub-headings is different than rest of text. This is good contrast.

Content is organized in a fashion that makes more sense to the reader; sub-titles and bulleted phrases are still used and some content was removed that was not needed.

Design Tips for Handouts

Handouts are helpful teaching and learning tools in both the digital and face to face classroom. They are useful for summarizing content from a complex topic, for presenting a specific set of steps or for giving to students in a 'gapped or skeleton' fashion to assist them in taking proper notes. On course web sites, instructors can easily share handouts with students in digital format. Handout design it isn't about 'decorating or prettying-up' material, it is about 'designing' materials that allow the student to learn the best. This page has some simple tips, which do not take much time, you can apply to making your handouts.

Step 1: Whole Handout Restructuring

Purpose: Focus on purpose of handout as that will lead the way for design choices.
- If students are to take notes - leave enough space for them to write
- If the handout is to capture key information that isn't in textbook, present material that is easily read and one can quickly grasp key points

Refine and Chunk Content: Look at content and determine what is necessary for student learning
- Establish what content is truly not needed and....get rid of it!
- Chunk (or group) content into sections that make sense and provide for better understanding

Headings: Use headings and sub-headings to show relative importance of points
- Aids learner in following the lecture and knowing lesson structure
- Change size of headings (to 2 pts larger than the text under the heading) to emphasize

Short Phrases/Bullets: Reduce number of proper sentences—use bullets or short phrases
- Reading much easier as people skim/scan things now and need to easily see sections/titles

Spacing: Good balance of 'white' space on page = Increased readability of document
- Use good margin width (at least 1 cm)
- Leave more space between sections of text that belong together
- Provide space for students to take notes if that is purpose

Before Handout

Heading

Content written in sentences with same space above and below text.

Heading

Content written in sentences with same space above and below text.

Heading

After Handout

Introduction

Heading
- Content in phrases/bullets – grouped
- Content in phrases/bullets – grouped

Heading
- Content in phrases/bullets – grouped
- Content in phrases/bullets – grouped

Page 1 of 2   Handouts: Design Tips v.3   Liesel Knaack, Date of Handout

Step 2: Applying Design Details

Bolding/Italicizing/Font Size and Face: Use 'style' features to emphasize items and design your document.
- Avoid use of underlining (it decreases readability)

Graphics: Add graphics when appropriate to handout (e.g., clip art, photographs, screen shots, etc.)
- Graphical elements must be directly related to content to be useful and enhance learning
- Avoid use of gratuitous graphics just for 'prettying up' a handout – no usefulness

Charts and Tables: Use a chart, graph or table to display information in a useful format
- Consider hiding the lines in a table to decrease busy-looking nature of chart lines

Alignment: Left justifying, centering or fully justifying your text
- Try to focus on just one alignment on your page (e.g., all left)
- Titles and headings do not need to be always centered – left justifying is great
- Best alignment is left justification with a ragged edge on the right
- Do not use full justification (like a newspaper) – very difficult to read

Contrast: When there is contrast on page, the eye can pick out key items easier. Create contrast by:
- Changing the size of font (larger for headings, smaller for content)
- Varying the fonts used (chunky font for main title, cleaner font for content)
- Using boxes and charts in some areas versus short text segments in other areas

> Change **Font Size** to add emphasis
>
> Mix 2 `font faces` to provide contrast
>
> **Bold** some words for added visibility
>
> Use italics *sparingly* but when it *helps*

Rounded rectangles contain examples of content to assist the reader in comprehending material.

The extra spaces between 'steps' makes each section more evident and easy to distinguish.

Step 3: Fine Tuning for Final Items

Title: Ensure you have a strong and relevant title
- Aids in organization of student papers and in preparing study materials

Footer: Include footer and include relevant information to present a professional document
- Put author's name of the material
- Include name of the course
- Use page X of Y is in the footer so students know how many pages they are
- Add date of the handout – it will help students organize and tie it to their class notes

Logo: a small graphic image you use on all of your handouts
- Students can easily sort through handouts – identify as belonging to your class
- Paste a symbol or graphics in footer or header of all your materials

Proofread: Ensure you proofread your work
- Spelling and grammar and sentence structure
- Proofread for proper layout and formatting – use this handout as a checklist!

Beside the content on using "logos" are some sample logos.

Footer content is improved.

Version 4 – This is the final version of the same handout from the previous pages. The title has changed again and so has the photo to more accurately reflect the purpose of the handout. The pages are now formatted into two columns. When you only have to read halfway across a page, you are not as overwhelmed with the material and are more likely to persist with reading. Sub-headings get a boost in bold and a slight font change to make them stand out more. Overall, this handout might have taken 20-25 minutes to format from the Version 1 state, but it provides greater readability and interest as a professional handout. Read through the tips in this final state to learn more about proper design of handouts.

Title is more specific. Part of title is in larger font size.

Content is further refined and edited for presenting the most important points.

Two columns present material in a more readable format.

Arrow between before and after examples gives movement to the page.

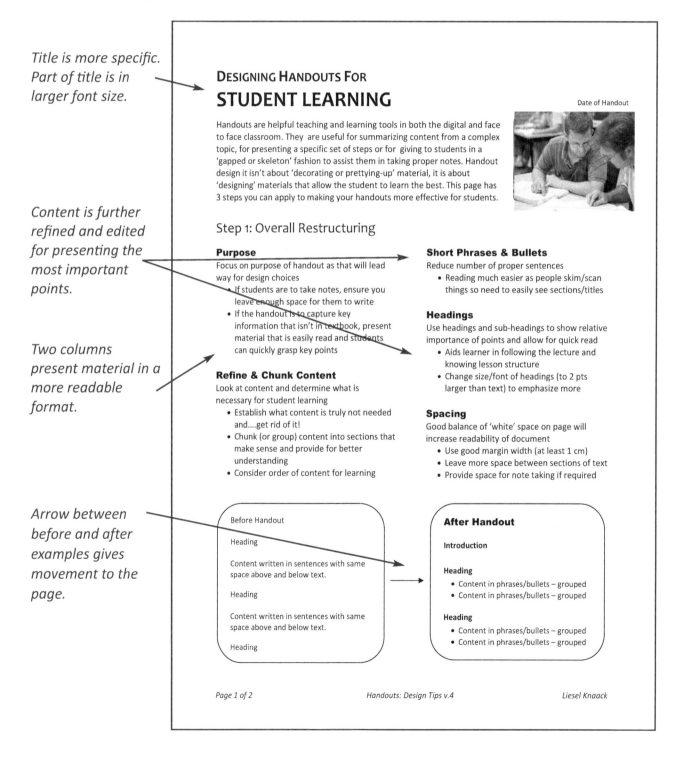

DESIGNING HANDOUTS FOR
STUDENT LEARNING

Date of Handout

Handouts are helpful teaching and learning tools in both the digital and face to face classroom. They are useful for summarizing content from a complex topic, for presenting a specific set of steps or for giving to students in a 'gapped or skeleton' fashion to assist them in taking proper notes. Handout design it isn't about 'decorating or prettying-up' material, it is about 'designing' materials that allow the student to learn the best. This page has 3 steps you can apply to making your handouts more effective for students.

Step 1: Overall Restructuring

Purpose
Focus on purpose of handout as that will lead way for design choices
- If students are to take notes, ensure you leave enough space for them to write
- If the handout is to capture key information that isn't in textbook, present material that is easily read and students can quickly grasp key points

Refine & Chunk Content
Look at content and determine what is necessary for student learning
- Establish what content is truly not needed and….get rid of it!
- Chunk (or group) content into sections that make sense and provide for better understanding
- Consider order of content for learning

Short Phrases & Bullets
Reduce number of proper sentences
- Reading much easier as people skim/scan things so need to easily see sections/titles

Headings
Use headings and sub-headings to show relative importance of points and allow for quick read
- Aids learner in following the lecture and knowing lesson structure
- Change size/font of headings (to 2 pts larger than text) to emphasize more

Spacing
Good balance of 'white' space on page will increase readability of document
- Use good margin width (at least 1 cm)
- Leave more space between sections of text
- Provide space for note taking if required

Before Handout

Heading

Content written in sentences with same space above and below text.

Heading

Content written in sentences with same space above and below text.

Heading

After Handout

Introduction

Heading
- Content in phrases/bullets – grouped
- Content in phrases/bullets – grouped

Heading
- Content in phrases/bullets – grouped
- Content in phrases/bullets – grouped

Page 1 of 2   *Handouts: Design Tips v.4*   *Liesel Knaack*

Step 2: Applying Design Details

Bolding/Italicizing/Font Size & Face
Use 'style' features to emphasize items and design your document.
- Avoid underlining (decreases readability)

> Change Font Size to add emphasis
>
> Mix 2 font faces to provide contrast
>
> **Bold** some words for added visibility
>
> Use italics *sparingly* but when it *helps*

Graphics
Add graphics when appropriate to handout (e.g., clip art, photographs, screen shots, etc.)
- Graphical elements must be directly related to content to be useful and enhance learning
- Avoid use of gratuitous graphics just for 'prettying up' a handout – no usefulness

Charts & Tables
Use a chart, graph or table to display information
- Consider hiding the borders in a table to decrease busy-looking nature of chart lines

Alignment
Left justifying, centering or fully justifying your text
- Use one alignment on your page (e.g., all left)
- Titles/headings do not need to be centered
- Best alignment is left justification with a ragged edge on the right (as we read L-R)
- Don't use full justification (e.g. newspaper) – very difficult to read

Contrast
When there is contrast, the eye can pick out key items easier. Create contrast by:
- Changing the size of font (larger for headings, smaller for content)
- Varying the fonts used (chunky font for main title, cleaner font for content readability)
- Using boxes and charts in some areas versus short text segments in other areas

Line between Step 2 and 3 makes the separation clear to the reader.

Step 3: Fine Tuning Final Items

Title
Create a well-worded and relevant title
- Aids in organization of student papers and in preparing study materials
- Sub-titles can help further define topic
- Create near end of process as handout purpose and content may have changed

Footer
Include footer and relevant information
- Author's name of the material
- Name of the course
- Page Numbers: Page X of Y allows students to know total pages
- Date of the handout – helps students organize and tie to class notes

Logo
Add a small graphic image on all handouts
- Students can sort through handouts to easily identify those from your class
- Paste a symbol or graphic in footer or header of all your materials

Proofread
Ensure you proofread your work
- Spelling, grammar and sentence structure
- Proofread for layout and formatting – use this handout as checklist!

G. Activity: Test Your Design Knowledge

This slide is part of a workshop about how to be an effective teacher. The content is included in bullets. A design template was chosen. The creator of this slide has not learned about design principles or suggestions for improving the presentation of information. Your help is needed!

What needs fixing? Jot your ideas here and consult the examples in the chapter for answers.

Steps to a Good Class

- Make sure you come to class organized and well prepared – students will appreciate it

- Include aspects of student involvement in the class

- Be clear, yet with enough details about what you expect for assignments and tests

- Continue to build good rapport with your students

- Share resources and notes with students online through your course web site

- Provide some study tips for mid-term and final exams – specifically what is covered and the types of questions

Top Ten Takeaways

1. **Digital and Print Materials are Used Frequently in Education:** They take on many forms from slideshow presentations and the creation of tests to handouts and supplementary materials for the course.

2. **Skimming and Scanning:** With the incredible amount of digital information available today, people are skimming and scanning text rather than taking the time to fully read every word. With less time and more information to sort through, it is wise to present content in a manner that makes it easy to access and comprehend useful information.

3. **Basic Design Principle: Preserve White Space.** Ensure you de-clutter a page as much as you can and put extra spacing between sections so that the eye can more easily scan for important information.

4. **Basic Design Principle: Group Similar Items**. When you chunk or group content that belongs together and you assign it a meaningful heading, you create a more accessible learning experience for the user.

5. **Basic Design Principle: Use Visuals.** When appropriate, try including more visual elements (clip art, photographs, charts, graphs, diagrams) into your slides and handouts. Pictures are often more effective for optimal learning.

6. **Basic Design Principle: Be Consistent.** Whether it be font style, size or color, bullet style, image type, or the alignment of text and titles, be consistent from page to page and slide to slide.

7. **Alternative Formats for Slide Presentations:** Not all slideshow presentations need to be bulleted text that comes in with its own animated entrance. More and more people are choosing to add activity slides, animated components, and interactive activities to eventually work toward a more visual and clutter-free presentation.

8. **Four Slide Progression:** Four slides are presented to show the progression from a cluttered slide to one that is more visual.

9. **Four Handout Progression:** Four handouts are presented to show the progression from a jam-packed handout to one that has less text and presented in a 2 column format.

10. **Taking the Time is Worth It!** Take 15-20 minutes of your time to consider a few design principles for improving your slides or handouts.

Next Steps

1. Find a slide presentation you have already created. Looking at a few of the slides, can you quickly change anything to make it a better design for increased readability and learning?

2. Try editing some of the information and making a slide or two less busy.

3. Find a handout you have in your files. Can you quickly change some element to make it more user friendly and easier to access information?

4. Try chunking or grouping content into sections with appropriate sub-headings.

5. The next time you need to create a slide or a handout, consult the tips in this chapter.

References and Resources

Alley, M., Schreiber, M., Diesel, E., Ramsdell, K., & Borrengo, M. (2007). Increased student learning and attendance in resources geology through the combination of sentence-headline slides and active learning measures. *Journal of Geoscience Education, 55*(1), 85-91.

Bartsche, R.A., & Cobern, K.M. (2003). Effectiveness of PowerPoint presentations in lectures. *Computers & Education, 41*(1), 77-86.

Duarte, N. (2008). *Slide:ology: The art and science of creating great presentations*. Sebastopol, CA: O'Reilly Media.

Harp, S. F. & Mayer, R.E. (1997). The role of interest in learning from scientific text and illustrations: On the distinction between emotional interest and cognitive interest. *Journal of Educational Psychology, 89*, 92-102.

Mackiewicz, J. (2007). Audience perceptions of fonts in projected PowerPoint text slides. *Technical Communication, 54*, 295-307.

Mahar, S., Yaylacicegi, U., & Janicki, T. (2009). Less is more when developing PowerPoint animations. *Information Systems Education Journal, 7*(82), 1-11.

Mautone, P. D., & Mayer, R. E. (2001). Signaling as a cognitive guide in multimedia learning. *Journal of Educational Psychology, 93*(2), 377-389.

Mayer, R.E., Bove, W., Bryman, A., Mars, R., & Tapangco, L. (1995). When less is more: Meaningful learning from visual and verbal summaries of science textbook lessons. *Journal of Educational Psychology, 88*(1), 54-73.

Paivio, A. (1990). *Mental Representations: a dual coding approach*. New York: Oxford University Press.

Reynolds, G. (2010). *Presentation Zen Design: simple design principles and techniques that enhance your presentations*. Berkley, CA: New Riders.

Vekiri, I. (2002). "What is the value of graphical displays in learning? *Educational Psychology Review, 14*(3), 261-312.

Chapter 15 – Ending the Last Class on a Strong Note

Chapter Overview

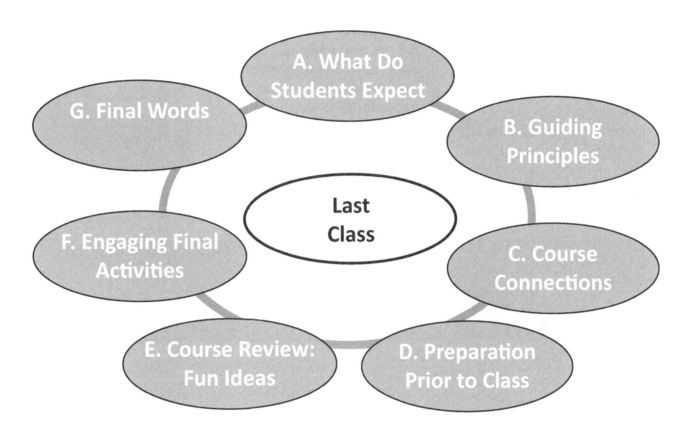

Just like the first class, the last class is a very important day. Instructors tend to spend a lot of time planning the first class and not so much time on the last class. It is often thought the last class is just for a few exam details and to wrap up course evaluations. But it could be so much more!

The last class is a time for the class to celebrate, to get some feedback on how the course has gone, and to answer questions. It is a day to review content, consolidate all the learning from the whole term, and ensure students leave feeling good about the course.

The last day is so important!

This chapter will provide you with ideas and components to consider on the last day of a course.

A. What Do Students Expect?

The last class of any course comes with a set of student expectations as to what the instructor will be doing, what information will be shared, and how the course will end. The following statements come from students about what they expect on the last day of a course. How do they meet with your expectations?

Often in our last classes we have to fill out the institution's course evaluations. I feel that my comments and ratings do not mean much as this is the last class and I will never have the professor again.

I once had an instructor who did this neat slideshow with music and voice to summarize the whole course. He put it up online for us to watch again after the class. He also showed us how all that we have learned is connected and will help us in the real world.

I like it when the instructor does a review session of the course material so that I am more prepared for the final exam.

Mostly, the last class of a course is a waste of time. I wish instructors would give us more help for the final exam. I wish we had a reason to attend the class.

I have some really good instructors who do great things in the last class. I like it when we play a game (like Jeopardy or Millionaire) and learn some sample questions for the exam. I also like having a lot of new material in the class as it makes it worthwhile to come to class.

The last class should be a time for the instructor to give us some tips for the final exam.

I usually skip the last class. I have my friend just tell me what happened and there usually isn't much. The instructor just shares a few tips for the exam and class ends early.

If the prof tells us what we are doing in the last class and there is some worthwhile stuff, I usually go. I like it when we end on a high note and everyone feels good about the exam and course.

B. Ten Guiding Principles

1. Provide a **well thought-out** last class.

2. Aim for a **positive last impression.**

3. **Connect** students to the learning and content from the term.

4. **Design** a class where students have time to ask questions.

5. **Encourage** students in an **active learning** environment.

6. **Review course material** through a fun game or activity.

7. **Consolidate the learning** with a memorable presentation.

8. Obtain **your own feedback from students.**

9. Provide **support to students** to aid them in studying for final exams or projects.

10. **Share personal** thoughts and experiences on the course.

C. Course Connections

The first day of class is about the connections being created between the students, the instructor, and the course. The last day of class is also about the connections students have made with the course content, their own learning, and the instruction.

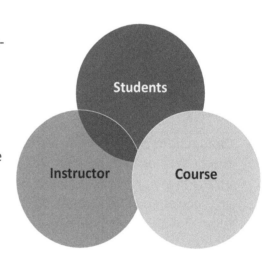

When you are planning your last day's activities, ensure you consider these three components and how they will connect with each other.

You want to leave a lasting impression with students, the relationship they now have to the course, and the new skills and knowledge they have gained.

D. Preparation Prior to Your Last Class

1. **Examine examples of final day activities.** Talk to colleagues about ideas, search the Internet, grab a few ideas from a book, etc.

2. **Ask students what they would like to see happen in the last class.** Poll them in a previous class as to what might benefit them the best. Getting student input is a great way to build your last class and make the students feel a part of the experience.

3. **Share with students your plan for the last class**. If students see a variety of activities that will help them further consolidate the content and feel more confident going into the exam, the more likely they will attend.

4. **Create an agenda** of what your last class will look like. Ensure you are not just going over the exam and conducting the course evaluation! Pack your agenda with a variety of activities that are similar to how you taught the course (e.g., include discussions, an engaging activity, etc.)

5. **Design you own course evaluation questions.** Even if you just ask a few specific questions, you will get important feedback on your course. Institutional course evaluations are more generic, so tailor a few questions about the value of assignments, what parts of the course students liked the most, what was the most challenging, etc. Assure students that their names are not to be on the feedback form and that you won't look at the forms until the marks are finalized.

6. **Be prepared.** Gather materials, arrive a bit earlier, and be ready for a great last class!

E. Course Review: Fun Ideas

You should spend some part of the last class reviewing course content. Here are some ideas:

1. **Student-Submitted Questions:** Have students submit questions anonymously via an online survey. Ensure you collect the questions at least a couple of weeks prior to the last class. Arrange the questions into categories. Project questions on a slide/screen and spend a few minutes answering them. Give students a copy of the questions to aid them in studying.

2. **Open Question and Answer Period:** If you have a small enough class, host an open question and answer period. Tell students to not specifically ask if X or Y is on the exam as you are unable to share that information. Instead, have students ask you questions about topics they need more detail on or concepts for which they would like another example or problem to solve.

3. **Connections Map:** In groups of 4-5 students, have students create a map of the core course topics. Provide each group with a piece of chart paper and a few markers. Ask them to access the course syllabus and use the topic list to prepare a map that shows how the topics are connected or have relationships to each other. Have students post maps around the room. For 10-15 minutes have students get out of their seats and walk around the room to look at all the maps.

4. **Jeopardy or Millionaire Templates:** Locate game show templates found on the Internet. Create a series of questions related to the course. Divide students into various teams and follow the game show format to award points to teams who answer questions correctly. Students always appreciate a fun way to review content.

5. **Practice Exam Questions:** Create a practice exam. Give students time to work through the questions either independently or in small groups. You could have small groups present answers to questions about which they are confident. Discussion time would allow students to defend their answers and probe deeper.

6. **Team Review Game:** Before class, create a variety of questions. Group students into teams of 3-8. Pose the same question to each team and give them time to ponder the answer as a group. This is a great time for students to work together and summarize what they have learned in the class. Randomly choose a group to answer. Correct answers warrant a point.

If a team answers incorrectly, randomly choose another team. Keep track of how many times you have asked each team. This will help you be fair in asking each team the same number of questions.

F. Engaging Final Activities: Consolidating the Course

In addition to providing a review activity, it is important to consolidate the course. You want to wrap up all the course content and leave students with a solid summary of the key points. You also want to have students see the relationships and connections within the course, so they leave with a reminder of the big picture of the topics. Try one of these ideas listed below. You want to engage students, have the activity be useful and meaningful to their learning, and provide some closure for your class. Consider doing your institution's course evaluation after these activities as they will be reminded of all that they have learned and have a better frame of reference for answering the questions.

- **Slideshow Summary:** Create a slideshow of images from the course with music/narration. Use movie or photo software to make something quickly that is sharable with students. The visuals and sound will surely be memorable and something students will appreciate.

- **Guest Speaker:** Invite a former student or two back to speak to your class. Ask them to talk about the most important or memorable parts of the course or how they took the concepts and applied them to other courses or a job. If former students aren't available to come to your class, possibly one or two of them could create a short video or audio presentation depicting the highlights they remembered from your class. It could be a wonderful and inspirational talk to motivate students to study and take what they've learned into other areas of their lives.

- **Note to Future Students:** Supply sheets of colorful paper and markers and ask your students to write a note that includes some tips and suggestions for future students taking the course. Share the notes with your students next term—they will appreciate reading them!

- **New Content:** Sometimes we need to have students learn new content in the last class. Be sure to include application activities and take up answers so they have a complete set of notes. Also try to weave the new content into the previous content so students immediately see connections.

- **Student Presentation Session:** Arrange students into small groups of 3-4. Give each group a topic studied throughout the term. Have each group provide a summary of the topic in any form they wish. Encourage them to try a dramatic routine, a visual or artistic format, or put it to a poem or song. They should be given about 2-3 minutes to share their presentation with the class. Students will appreciate the fun aspect along with the challenge in summarizing the content in an alternative format.

- **Video:** Show a video or part of a video that nicely consolidates your course. Maybe it might be a video about a career or a research experiment related to your course. Students will appreciate seeing the video and discussing the relevance to the course.

- **Consolidation Story:** As the instructor, prepare a 10-15 minute summary highlighting the key points and big ideas you want students to remember. Try formatting it within a story format weaving together experiences, experiments, and activities you or others have done with the course topics. Students will appreciate listening to a story rather than a series of points flying by on the screen in a PowerPoint presentation.

- **Course Feedback Form:** From questions you have previously prepared, give students some time to fill out a feedback form. Ask questions about topics, assignments, and class format. This will help you reflect on the course and adjust accordingly. Ensure you ask a responsible student to collect the responses and put them in a sealed envelope. Have the student drop off the envelope to a pre-selected administrative assistant in your department who will give you the envelope after marks have been finalized. Tell students the procedure so they will feel more comfortable in giving good feedback.

- **Puzzle Pieces:** In a word processing program, create a set of terms/concepts/key words from the course. Put each word or phrase a few lines apart from each other as you go down the page. Copy the sheets of paper and with a paper cutter slice each word or phrase. Put the slices from a whole set into an envelope. Make enough sets for teams of 3-4 in your class. Give each team the envelope with the complete set of terms/concepts/key words. Ask them to arrange them in a meaningful format that shows their understanding of the course. Give them a piece of newsprint and a glue stick to affix their final product. This is an excellent activity for students to work together to come to a shared understanding of the course material and the relationships they see between concepts. Ask each group to briefly share with the rest of the class.

G. Final Words

Have a proper ending to the class. You have just spent the whole term with a group of students and so it is fitting to make the final moments positive and informative. Here are some suggestions:

1. Share your personal thoughts on what you learned in this course. Share highs and lows and where you feel you might tweak or change things the next time you offer the course.

2. Give final reminders and details on the final exam location, time, and approved items that can be brought into the exam.

3. Remind students about other courses that are offered that will work nicely with the course they have just completed. Share how the concepts and content are related. Students may

make some last minute changes to their schedule for next term given this information. You can also get students excited about new courses or other offerings you feel will complement their program.

4. Thank the students for their participation and hard work in the course. Acknowledge the challenges they faced and the rewards that they received for their efforts.

5. Invite students to your office should they have any questions about the course or the exam. Encourage students to drop by in the future should they have any questions about careers, research, or graduate work.

Top Ten Takeaways

1. **Plan an Effective Last Class:** While most instructors have run out of energy by the end of the term, it is important to plan an effective last class to make use of the time and provide students with a solid summary.

2. **Meet Student Needs:** Students sometimes tell us that the last class is often a waste of time to attend. Instructors should design a final class that meets students' needs and provides a solid reason for attendance.

3. **Consider the Ten Guiding Principles:** Keep things positive, engaging, and celebratory in nature.

4. **Connections:** Like the first class, the last class involves the connections between the course, the students, and the instructor. Plan activities that strengthen these connections.

5. **Preparation:** Take some time to prepare your last class. Let students know about the agenda so they see it is important to attend.

6. **Review:** A good portion of the final class should contain a review component. Play a Jeopardy or Millionaire game, have students do short presentations or engage them in a quick question and answer session. Create practice exam questions to take up in class. Students will see value in attending when a worthy review session is held.

7. **Interactive Activities:** The final class should contain fun and interactive activities that help students consolidate the course and its concepts. Invite in a guest speaker, have students write notes to future students, show a video, create a short photo/music summary of the course, or have students build concept connections.

8. **Feedback:** In addition to the institutional evaluation form, try asking the students a few questions about what they liked or will remember the most from your course.

9. **Share Benefits of Course:** Share a story about what students have learned and how this new knowledge and skills will benefit them. Students will appreciate seeing how the content will help them in the future.

10. **Final Words:** Make sure you leave a few minutes to share some final words. Wish students well on their courses and career paths, share some last minute details about the exam, and indicate how your course connects to other courses offered by your department.

Next Steps

1. Make a pact with yourself to do something different for your final class this year.

2. As the term draws to an end, poll students through an online survey about what topics or concepts require review or additional class work. Categorize these responses and build your last class around those areas where students want more help.

3. Create a few questions you can ask students during the last class. You may wish to know a bit more about a new assignment or what teaching and learning strategy worked best for them.

4. As you near the end of term, start collecting some photos, quotes, or videos that would be great to share during the last class.

5. Advertise what you are going to do the last class a few weeks prior. It will let students know they should attend and that there will be useful material presented.

References and Resources

Davis, B. G. (2005). *Tools for Teaching.* San Francisco, CA: Jossey-Bass.

CPSIA information can be obtained at www.ICGtesting.com
Printed in the USA
LVOW012038240113

316987LV00003B/11/P

9 781897 160473